FOOTBALL AND PHILOSOPHY

The Philosophy of Popular Culture

The books published in the Philosophy of Popular Culture series will illuminate and explore philosophical themes and ideas that occur in popular culture. The goal of this series is to demonstrate how philosophical inquiry has been reinvigorated by increased scholarly interest in the intersection of popular culture and philosophy, as well as to explore through philosophical analysis beloved modes of entertainment, such as movies, TV shows, and music. Philosophical concepts will be made accessible to the general reader through examples in popular culture. This series seeks to publish both established and emerging scholars who will engage a major area of popular culture for philosophical interpretation and examine the philosophical underpinnings of its themes. Eschewing ephemeral trends of philosophical and cultural theory, authors will establish and elaborate on connections between traditional philosophical ideas from important thinkers and the ever-expanding world of popular culture.

Series Editor

Mark T. Conard, Marymount Manhattan College, NY

Books in the Series

FOOTBALL AND
PHILOSOPHY
GOING DEEP

EDITED BY **MICHAEL W. AUSTIN**

WITH A FOREWORD BY **JOE POSNANSKI**

THE UNIVERSITY PRESS OF KENTUCKY

Scholarly publisher for the Commonwealth,
serving Bellarmine University, Berea College, Centre
College of Kentucky, Eastern Kentucky University,
The Filson Historical Society, Georgetown College,
Kentucky Historical Society, Kentucky State University,
Morehead State University, Murray State University,
Northern Kentucky University, Transylvania University,
University of Kentucky, University of Louisville,
and Western Kentucky University.
All rights reserved.

Editorial and Sales Offices: The University Press of Kentucky
663 South Limestone Street, Lexington, Kentucky 40508-4008
www.kentuckypress.com

12 11 10 09 08   5 4 3 2 1

Library of Congress Cataloging-in-Publication Data

Football and philosophy : going deep / edited by Michael W. Austin ;
with a foreword by Joe Posnanski.
    p.   cm. — (The philosophy of popular culture)
  Includes bibliographical references and index.
  ISBN 978-0-8131-2495-7 (hardcover : alk. paper)
  1. Football—Philosophy. 2. Football—Social aspects. I. Austin,
Michael W.
  GV959.F55 2008
  796.332—dc22
                                        2008007853

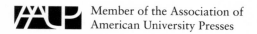

CONTENTS

FOREWORD

As a sports columnist, I often write about philosophy. Why, just the other day I was discussing philosophical theories with Kansas City Chiefs football coach and NFL Nietzsche Herman Edwards. "My philosophy," Edwards said, "is that you've got to hit the quarterback." Among moral philosophers, this quote may not rank with "Man is the cruelest animal." But couldn't you argue that both say the same thing? This is the wonderful thing about football. While coaches and players are constantly talking about their particular brands of football "philosophies" (for example, "We want to run the football," "We play our corners in bump and run," "Only the best players will make this team," "I just want to earn my respect"), it seems they are, in their own way, touching on some of our larger questions.

After all, while Stobaeus may have asked, "What use is knowledge if there is no understanding?" it was that tough coach Bill Parcells who said, "If you don't quit making that same [bleeping] mistake, I'm going to cut you and send you to a truck stop in New Jersey." It seems to me that Parcells was just taking the next logical step.

Apparently, I'm not the only person to think this way. Mike Austin and his group of talented philosophers, writers, and teachers have taken that next step here. The difference is that Mike Austin and his group of talented philosophers, writers, and teachers are a lot smarter than I am. In this fine book, they use football as an opportunity to discuss some of life's biggest topics, bold and important ideas that philosophers have studied through the years. Some of the chapters that follow delve into questions of our time that seem quite simple until you actually think about them: What *is* wrong with using performance-enhancing drugs, anyway?

Some of these essays use philosophical principles and ideals to take on sports-bar questions: Is the NFL's salary cap fair? Where does Vince Lombardi, surely the most celebrated philosopher in the history of professional football, fit into the larger philosophical world? Have athletes become too egotistical? And what would Marx think of a college football playoff anyway?

Then, of course, there are chapters dealing with football and God. I recently saw a punter kick a ball high and far; the ball soared, a beautiful spiral that seemed to linger and dangle in the air for a half hour. The football then hit the ground and pitched forward into the end zone. At that point, the television camera pointed back to the punter, and it showed him point up to the heavens, a tribute to the being that allowed him to punt a ball so magnificently. I could not help but wonder, though: If there is a just and fair God looking over this world, wouldn't he have made the ball stop at the 1?

Most of all, this book is thoughtful and more than skin deep and a lot of fun, and if it gets you to think about how college football players are similar to Roman gladiators, so much the better.

After all, as football coaches will tell you, everybody has a different philosophy. I am reminded of the words that longtime professional football coach Gunther Cunningham wrote in a letter to my daughter on the day she was born. He wrote, "Always play the game like there is no scoreboard."

I don't know what Plato would have thought of that, but it makes sense to me.

Joe Posnanski
Kansas City Star

ACKNOWLEDGMENTS

First, I would like to thank each of the contributors for their hard work on this book. Thanks also to Anne Dean Watkins, Steve Wrinn, and everyone else at the University Press of Kentucky, all of whom were great to work with throughout each phase of the production of this book. I also appreciate the feedback from two anonymous referees for the press, including the one who provided the phrase "going deep," which found its way into the title. Thanks also to my wife, Dawn, and our daughters Haley, Emma, and Sophie for their encouragement and love, and for enduring my rants about my beloved Kansas City Chiefs! Finally, I would like to thank my parents, who, by their time, money, effort, and love, helped me come to love this great sport. It is to them that I dedicate this book.

Michael W. Austin

INTRODUCTION

The Pregame Warm-up

One event dominates the consciousness of America every year in early February. The two weeks leading up to the Super Bowl are filled with interviews, stories of football greatness, predictions, and, unfortunately, the occasional scandal. On Super Bowl Sunday fans gather around television sets at the local bar or in their living room to watch two teams play for the Lombardi Trophy. Those who aren't fans of the game and don't watch it much during the regular season often tune in to the Super Bowl (or at least the high-priced commercials that have become a part of the spectacle).

Football is a part of popular culture not only on Super Bowl Sunday but also throughout the rest of the year. Joe Namath famously appeared in a commercial for pantyhose. Football movies like *Brian's Song* and *Remember the Titans* have enjoyed wide popularity. Perhaps the most well-known involvement of football players in pop culture happened in 1985. Members of the 1985 Super Bowl Champion Chicago Bears released a rap song (okay, maybe that's being a bit generous) called "The Super Bowl Shuffle," with a music video appearing on MTV that included Walter Payton, Mike Singletary, Jim McMahon, and several other members of the team. Surprisingly, this was the Chicago Bears Shufflin' Crew's only hit song. Pop culture and football mix on the field as well. When Kansas City Chiefs running back Larry Johnson scores a touchdown, he makes a symbol with his hands promoting Rocawear, a clothing line founded by rapper Jay-Z and endorsed by Johnson.

While football is a part of pop culture, it is more than that. It is also the most popular spectator sport in the United States, with high-impact collisions, feats of great athletic skill, and meticulously developed strategies played out before the eyes of millions. What does all of this have to do with philosophy? Good question. As it turns out, and as the chapters in this book show, plenty. One thing that football fans and philosophers have in common is that they love to argue and often do so with great passion. If you want to see a good debate, get a group of diehard football fans together and ask them who the greatest quarterback in NFL history is. Joe Montana? John Elway? Johnny Unitas? Philosophers also love to argue and often focus their attention on some of life's big questions: What is the meaning of life? Is there a God? What is true happiness? How should we live? What is beauty?

Philosophy literally means "the love of wisdom," so one of the aims of this book is to offer some valuable insights that can be gained when thinking deeply about football and philosophy. In pursuit of such insights, this book's lineup of contemporary philosophers turn their attention to the game of football and the game of life and try to answer several questions that are important to fans, players, and coaches. What is wrong with performance-enhancing drugs? Should we have a playoff in Division I-A college football? Is there really such a thing as momentum? Does the NFL salary cap promote fairness? What is the significance of forgiveness for the game of football and the game of life? What can we learn from Vince Lombardi's philosophy of winning? Whether or not you agree with the answers given, you'll definitely have some food for thought.

While this book is published by an academic press, it is not an "academic" book, though it does contain some serious philosophical reflection. Academic books are usually written by professional philosophers for other professional philosophers, whereas this book is written by football fans (who happen to be philosophers) for football fans, coaches, and players. So if you're looking for something to do on a Sunday afternoon during the off-season, or when your favorite team has a bye week, read a chapter or two. If you do, the next time you and your friends start debating the pros and cons of instant replay, whether or not we should replace the BCS with a playoff, or whether it is good to mix football and religion, you'll be warmed up and ready to go.

FIRST QUARTER

FOOTBALL'S LESSONS FOR THE GAME OF LIFE

Raymond Angelo Belliotti

VINCE LOMBARDI AND THE PHILOSOPHY OF WINNING

> Each man must make a personal commitment to excellence and victory, even though we know deep down that the ultimate victory can never be completely won. . . . It is the spirit, the will to excel, the will to win: these are the things that endure.
>
> —Vincent Thomas Lombardi, football coach

Vince Lombardi was born on June 11, 1913, in Sheepshead Bay, Brooklyn, New York. His father, Enrico ("Harry"), was born in Italy. His mother, Matilda Izzo, was born in Sheepshead Bay to Italian immigrants. Enrico and his brother operated a wholesale meat store.[1] Vince grew up under two overpowering, unconquerable forces: *l'ordine della famiglia*, the unwritten but deeply ingrained system of social relations Southern Italian immigrants brought to America, and the Roman Catholic Church when it was in its heyday in America. Both forces converged on core values: acting from duty, relishing hard work, refusing facile excuses, celebrating successful struggle, paying the price to attain goals, committing to obsessive promptness, glorifying discipline, adhering to principles, and sacrificing for the common good (as defined by your family or immediate circle of believers).

After graduating from St. Francis Prep, Vince enrolled at Fordham University in the fall of 1933 on a football scholarship. He gained a measure of regional celebrity as an undersized guard on the "Seven Blocks of Granite" offensive line that animated the fine Fordham teams of the mid-1930s. Upon graduation, he dabbled at Fordham law school for one semester, later accepting a teaching job at St. Cecilia High School in Englewood, New Jersey. He there began his football coaching career, running off thirty-two unbeaten games at one point. By 1947, he had landed an assistant coaching position at Fordham, which proved to be a springboard to another assistant coaching job at West Point under the renowned Colonel Earl "Red" Blaik. In 1954, Vince entered professional football as offensive coordinator of the New York Giants. With Lombardi guiding the offense and Tom Landry in charge of the defense, the Giants, under head coach Jim Lee Howell, rose to prominence. They won the 1956 NFL championship and lost the famous sudden-death championship final in 1958 to the Baltimore Colts.

Lombardi became head coach of the hapless Green Bay Packers in 1959. The Packers had won only four games in their previous two seasons and had suffered through eleven consecutive losing seasons. Vince Lombardi arrived with one startling message: he had never been associated with a losing team and he was not about to break that streak in Green Bay. Driving, cajoling, threatening, laughing, extolling, demanding, and willing his team to success, Lombardi finished with a 7–5 record in 1959. The next year, the Packers lost a closely played championship game to the Philadelphia Eagles. Lombardi promised his team they would never drop another championship game under his watch. Astoundingly, they did not. Over the next seven years, the Packers won five NFL championships, including the first two Super Bowls. Vince Lombardi retired from coaching after the 1967 season, the greatest winner in professional football. In 1969, the restless Lombardi took control of the lowly Washington Redskins. Even though he inherited a defense more porous than a colander, Lombardi's Redskins finished with a winning record. Continued progress was expected the following season, but Lombardi was hospitalized with an especially pernicious cancer of the colon. He died on September 3, 1970. The championship Super Bowl cup was renamed the Lombardi Trophy. Vince the Winner would be commemorated annually.

The Philosophy of Winning

His players celebrated Vince Lombardi as a role model who exemplified the values he preached. Willie David, a Hall of Fame defensive end, gushed, "He is all the man there is." Emlin Tunnell, the greatest defensive back of his period, declared admiringly, "You had to walk proud when you were with him because he walked that way." His players also recalled Lombardi's pitiless crusade for excellence. Hall of Fame running back Jim Taylor wistfully reflected, "All he wanted from you was perfection." Defensive tackle Henry Jordan captured Lombardi's unique mix of egalitarianism leavened with ruthlessness: "He treated us all the same—like dogs."

Contrary to legend, Lombardi was not the first person to bellow, "Winning isn't everything, it's the only thing." Former Vanderbilt and UCLA football coach Henry "Red" Sanders probably coined the expression in the 1930s. John Wayne played a small-time college football coach in a 1953 film, *Trouble along the Way,* in which the line was uttered. A 1955 *Sports Illustrated* article attributed the quote to Red Sanders. The 1961 San Diego Chargers yearbook fastened the line to head coach Sid Gillman. None of this matters, though. Vince Lombardi will forever be linked to the quote because he did not merely spew it, he seemed to live it.

The slogan is less impressive and not as profound as one might first suspect. Does it suggest that winning is the only value in sports? That winning by any means necessary is recommended? That only if a team wins can it gain anything? That the only reason to participate in sports is to seize victory? Under any of these interpretations, the adage is incontestably false.

Lombardi's Seven Blocks of Granite

Only by understanding Lombardi's deeper philosophy of winning, depicted in seven themes, or seven conceptual blocks of granite, can we appreciate the substance of "Winning isn't everything, it's the only thing."[2]

1. *The meaning of football:* The contest is inherently violent and demands 100 percent determination and resolve. Victors are rewarded with full elation and fun. The game requires sacrifice, self-denial, dedication, and courage. Football transcends social and racial barriers. To renege on the physicality, commitment, virtues, or universality of football is to misconstrue its meaning and to compete inadequately.

2. *The value of competition:* The test of competition spurs the pursuit of personal excellence. Only through competition can we maximize our higher capabilities. We must conquer ourselves before we can master others, and competitive contexts are exercises in self-discovery and self-mastery.

3. *The pursuit of perfection:* Winning is only part of the quest. The

greater ideal is actualizing our talents to their fullest. Victory can often be seized by falling short of this ideal. But it is our pursuit of perfection that vivifies our character: "The spirit, the will to excel, the will to win, they endure, they last forever. These are the qualities that are larger and more important than any of the events that occasion them."[3]

4. *A conviction that individual freedom has turned to wrongful license:* Sensing social change in the 1960s, Lombardi suspected the centuries-old struggle against dogmatism, authoritarianism, and tradition had gone too far. The relentless rise of individual freedom had undermined rightful authority in the family, salutary discipline in education, and codes of decency in conduct. The result would be impending chaos instead of unambiguous social progress.

5. *The value of discipline:* Social unrest is in large part a reaction to ineffective leadership: "While most [people] shout to be independent, [they] at the same time wish to be dependent, and while most shout to assert themselves, [they] at the same time wish to be told what to do."[4] Strong leaders must emerge if the value of freedom is not to disintegrate into wrongful license.

6. *The belief that leaders are made, not born:* Hard work, the ground of all worthwhile attainments, is critical to leadership. A balance must be struck between love and mental toughness. The toughness—sacrifice, self-denial, dedication, and fearlessness—is typically the easier part of the equation. Love flows from the bonding of teammates: "The love I'm speaking of is loyalty. . . . Teamwork, the love one man has for another and that he respects the dignity of another. The love that I'm speaking of is charity. . . . [A leader] must walk a tightrope between the consent he must win and the control he must exert."[5]

7. *The primacy of character and strong will:* The strong will is character in action. Our pursuit of victory and desired goals reflects and sustains our characters: "While it is true the difference between men is in energy, in the strong will, in the settled purpose, and in the invincible determination, the new leadership is in sacrifice, it is in self-denial, it is in love and loyalty, it is in fearlessness, it is in humility, and it is in the perfectly disciplined will. This is the distinction between great and little men."[6]

At first blush, the line is fine between Lombardi's credo taken as an inspiring call for glorious self-creation and as a celebration of fascism.

The Dark Side of the Relentless Competitor: The Dangers of Winning at All Costs

Even at the professional sports level, ruthless competition and unwavering striving for victory can exact an unappealing price. Critics of zealous competitors who supposedly overemphasize the importance of winning lodge several challenges.[7]

Zealous competition is physically and mentally unhealthy.

Overly combative, impatient, hypertense strivers are more vulnerable to high blood pressure, heart attacks, and strokes. The impulse to reach and remain at the mountaintop of victory is unhealthy. For example, Bob Cousy, Hall of Fame NBA basketball player and coach, eventually came to doubt the value of the hypercompetitive life:

> As you rise to higher levels you compete against other people who are equally talented. Then you need intensity, a killer instinct that impels you to keep going the extra mile to reach a goal when others slow down or stop. . . . I had always wanted to be a success in anything I tried. In any competition I had an almost uncontrollable need to win. This killer instinct had brought me success as a player and as a coach, but it also tempted me to run over people, to break rules, to neglect my family, to neglect myself to the point where I was on the edge of physical and emotional breakdown.[8]

While this criticism of zealous competition has merit, several rejoinders are available. The pivotal modifier is "overly." If a person is ultra-competitive in all or most aspects of her life, then her susceptibility to health problems increases. But this need not be true if she is strongly, but not overly, competitive in most aspects of life, or if she is overly competitive in only one dimension of her life. Moreover, even if a person's combativeness does invite health problems that shorten her life, it does not follow that a calmer, more contented life would have been preferable. Prizing intensity, adventure, risk, boldness, and conquest over obstacles more than serenity, safety, peace, and compromise is not automatically misguided.

Those of us who are prone to hypercompetitiveness must understand the possible trade-offs and, as ever, choose under conditions of uncertainty. Whether Lombardi's roaring appetite for victory contributed to the disease that killed him is purely speculative. Even if it did, to assume that Lombardi would have been willing to pay even that price for the life he led is reasonable.

Overemphasizing winning leads us to classify participants into a few winners and many losers.

Lionizing the Super Bowl and World Series champions as ultimate winners causes us to tend to feel contemptuous toward runners-up and also-rans. We judge "winners" as excellent, valuable, and strong. We judge "losers" as weak and mediocre. The implication is that by judging athletes and teams by their accomplishments—as defined only by the outcomes of their performances—we devalue more important human attributes such as character and personality. This conclusion, though, does not follow. First, Lombardi would not so easily separate performance from character. He was thoroughly convinced that victory flowed from strong, disciplined character joined to appropriate athletic skill. He prized the pursuit of excellence, the futile but rewarding quest for perfection, over victory as such. "Winning in and of itself was not enough for him. His players knew that he was more likely to drive them mercilessly after they had played sloppily but won than when they had played hard but lost. . . . Winning wasn't everything to him, he wanted excellence."[9] Second, we should classify athletes as winners only as athletes, not as human beings. St. Louis Rams coach Dick Vermeil, for example, described Lawrence Phillips, sixth overall pick in the 1996 NFL draft, as potentially the best running back he had ever coached. As a human being, though, Phillips was coarse, insensitive, selfish, fraudulent, and loutish. He was arrested numerous times for felony assault, domestic violence, and child abuse. Third, sports fans and commentators feel contemptuous toward individual athletes or teams only if they judge that the athletes' performances, not necessarily their outcomes, are subpar. If players perform below their capabilities, if they make mental errors, if they fail to hustle, if they act out wrongly, then criticism, even temporary contempt, may follow.

But negativity does not automatically dog defeat. Sometimes defeated athletes garner as much glory as victors, or even more. Think Joe Frazier at Manila, Arturo Gatti in several battles, the Packers in the 1960 NFL championship game, or the New York Giants in the 1958 final game.

Process values—the texture and quality of the pursuit of excellence—always resonate, even in the highly competitive context of professional sports. Process values include maximization of athletic potential, the joy of participating in sport for its own sake, the experience of intense competition, and development of virtues such as discipline, focused preparation, and commitment to hard work. Process values can usually be attained independently of scoreboard results.

Relentless competition overwhelms more important values such as cooperation and, instead, sharpens predatory instincts.

Single-minded striving hones our instincts for domination and conquest while dulling our yearning for cooperation and community. We risk isolation and estrangement as paramount social bonds grow weaker.

Again, Bob Cousy's words are instructive: "Perhaps I had put too much stock in competition. If I had to do it over again, I told myself, I would look for a better balance between the competitive and noncompetitive sides of life, giving more time and attention to my family, and to . . . reading, reflecting, helping others."[10]

Whatever force this objection has in the context of individual sports is muted in team sports such as football. Cooperation, loyalty, and mutual respect and dignity were the cornerstones of Lombardi's notion of love: "You might have a guy playing next to you who maybe isn't perfect, but you've got to love him, and maybe that love would enable you to help him. And maybe you will do something more to overcome a difficult situation in football because of that love."[11] Cousy here ignores the values of teamwork and group bonding in professional athletics. Also, strongly competitive athletes need not ignore the noncompetitive aspects of life that Cousy lists. Time away from the playing field can be used for such purposes where the will to do so is firm. For example, Nick Buoniconti, Cris Collinsworth, and Alan Page are among numerous NFL players who earned law degrees during their off-seasons.

Focusing only on winning supports an "ends justify the means" mentality.

When outcomes become paramount, athletes rationalize their use of underhanded means. Breaking the rules of competition, through use of performance-enhancing drugs or outlawed methods of gaining an edge, is spun as gamesmanship. Paying student-athletes to enroll or remain in an institution of higher learning, in violation of NCAA rules, is packaged as humanitarian aid to the disenfranchised. As long as athletic success follows and the chicanery remains undetected, contentment reigns.

This is, of course, a legitimate concern, because so many moral transgressions pervade the relentless crusade for victory. But this results only when process values are completely cast aside, when victory becomes an end in itself. Certainly, Vince Lombardi's philosophy of winning did not approach that point. David Maraniss writes: "There was a crucial distinction in his philosophy between paying the price to win and winning at any price. [Lombardi] did not believe in cheating to win, and he showed no interest in winning the wrong way, without heart, brains, and sportsmanship. . . . Winning in and of itself was not enough for him."[12]

Relentless competition nurtures a "crush the opposition" mentality and ignores the deeper value of athletic contests.

Opponents may be viewed as mere obstacles to be overcome, as objects to be used for our purposes, as pesky intruders trying to frustrate our ends. Worse, such an attitude can corrupt the better angels of our nature. Again, Cousy warns us: "I'm no longer so proud of the killer instinct. It may be a drive that makes a superstar in sports, sells a product or wins a war. But it can do more than blow away an opponent. It can kill the moral sense, the happiness of a family, even the man himself."[13]

With most human beings, our worst attributes are just our best attributes exaggerated. The gregarious extrovert can become an obnoxious annoyance merely by ratcheting up the intensity of her concern. The strong, silent type can become a self-absorbed sphinx, imperious to the interests of others. The erudite professor can morph into an insufferable know-it-all. Yes, the zealous competitor can come to despise and demean opponents and become an unwitting collaborator in his own self-destruction.

But such a fall from grace was not part of the Lombardi philosophy of winning. In his biography of Lombardi, Michael O'Brien notes: "Vince honored football with his sportsmanship, which was one reason his peers admired him. When he lost, he seldom offered excuses or alibis. He complimented the opposition and often praised his own players. Usually when a coach excelled for long in sports there were insinuations that he engaged in unsportsmanlike practices. Losers drop hints or spread suspicions. But none of his peers questioned Vince's conduct. No one said that he had been dishonorable or unethical. Moreover, for him to win any other way than fairly would take all the pleasure out of his victory."[14]

Sports promote numerous excellences beyond victory on the scoreboard: physical skill, strength, discipline, self-sacrifice, effort, maximization of potential, strategy, intelligence, judgment, craftiness, understanding, perseverance, resilience, and the like. Having worthy opponents is necessary for the righteous challenges that form the context for attaining these excellences. Muhammad Ali could not have been the prizefighter that he was without Joe Frazier. Tony Zale would have been the obscurest of middleweight champs without Rocky Graziano. The shining playoff comeback of the Boston Red Sox in 2004 would not have been the same without the New York Yankees. The Packers' Ice Bowl triumph in 1967 required the gallant Dallas Cowboys for its luster. Lombardi never lost sight of the truth that the pursuit of excellence and the glory of competitive success require worthy, respected opponents.

The values of the unyielding striver mirror and sustain the worst excesses of capitalism.

From a Marxist standpoint, sports are part of the ideological superstructure—the ideas, understandings, and practices that strongly structure how we perceive and act in the world. Capitalist economics has needs that are promoted by sports that are organized in certain ways and that promote values of certain sorts. Critics claim that competitive sports support patriarchy, authoritarian and hierarchical organization, the performance principle, and meritocracy; overemphasize winning; and train participants to accept the prevailing social structure and their fate as future workers within advanced capitalist enterprise.[15] If correct, sports perform important ideological functions in service of capitalist economics. From a Marxist standpoint, the same can be said of every major socializing force in our society: family, schools, religion, and the media.

Much depends on how a person views the dominant social order. If we strongly favor advanced capitalist economics and the ideology that supports it, we may well celebrate their supposed connection to American sports. If we advocate significant social change, including thoroughly restructuring or even eliminating capitalism, we may also prefer transforming the culture of sports.

In any case, the criticism is an important reminder that we should continually evaluate the lessons, messages, and values transmitted by sports. Sports are often fashioned in ways that correlate with patriarchal, hierarchical, authoritarian themes. But they can also nurture character traits that go beyond the needs of economic systems and honor human attributes that are worthy in themselves.

Consider the idea of taking responsibility for our choices and actions, unchaining ourselves from the false consolation of easy excuses. Maybe this is a value useful to this or that economic system. I would argue, though, that the notion of taking responsibility for one's choices and actions is valuable for its own sake and for its role in developing strong character. Some character traits are praiseworthy in every economic system.

Consider also the much-maligned Puritan work ethic. Giving a nod of respect to the likes of Cotton Mather and Miles Standish, the human need for creative labor need not be tied to religion or capitalism. Karl Marx (1818–1883), for example, criticized both capitalism and religion. Yet he insisted that human beings are fulfilled mainly through hard work and creative labor. He did not believe that we share a fixed, universal human nature. He claimed that we are neither naturally selfish nor unselfish. We do share, though, one general trait: we shape our identities and satisfy our spirits through work. Labor is a primary human activity because it is only through free and creative activity that a person realizes unalienated being, a condition in which a person maximizes her most glorious human possibilities and capabilities, because productive work is liberating, social, challenging, stimulating, and personally transformative.[16] Creative labor is done for its own sake, not merely to survive. Picture an artist, completely engaged in her work, who is fulfilled by the process of creating. She does not watch the clock, mark off the days until her next vacation, or pray for days off. She is fulfilled by hard work because she has control over what she creates, how she creates it, and what happens to her product. Work, under such conditions, is fulfilling for its own sake. My point is that the value of hard work need not be tied in with accepting the demands of advanced capitalism or the rules of religions. Hard work, under the appropriate circumstances, can be seen as worthy for its own sake and as a way of creating a meaningful, valuable life.

Friedrich Nietzsche (1844–1900), a German philosopher, also glorified unalienated labor. Nietzsche, like Marx, viewed exertion, energy, enthusiasm, and hard work as valuable. These values need not be taken merely as requirements of advanced capitalist economics or religions, but as human needs. Marx rebelled against capitalism, religion, and the dominant social ideas of his day. Nietzsche criticized democracy, egalitarianism, Judeo-Christian religion, social conformity, and much more. Yet Marx and Nietzsche celebrated character traits and activities glorified often in sports.

That sports promote the values of exertion and hard work (the "Puritan work ethic") is hardly an indictment and should not be taken as evidence that sports in our culture are closely tied to the excesses of advanced capitalism. If sports promote social conformity, blind obedience, loss of freedom, happy acceptance of absolute hierarchy, patriarchy, and the like, that is a greater concern. Values such as accountability, mutual respect, the pursuit of excellence, interrogation of the conditions of choice, initiation and pursuit of meaningful projects, joyful exertion, and intense engagement with life exude their own vitality. Their widespread acceptance outside athletics would probably facilitate material production in a capitalist system and most other economic systems. But such values are neither fully generated by nor totally dependent upon a particular economic context.

Lombardi and the Grand Transcender

Lombardi's philosophy of winning embodies the image of the grand transcender: pursuing the futile goal of excellence defined by perfection, engaged in recurrent self-discovery and self-creation, taking no goal as final, and committed to paying a heavy price for enduring values. Grand transcenders live intensely, joyfully, with great expectations, although they understand human limitations. Grand transcenders luxuriate in the immediacy of life, immerse themselves in the flow of experiences, and value the process of life for its own sake. They aspire to go beyond their past and current self-understandings to more glorious conceptions.

While I doubt that the image of the grand transcender captures the entire deep truth about human personality and that it shows the only way to a meaningful life, it highlights important insights. Human beings are not static creatures. We flourish through ongoing creative development. The image of the grand transcender, heroic and romantic, is appealing. It attracts us because it speaks to our sense of adventure, our individualism, our need to experience intensely. But we are much more than grand transcenders. Our sense of community, our needs for peace and respite, and our yearning for narrative structure are also part of human personality. Grand transcenders should also acknowledge and relish their interdependence with others and appreciate how self-identity is linked to social contexts.

In sports, grand transcenders strive heartily to improve their performance and maximize their capabilities. They understand that competing against worthy opponents and bonding with committed teammates invigorates the process and enhances the value of the sport. They intuit that athletic participation at its best can nurture grand creativity and fuel our ongoing efforts at sculpting worthy selves. They refuse to collaborate in their own defeats, make no excuses, and arise from temporary disappointments with full spirits.

Vince Lombardi was seduced by the lilt, not the substance, of "Winning isn't everything, it's the only thing." He understood acutely that many of the process values of football—maximizing potential, striving for excellence, attaining superior physical condition, nurturing mental toughness, fostering an indomitable spirit—are animated by the outcome value of victory. Only when winning is wrongly taken to be an end in itself does the dark side of zealous competition emerge and the tinny echo of fascism sound.

These are ever-present dangers, but not natural consequences, of Lombardi's perspective on winning. Incidentally, Vince Lombardi's favorite subject as an undergraduate at Fordham was philosophy.[17] No accident, this.

Notes

1. Vince Lombardi Jr., *The Essential Vince Lombardi* (New York: McGraw Hill, 2003), 5–10.

2. David Maraniss, *When Pride Still Mattered: A Life of Vince Lombardi* (New York: Simon & Schuster, 1999), 400–406.

3. Maraniss, *When Pride Still Mattered*, 402.

4. Maraniss, *When Pride Still Mattered*, 405.

5. Maraniss, *When Pride Still Mattered*, 405.

6. Maraniss, *When Pride Still Mattered*, 406.

7. Joan Hundley, "The Overemphasis on Winning," in *Philosophy of Sport*, ed. M. Andrew Holowchak (Upper Saddle River, NJ: Prentice Hall, 2002), 206–19; D. Stanley Eitzen, "The Dark Side of Competition," in Holowchak, *Philosophy of Sport*, 235–40; Torbjorn Tannsjo, "Is Our Admiration for Sports Heroes Fascistoid?" in *Ethics in Sport*, ed. William J. Morgan, Klaus V. Meier, and Angela J. Schneider (Champaign, IL: Human Kinetics, 2001), 393–408.

8. Bob Cousy, *The Killer Instinct* (New York: Random House, 1975), 4, 10–11.

9. Maraniss, *When Pride Still Mattered*, 366.

10. Cousy, *The Killer Instinct*, 204.

11. Maraniss, *When Pride Still Mattered*, 374.

12. Maraniss, *When Pride Still Mattered*, 366.

13. Cousy, *The Killer Instinct*, 211.

14. Michael O'Brien, *Vince: A Personal Biography of Vince Lombardi* (New York: William Morrow, 1987), 200.

15. George H. Sage, *Power and Ideology in American Sport* (Champaign, IL: Human Kinetics, 1990), 199–201.

16. Raymond Angelo Belliotti, *Justifying Law* (Philadelphia: Temple University Press, 1992), 145–61.

17. O'Brien, *Vince*, 39.

Jeffrey P. Fry

ON FUMBLING THE BALL

On January 6, 2007, the Dallas Cowboys appeared on the verge of defeating the defending Super Bowl champion Seattle Seahawks in a National Football League wild-card playoff game.[1] A victory by Dallas would solidify claims that the Cowboys, led by veteran coach Bill Parcells and Pro Bowl quarterback Tony Romo, were once again an NFL team to be reckoned with.

With 1:19 left in the contest, Seattle led 21–20. But Dallas had possession of the football on the Seattle 2-yard line with fourth down and one yard to go for a first down. Veteran placekicker Martin Gramatica entered the game for what should have been an easy field-goal conversion. Quarterback Tony Romo, a darling of the fans and media, who had replaced the injured Drew Bledsoe earlier in the season and had performed brilliantly as Bledsoe's replacement, positioned himself to hold the ball for the kick. It appeared that another chapter was about to be written in the history of the Dallas Cowboys.

But then, after what appeared to be a good snap of the football from the center, the unthinkable occurred. Dallas holder Romo fumbled the ball. After retrieving the football, he scrambled for the end zone, but he was tackled at the 2-yard line, short of a first down. Seattle took over possession of the ball. Seattle eventually turned the ball over to Dallas at the 50-yard line, where Romo heaved a desperate last attempt toward the end zone. The attempt was unsuccessful. Dallas had not only lost but had also been eliminated from the playoffs. In a single play the Cowboys' fortunes had suffered a dramatic reversal.[2]

Following the game, Romo was distraught. "I know how hard everyone in the locker room worked to get themselves into position to win that game today and for it to end like that, and for me to be the cause is very tough to swallow right now," he said. "I take responsibility for messing up at the end there. That's my fault. I cost the Dallas Cowboys a playoff win, and that's going to sit with me a long time." Romo added, "I don't know if I have ever felt this low."[3]

Whether Romo actually should have shouldered so much responsibility for the Dallas loss is open to debate. But of the numerous ways that one may become the "goat" of a game of football, fumbling the ball is surely one of the most poignant. When the ball is in your hands and all eyes are trained on you, a fumble frequently results not only in a lost opportunity but also in a significant loss of momentum. The fumble is a mistake that can be very costly to the team as a whole.[4]

That being said, in this chapter I want to highlight the fact that not all fumbles are alike. There are numerous contributing causes of fumbles. There are also various outcomes of fumbles, linked to different ways of responding to them. I argue that it is instructive to examine these differences, not only because of what they teach us about the game of football, but also because of how they illuminate the larger game of life. Among other things, these significant differences can teach us important lessons about contingency, responsibility, humility, courage, solidarity, redemption, and grace. In reflecting on the game of football, we may also be led to contemplate a philosophical theme that has continuing relevance as well as ancient roots: the fragility of the good life.[5]

It should not be too difficult for us to make connections between football and life. "Fumbling the ball" is a locution that has crossed over into everyday parlance. We all know what it is like, *in a symbolic sense,* to fumble the ball. Indeed, I want to claim that, due to their symbolic link with our own life experiences, sporting events such as football games have a *representative* function. They are *psychodramas* as well as athletic contests. When players and fans participate in or observe sporting events such as football games, they are not simply in a state of forgetfulness about their lives. Instead, they bring with them an awareness of their own histories. This backdrop of meaning adds poignancy to the events on the playing fields. At the same time, sporting events can illuminate our own lives.

This interplay between sport and life in our imaginations is illustrated in a novel entitled *Number 6 Fumbles,* by Rachel Solar-Tuttle. As the book opens, college coed Rebecca Lowe is attending a football game between her own University of Pennsylvania and Ivy League foe Cornell.

> It's the Penn/Cornell game and we're sitting above the fifty-yard line up on the second tier with all the Sigma Chi brothers and everyone has their screwdrivers in their Hood orange-juice containers as usual and it's cold. This one player, Number 6, fumbles the ball, and I see it tumble on the field like a dropped baby and I hear the blur of the announcer and the Sigma Chi guys getting up and slapping their thighs and swearing, but what I feel is not anger but sadness, I mean, thinking of this guy who fumbled. Were his parents watching him today? Will his girlfriend comfort him tonight? Will he try to work a calculus problem and keep thinking back to this moment?[6]

Rebecca's thoughts then turn to her telephone conversation with her mother that morning. Her mother had called into question Rebecca's savvy in scholarly matters. The conversation had lasted a mere five minutes, but when it ended, Rebecca was exhausted and let out a scream. Rebecca continues: "Thinking about this and about Number 6 fumbling the ball suddenly makes me feel some generic negative way I can't quite pin down, except to show that I need to be somewhere else."[7] In the course of the book it becomes clear that the author of *Number 6 Fumbles* connects Rebecca's negative feelings to her fears that the fumble on the football field might become an apt symbol for her own life. In reciprocal fashion, Rebecca's sense of her own life also clearly colors her sympathetic response to player number 6. Rebecca's reactions display her gnawing awareness of the fragility of the good life.

Rebecca's experience is surely not unique. We too can relate in some way to the player on the field who fumbles the ball. We know that we too are capable of fumbling the ball. Indeed, *we have all fumbled the ball,* and we have faced the sometimes painful, sometimes comical consequences. Sometimes our fumbles are public events, and we feel the weight of public censure. At times we have also known what it is like to experience redemption, through our own efforts, through luck, and through something like acts of grace.[8]

In part 1 of this chapter I examine further the significance, literal and symbolic, of fumbling the ball and outline some of the contributing factors to fumbles. I locate these factors in the game of football and then discuss their analogues in the game of life. While I cannot offer an exhaustive list of such factors in either football or life in general, I hope that by discussing a range of such factors I can make a convincing case for the need for discrimination in our responses to fumbling the ball, whether as fumblers or as observers. In part 2, I discuss some possible outcomes and responses to fumbling the ball, both on and off the playing field.

Part 1: Fumbling the Ball

Hard Knocks

In the novel *Number 6 Fumbles,* few details are given about the causes of the fumble. The text merely says that number 6 fumbled the ball. This leaves the cause of the fumble open to speculation. We are told that some of the fans reacted in anger; later, when Rebecca meets number 6, he acknowledges that he made a mistake.[9]

But not all fumbles are alike. Surely football players can be *more or less* culpable for fumbling the ball. As a result, our responses should be discriminating and measured. For example, when a ball carrier is blindsided by a defensive player who attempts to strip the ball away while two other tacklers are hanging on to him, or when a receiver has caught a pass a moment before being crunched between two bone-jarring tacklers, holding on to the ball could be considered an act of athletic supererogation—an act above and beyond the call of duty.

While it is true that in a sense the fumbler is responsible for fumbling the ball in such cases, we ought not to hold him responsible in the same way that we would in different circumstances. Perhaps the opposing team recovers the football and the fumble becomes a very costly mistake. Still, we may have some sympathy for the offensive player who fumbles the ball in circumstances such as I have described. There are mitigating, exculpatory factors at play. The player has taken reasonable precautions against fumbling, but in spite of this, the hard blows have knocked the ball free. Bone-jarring tackles or strategic maneuvers by the defense are in the realm of contingencies over which one has little or no control. In such cases the fumble is attributable at least as much to the skill of the tackler(s) and to physics as to culpability on the part of the fumbler.

Often in life we find that "the ball is in our hands." On many occasions, we are entrusted with opportunities and responsibilities that affect our own and others' lives in more or less significant ways. As a result, we may feel (and others may concur) that at times we have dropped the ball and in doing so have let others down. As a result, our self-concept and our sense of well-being may be shaken. But there may have been contingent factors at play over which we had little control that should mitigate harsh assessments of blame.

Imagine a father who works hard on a construction site to help support his family. There is an announcement that there will be cutbacks at the job site. On the day that cutbacks are announced, the father receives a pink slip. The father has been responsible in the performance of his job-related duties. He has shown up for work on time and worked diligently and skillfully. He did need two weeks off at one point because of a back injury, which he had incurred on the job site. As a result, his bosses are concerned that he is injury prone and thus conclude that he is expendable.

The father feels that he has let his family down. He has "dropped the ball." He engages in self-recriminations. If only he had worked harder, or longer, or had not been injured, he might have retained his job. We can understand this response. At the same time we would want him to realize, after the initial shock has worn off, that there were mitigating factors that call for compassion. He had worked hard. He was not culpable for the injury he had sustained. A number of jobs were going to be cut in any case. He had experienced a bad break, or one of the "hard knocks" of life. Perhaps he was even treated unjustly.

Of course, an important issue remains in play. What will the father do now in an attempt to *recover*? As I will show later, there can be a variety of responses at this point, some of which involve expressions of solidarity from other individuals. In some cases help comes from unlikely sources. For the moment, however, I turn to another factor that is often implicated in fumbling the ball: a breakdown in communication.

A Failure to Communicate

Sometimes the responsibility for fumbling the ball in football is justly allocated among a number of individuals. A primary example of this occurs where miscommunication results in a fumble. For example, lack of clear communication may foul up a snap from the center. While at times the fault may lie principally with one individual, on some occasions it seems plausible to attribute shared responsibility to the center and the quarterback. If there is sloppiness in executing the snap from the center owing to miscommunication, this may be attributable to a failure to pay attention or distractedness, weariness, nervousness, or other factors, perhaps compounded by the noise of the fans. Both the quarterback and the center may contribute to the confusion. In some cases, we may even call into question *who* has actually fumbled the ball. Again, unless we hold unrealistic expectations of perfection from athletes, we may feel some sympathy for these all-too-human foibles. This example also calls attention to the importance in football of focus, concentration, and attention to detail.

As human beings, we exist in a web of connections with other people. As a result of this interdependence, good communication and mutual understanding play important roles in the quality of our relationships and in our own happiness. It comes as no surprise, then, that miscommunication is frequently implicated in fumbling the ball in our daily lives. As in the game of football, the background noise (both literal and figurative) of bustling life in the twenty-first century can complicate matters.

Picture the following. A mother and father are speaking with each other over a cell phone. The topic of the conversation is who is to pick up Johnny from Pop Warner football practice and at what time, and who will be responsible for picking up Angela from her soccer game. Both mother and father are distracted at the time of the conversation. The mother is driving nervously in heavy traffic en route to a meeting with her boss and a discussion about a possible promotion. The father is standing in line in a hot and crowded grocery store with pushy patrons who seem to be about to break out into a wrestling match. In the confusion, each parent understands that the other has agreed to pick up Angela. As a result, both fumble the ball, and after a lengthy wait, Angela winds up having to get a ride home from her soccer coach.

This is not to say that one should have no empathy for the parents' plight in cases such as this. Parents, in particular, will understand such scenarios. But as in the game of football, so too in the game of life, playing well requires concentration and attentiveness.

These cases illustrate how easy it is to fumble the ball. Indeed, some people, in football or in life, seem to have a propensity to fumble.[10] But in some cases there are clearer signs of personal culpability and even self-destruction than in others.

Taking Care of the Ball

During Super Bowl XXVII, Dallas Cowboys defensive lineman Leon Lett recovered a fumble and appeared to be on his way to running the ball in for a touchdown. But instead of simply charging into the end zone, Lett actually *slowed down* and taunted the Buffalo Bills' Don Beebe with the ball. As a result, Beebe was able to knock the ball out of Lett's hands. Dallas still won the game but lost opportunities to set records for most points and biggest victory margin in a Super Bowl game.[11]

In a case like this we have reason to be less sympathetic to the fumbler. Having just recovered a fumble himself, Lett had not, with due humility, taken note of how easily and quickly one's fortunes can be reversed. This incident is an example of poor sportsmanship encompassing a kind of nonchalance that led to fumbling the ball. It is perhaps at times when things seem easy enough—after, as in the case of Leon Lett, the ball seems to fall into our hands—that we need to be vigilant against complacency, lest we fumble the ball.

This example also has analogues in the realm of human relationships. For example, when a marriage or relationship with a significant other becomes "old hat," it becomes all too easy to take a partner for granted. The stale routines with which one becomes comfortable replace the attentiveness that a thriving relationship requires. Complacency sets in. The relationship is permeated with a kind of *carelessness*. One forgets an anniversary or other significant marker of the relationship. Common courtesies and simple acts of kindness are abandoned. In these and other ways one fumbles the ball. Then, sadly, one is blindsided (though in fact the results could have been foreseen) when a partner announces his or her lack of fulfillment or, worse yet, an intent to leave the relationship. In such cases, the road to recovery from carelessness may be long and difficult.

The philosopher Harry G. Frankfurt claims that what we care about reveals much about who we are. Frankfurt writes: "A person who cares about something is guided, as his attitudes and actions are shaped, by his continuing interest in it. Insofar as he does care about certain things, this determines how he thinks it important to conduct his life. The totality of the various things that a person cares about—together with his ordering of how important to him they are—effectively specifies his answer to the question of how to live."[12] In other words, what we care about determines how we play the game of life.[13] As will now become apparent, failure to play well until the end of the game may be consequential.

Hanging On in the Second Half

Finally, think about fumbling the ball when your legacy is at stake. Put yourself in the shoes of Jerome Bettis of the Pittsburgh Steelers during an NFL playoff game against the Indianapolis Colts in 2006. After a stellar career as a running back, Bettis was playing in what might well have been his last game as a professional football player. With just over a minute to go in the game, and with the Steelers leading the Colts by three points and seemingly about to put the game out of reach, Bettis fumbled the football at the Indianapolis 2-yard line. The Colts' Nick Harper recovered the ball and headed for the opposite end zone and glory. But Pittsburgh averted a touchdown and a probable loss of the game when quarterback Ben Roethlisberger made an *improbable* open-field tackle.[14] Having been rescued from the brink of disaster, the Steelers then went on to win the Super Bowl.

The ancient Greek philosopher Aristotle (384–322 B.C.) was keenly aware of the way contingencies can impinge on our lives. As a result, he pondered whether one can truly pronounce an individual happy before the individual's life is complete.[15] I want to suggest that there are myriad ways that individuals can fumble the ball even in the mature stages of life and thereby alter the quality of their lives.

Think of the seasoned politician who, at the peak of her career and facing retirement, succumbs to a lobbyist's offer of payment for "special" considerations. Or consider the middle-aged man who, in a midlife crisis, engages in a sexual indiscretion that threatens to destroy a long-standing relationship. Or think of the alcoholic who, after years of sobriety, relapses under stressful conditions. Occasions for fumbling the ball—tailor-made to our personal circumstances—are present throughout our lives, and sometimes the associated costs are high.

I have outlined only a few parallels between fumbling on the football field and fumbling the ball in the game of life. To be sure, many other parallels could be drawn. When, in *Number 6 Fumbles*, Rebecca Lowe reacts to the misfortunes of number 6, she responds from a sense of her own life spiraling out of control and her fears of failure and humiliation.

The legendary football coach John Heisman, in whose name the Heisman trophy is awarded each year to the outstanding Division I-A college football player, reportedly said, "Gentlemen, it is better to have died as a small boy than to fumble this football."[16] While these sentiments are hyperbolic, fumbles do have consequences, both on the playing field and in the game of life. This raises a critical question. What happens after we fumble the ball? Indeed, what transpires after the fumble is revelatory and may be as important as, if not more than, the actual fumble. We may find ourselves spiraling downward into yet further complications. Or paths to redemption may open up.

Part 2: Recovering (from) a Fumble

Picking Up the Ball

The typical, almost instinctive, reaction to fumbling the football is to make an attempt to recover the ball. Were no such attempt made, we would hold the fumbler doubly accountable. We want to see the fumbler make an effort to redeem himself and reverse the team's ill fortune. In the case discussed at the beginning of this chapter, Tony Romo recovered his own fumble. He then found himself in a do-or-die situation, and he scrambled toward the end zone. But although he had recovered the football and then attempted to redeem himself, he was unable to atone for his mistake. He did receive another chance at the end of the game, but he was unable to prevail against the long odds. In the short term, all that Romo could do was to acknowledge his responsibility and express his regret.

Sometimes, however, fumbles have happier endings. One may recover one's own fumble and, in doing so, advance the football. This is most likely to occur when, instead of giving up on the play, one puts forth a second effort in an attempt to redeem oneself.

So too in life when we fumble the ball, we are presented with a choice. This choice represents both a test of our character and a revelation of it. We may seek to redeem ourselves in light of what we have learned from our mistakes. Or we may do things that compound our mistakes. We can also choose to do nothing. If we attempt to make amends in light of what we have learned from our mistakes, a process of redemption has already begun. If we repeat or compound our mistakes, we show that we have not learned from our previous errors. If we stand idly by, we depend on the labors of others or on luck.

Lucky Bounces

In the topsy-turvy world of football, sometimes the fumbler receives aid from the most unlikely of places. In October 1964, in a game against the Minnesota Vikings, the San Francisco 49ers fumbled the ball. The Vikings' Jim Marshall recovered the fumble and ran sixty-six yards into the end zone. Unfortunately for Marshall, he had run in the wrong direction and thus into the wrong end zone. Thinking he had scored a touchdown, he celebrated by throwing the ball away. This resulted in a San Francisco safety. Fortunately for Marshall, the Vikings won the game in spite of his malfunctioning inner compass.[17] But at the time of the fumble, the San Francisco 49ers experienced what is expressed in German by the phrase *Glück im Unglück* ("luck in bad luck").

So too in life we are at times aided by an undeserved bit of luck that covers our blunders. This is illustrated by what philosophers call "moral luck."[18] "Moral luck" refers to various kinds of factors that individuals do not control but that nevertheless influence our moral assessments of these individuals. One kind of moral luck pertains to the circumstances in which one finds oneself. Thomas Nagel has us consider a truck driver who negligently fails to have his brakes checked. He then runs over a child in a situation in which his negligence is a contributing factor. He has fumbled the ball. But note that the driver has no control over whether the child runs across his path. Had the child not done so, the driver would still be negligent; we could still say that in some sense he had fumbled the ball. Yet by sheer circumstantial luck the driver's life would not be altered forever.[19]

Saved by Grace

Fumbling the ball is sometimes redeemed through our own effort. Luck also plays a role in covering our sins. But sometimes a path to redemption requires an act of grace—a gift bestowed at just the right moment—to which the appropriate response is one of thanks. When Jerome Bettis fumbled the ball at the 2-yard line against the Indianapolis Colts and the

Colts' Nick Harper streaked toward the opposite end zone, Bettis was redeemed by the improbable tackle made by the Steelers' quarterback, Ben Roethlisberger. It was in some respects an act of grace. To be sure, the analogy is imperfect. It is true that we would have expected Roethlisberger to make the effort. A good teammate would do so. But the point is that Bettis did not redeem himself for his own mistake. Rather, because of his teammate's effort, the Steelers advanced in the playoffs and Bettis concluded his career with a happy, storybook ending.

In the game of life, recovery after fumbling the ball is often aided by an act of grace. Redemption may involve an act of forgiveness by a significant other. It may be aided by a word of encouragement from a friend or counselor. It may come as a gracious act of timely intervention by a member of a support group. In myriad ways recovery and redemption depend on, and sometimes require, gracious acts. Those who have family, friends, acquaintances, and even strangers who help redeem their mistakes would do well to consider themselves blessed. Finally, but not least of all, whether on the football field or in the game of life, those who are graced with the ability to forgive themselves have inner resources to help them come to terms with fumbling the ball.

Conclusion: Mercy for Fumblers

In the book *Number 6 Fumbles,* Rebecca is fraught with anxiety over the prospects of fumbling the ball. But as we have seen, one can take steps to help prevent a fumble. When we do fumble the ball, both in football and in the game of life, there are also roads to recovery. Through our own efforts, through luck, and through acts of grace, paths to redemption open up. Even then the rest of our life's adventure looms before us, but we can carry with us the lessons of the past.

In the game of football, the rules enshrine some leniency to those who fumble the ball. According to the rules, the ground cannot cause a fumble. Some mercy is thus provided for a player who is brought down despite his efforts. Beyond that, piling on is prohibited. Perhaps there are lessons here too for the game of life. We have all fumbled the ball, and thus we are all at times in need of mercy. Given that this is the case, it is fitting that we extend this mercy to others in a spirit of humility.

Notes

1. See "Romo's Botched Hold Grounds Cowboys, Lifts Seahawks," ESPN.com, http://sports.espn.go.com/nfl/recap?gameId=270106026. Accessed 25 June 2007.

2. It is difficult to resist speculating about the ramifications of the Dallas loss. Had Romo fielded the ball cleanly, would Gramatica have successfully kicked the field goal? Would Dallas then have gone on to win the game (and perhaps further games in the playoffs)? Had Dallas defeated Seattle, would Bill Parcells still have resigned at the end of the season? "For want of a nail . . . "

3. "Romo's Botched Hold."

4. The qualification of the statement is necessary since a fumble sometimes results in a net gain of yardage. There are also intentional uses of the fumble. Rule changes have reportedly curtailed this play, but in a game between the Oakland Raiders and the San Diego Chargers in 1978, quarterback Ken Stabler of the Raiders apparently intentionally fumbled the ball forward. It was eventually batted into the end zone, where the Raiders recovered it for a touchdown. The play has been referred to as the "Immaculate Deception." During the 1984 Orange Bowl, on a play known as the "Fumblerooski," Nebraska's All-American guard Dean Steinkuhler scored a touchdown on a play that involved a fake fumble. See "Fumble," Wikipedia.org, 25 May 2007, http://en.wikipedia.org/wiki/Fumble. Accessed 6 June 2007.

5. See Martha C. Nussbaum, *The Fragility of Goodness: Luck and Ethics in Greek Tragedy and Philosophy* (Cambridge: Cambridge University Press, 1986). . See also Jeffrey P. Fry, "Sports and 'the Fragility of Goodness,'" *Journal of the Philosophy of Sport* 31 (2004): 34–46.

6. Rachel Solar-Tuttle, *Number 6 Fumbles* (New York: Pocket Books, 2002), 2.

7. Solar-Tuttle, *Number 6 Fumbles*, 2–3.

8. For a treatment of some similar themes related to sports in general and life, see Jeffrey P. Fry, "Sports and Human Redemption," *Contemporary Philosophy* 26, nos. 3 & 4 (2004): 50–57.

9. Solar-Tuttle, *Number 6 Fumbles*, 218–23.

10. Quarterback Warren Moon fumbled an NFL-leading 161 times during his career. But there is an upside to this story. He recovered fifty-six fumbles, which is also a league best. See "Records & Factbook. Individual Records: Fumbles," NFL.com, http://www.nfl.com/history/randf/records/indiv/fumbles. Accessed 26 June 2007.

11. See "Top 10 Embarrassing Performances," *Winnipeg Sun*, 3 December 2006. Available at winnipegsun.com.

12. Harry G. Frankfurt, *The Reasons of Love* (Princeton, NJ: Princeton University Press, 2004), 23.

13. For an approach to ethics that has caring as the centerpiece, see Nel Noddings, *Caring: A Feminine Approach to Ethics & Moral Education* (Berkeley: University of California Press, 1984).

14. For details of the fumble by Bettis, see Ed Bouchette, "Steelers/NFL: Bettis' Mom Sought Divine Help after the Fumble," *Pittsburgh Post-Gazette,* 19 January 2006. Available at http://www.post-gazette.com.

Pittsburgh fan Terry O'Neill had a heart attack just after Bettis fumbled the ball while O'Neill watched the game from a Pittsburgh bar. O'Neill stated: "I was upset because I didn't want to see him end his career like that. A guy like that deserves better. I guess it was a little too much for me to handle." See "Fan Had Heart Attack Seconds after Bettis Fumble," ESPN.com, 17 January 2006, http://sports.espn.go.com/nfl/news/story?id=2295603. Accessed 6 June 2007.

15. See Aristotle, *The Nicomachean Ethics,* Oxford World's Classics, trans. David Ross, rev. J. L. Ackrill and J. O. Urmson ([1925] Oxford: Oxford University Press, 1980), 11–23.

16. See John Rolfe, "Magic Words: These Quotes Will Always Stay with Me," SI.com, 2 August 2005, http://sportsillustrated.cnn.com.

17. See "Jim Marshall (American Football)," Wikipedia.org, 19 May 2007, http://en.wikipedia.org/wiki/Jim_Marshall_(American_football). Accessed 6 June 2007.

18. See, e.g., Daniel Stedman, ed., *Moral Luck* (Albany: State University of New York Press, 1993).

19. See Thomas Nagel, "Moral Luck," in Stedman, *Moral Luck,* 57–71, esp. 59, 61.

Daniel B. Gallagher

FOOTBALL AND ARISTOTLE'S PHILOSOPHY OF FRIENDSHIP

After his induction into the Pro Football Hall of Fame in 1990, running back Franco Harris explained one of his team's secrets to winning four NFL championship rings during the powerful reign of the Pittsburgh Steelers in the 1970s. "Halfway through the decade," he said with a smile, "we realized that we had a great team and that we could do great things." So how did they bring that potential to reality? "We said to our-selves, 'let's make sure that we do enjoy these moments and let's try to share as many things as we can together.' And we did. We just did a lot of things together as a team off the field and we really shared a lot of special moments off the field just as much as on the field."[1]

Friendship. It was a key factor in building one of the greatest dynas-ties professional football has ever seen. It was also a key component in Aristotle's (384–322 B.C.) elaborate and enduring ethical philosophy. The Steelers had talented individuals, a competent coaching staff, and dedi-cated management, but they never would have racked up the wins if it had not been for the bond of friendship. Aristotle would hardly have been surprised at this. Though he had never laid eyes on a pigskin, the sage from Stagira predicted exactly the attitude that would thrust the Steelers out of mediocrity in the 1960s and into four Super Bowls during the 1970s. Aristotle could have practically written Franco Harris's script: "Since they wish to live with their friends, they do and share in those things which give them the sense of living together."[2]

But we must not to be too syrupy about friendship—or football, for that matter. Aristotle knew well the imperfections of friendship and its limited role in living a happy life. Indeed, as Terry Bradshaw reveals in his autobiography, there were plenty of tense relationships between players, coaches, and management that the Terrible Towels kept covered only for so long.[3] Aristotle was astute to observe that "doing," "sharing," and "living" together means more than going out for a postgame beer and an off-season round of golf. Some of the best teams were composed of players who spent little time with one another beyond the interminable summer-camp sessions and coast-to-coast air travel. Aristotle's notion of friendship was much broader and deeper than the one we hold today. A taxonomist by training, this student of Plato was a master of distinctions. In books 8 and 9 of his *Nicomachean Ethics,* he attempts to delineate and describe the many ways in which humans relate to one another as friends. To appreciate what football can teach us about friendship, and what friendship can teach us about football, we'll have to take a closer look at both.

Aristotle's Approach to Friendship

Today, we tend to think of "friends" only as those with whom we pass our spare time. However, Aristotle had in mind everybody to whom we relate on a day-to-day basis with some regularity and with some degree of dependency or intimacy: husbands, wives, parents, children, neighbors, business partners, bowling-league buddies, and fellow Democrats or Republicans (whatever the case may be). Broadly speaking, we relate to such people through *philia* (the Greek word for "friendship" or "love"), which is the natural affinity moving us to enter into a life of community. Aristotle believed that the need for philia in a happy life is so obvious that no argument is needed to justify it. "For without friends, no one would choose to live, though he had all other goods."[4]

We must also keep in mind that the verb "to love" *(philein)* had a much broader connotation in ancient Greece than it does today. Philein is the action one performs toward a friend regardless of the type of philia involved. Whereas today we limit the use of "love" to romantic and familial relations, Aristotle would not have hesitated to apply it to coworkers, gas-station attendants, and hotel receptionists. Similarly, according to Aristotle's broad meaning, every player on a football team needs to "love" his teammates and coaches even if, deep down, he really does not "like" them. Quite frankly, football would not exist without philia. It takes eleven men (or at least two in the case of backyard ball) to field a team. At the very least, each of the members shares a love for the sport and a willingness to associate with others who have the same love.

We can think of it this way: With a bit of training (okay . . . with a whole lot of training), I could run the Boston Marathon or swim the English Channel by myself. Alone on the gridiron, I can't do much more than run a few wind sprints (if that). You need only one opponent to play a set of tennis or a game of hoops. But one-on-one football gets old fast. It was philia that gave birth to football, and the great American game still needs it today.

So just what was Aristotle's revolutionary philosophy of friendship? It was all based on a set of three fundamental categories regarding the object of love. Broadly speaking, friendship is based on utility, pleasure, a shared commitment to the good, or some combination of the three. Though there is a hierarchical ordering among these three, each contributes in its own unique way to the good life. Aristotle was convinced that "man is by nature a political animal."[5] He meant that human beings naturally need each other even before they go out of their way to seek one another's company.

QBs and Offensive Linemen: Friendship Based on the Useful

According to Aristotle, the most basic form of friendship is based on utility. It is useful and desirable for two human beings to associate with one another if each derives some benefit from the relationship. The object of love in the case of friendship based on usefulness is not the person per se but some quality, benefit, or advantage gained from the relationship. This is precisely why opposites attract.

From the point of view of usefulness, a 165-pound quarterback is naturally attracted to five 300-plus-pound offensive linemen. He finds them useful as he gazes into the eyes of the menacing defensive linemen and blitzing linebackers glaring at him across the line of scrimmage. On the other hand, friendships based on utility are short-lived. Unless he needs them to fend off swarming fans waiting outside the clubhouse, a superstar quarterback can bid farewell to his linemen as soon as the game is over. Similarly, a coach might easily replace the offensive line with five other able bodies and the quarterback would be just as happy—provided they have studied the playbook and know when to block right rather than left. More often than not, friendship based on utility seems to revolve around some element of inequality. In fact, in the *Politics,* Aristotle argues that a fair and just society must acknowledge and esteem the differences that distinguish various classes of citizens and the role they play in preserving the well-being of the state.[6] Such differences are based more on a specialization of competency than on degree. Each needs the other in order to excel.

The same could be said of a football team. A quarterback, as we've already noted, would find it very difficult to perform any of his tasks without an offensive line. But does the offensive line need the quarterback? We could imagine a rather absurd situation in which an offensive line springs into action with no quarterback behind it. The team probably would not score too many touchdowns, but the linemen would still be able to execute their blocks perfectly. From one point of view, a quarterback needs his linemen more than they need him (i.e., to keep from getting sacked), but from another point of view, the linemen need the quarterback more than he needs them (i.e., to advance the ball up the field). In Aristotle's words, they "do not love each other for themselves but in virtue of some good which they get from each other."[7]

We can contrast the relationship between a quarterback and his linemen with that between a quarterback and his receivers. Does a quarterback need them? If he is going to pass, yes. But does he really *need* to pass? If you put a running back like Barry Sanders together with an all-pro line, probably not much. After all, college football had been in existence for over forty years before a rules committee finally authorized the use of the forward pass in 1912 (to spice things up, of course) and saved the game from imminent extinction. Does a receiver need his quarterback? If we assume that the quarterback is the primary passer, and that what the "receiver" receives is a football in flight, then yes. On one level, there is a disproportionate need between the quarterback and his receiver. On another level, there is perfect reciprocity between them (i.e., a quarterback needs someone to throw the ball to).

These examples help us to see how Aristotle perceived characteristics of both equality and inequality in friendships based on utility. Every unequal friendship still needs reciprocity. There is usually about a 150-

pound difference between a quarterback and an offensive tackle, yet due to a certain proportion between them, their friendship remains intact. "Each party neither gets the same from the other, nor ought to seek it."[8] Whereas the quarterback can nail a receiver in the numbers from thirty yards out, a lineman can bench three hundred pounds thirty times. The great chasm separating their respective talents and abilities is precisely the thing that establishes the proportion upon which their friendship is based. "For when the love is in proportion to the merit of the parties, then in a sense arises equality."[9]

Friday Night Lights: Friendship Based on the Pleasurable

Aristotle's second basic category of friendship is based on pleasure. As every thirty-second Sunday commercial spot reminds us—whether it be for cars, beer, or Caribbean cruises—football is all about pleasure. Aristotle associates pleasure-based friendships primarily with the young, "for they live under the guidance of emotion, and pursue what is pleasant to themselves and what is immediately before them."[10] High school players look forward to the thrill of another Friday night and one more chance to win. College football rides on the pleasures of tradition and fraternity.

Yet once again, good philosophy and good football both need a good dose of sobriety. As any rookie will tell you, everything changes in the big leagues. Youthful pleasures quickly fade into the grueling routine of mature adulthood.

"It was a different ball game," Terry Bradshaw writes of his rookie season. "The game had always come so easily to me that I had never studied it."[11] Bradshaw consequently spent much of his first season in the Steel City on his butt, either because he had been sacked or because he was on the bench. Bradshaw is one of countless rookies who struggled through the transition from the simple pleasures of high school and college ball to the serious business of the big leagues. "It doesn't matter how good you are or what your loyalty is to a team," explains Jerry Rice. "Professional football is a business and you will get replaced. It was a business back when I broke in and it has grown tenfold since."[12]

Aristotle explains that with increasing age, the pleasures of friendship mature. At the professional level, players are happy if they can find just a few close friends who can understand them and whom they can understand. One takes great pleasure in getting mobbed by his teammates after the big score against the crosstown high school rival. But in the pros, one is more likely to take pleasure in finding an agent he can trust.

Schembechler and Carter: Friendship Based on a Shared Love of the Good

The third and highest form of friendship can be formed when two people discover in each other a similar goodness that motivates them to imitate one another as closely as possible. "For these wish well alike to each other *qua* good, and they are good in themselves."[13] In such a friendship, one does not love the other solely on account of a useful quality or the sense of pleasure he derives from the other, but rather because he recognizes that what his friend pursues, what he himself pursues, and what each of them wants to pursue for the sake of the other are *truly* good.

Interestingly, this opens the door to the importance of self-love in Aristotle's theory of friendship. In order for you to recognize what is truly good for your friend, you must already know—however imperfectly—what is truly good for yourself. Unlike the other two forms of friendship, this third form is permanent, "since there meet in it all the qualities that friends should have."[14]

Friendship based on a shared love for what is good endures long after one retires from football. Aristotle observes that such friendship is "rare" and requires "time and familiarity." Though it usually exists between two people close in age, it can also span generations and even bridge the gap between players and coaches.

Longtime University of Michigan coach Bo Schembechler speaks of wide receiver Anthony Carter in these terms. Bo, like everyone else at Michigan, was awestruck by Carter's dazzling catches and lightning-quick moves between the years of 1979 and 1982. Such feats easily won Carter many friends on the basis of usefulness and pleasure. What galvanized his enduring friendship with Coach Schembechler, however, were his virtues of humility, prudence, and deference to teammates.

Bo tells the story of how he spied Carter sitting alone in the locker room after the Wolverines' 1981 Rose Bowl victory over the Washington Huskies. "Anthony," he asked, "what are you doing in here? There's all those reporters out there. They all want to talk to you." "Coach," he answered, "they talk to me enough. If I stay in here, then they'll have to talk to some of my teammates and give them some credit."[15] Schembechler says there was no greater testimony to Carter's character. The mutual admiration between coach and player illustrates precisely the type of friendship Aristotle placed above utility and pleasure.

Aristotle also contrasts friendship based on a shared love for what is truly good with the two inferior sorts of friendship in that the former is had only by those who are truly good themselves. "For the sake of pleasure or utility, then, even bad men may be friends of each other . . . but for their own sake clearly only good men can be friends; for bad men do not delight in each other unless some advantage come to the relation."[16]

Corruption within a football franchise can be contagious. If the only shared goal is to chalk up the victories, then friendship never rises above the level of the useful or the pleasurable. But if a team strives to cultivate virtues that will shine just as brightly off the field as they do on, they will reach Aristotle's third and highest level of friendship in which friends love one another "without qualification" and "in virtue of their goodness."[17]

True Teammates: The Concord of Friendship

Aristotle speaks of "concord" as one of the fruits of friendship in the sense that two friends who love and strive after the same things tend to agree in mind and heart, so much so that they seem to be one.[18] "What is a friend?" he asks. "A single soul dwelling in two bodies."[19]

This is the way former Chicago Bear fullback Roland Harper describes the relationship both he and his successor Matt Suhey had with legendary halfback Walter Payton. "I think what made Matt and Walter such good friends was an extension of what happened between me and Walter. When you've got the right guy in front of you, there's this telepathy that goes on that connects you. He had to know which way I was going to block someone so he could set that block up and cut off it."[20] According to Aristotle, this type of concord—or "telepathy" in the words of Harper—is unique to the third type of friendship since it is not based on an exchange of one thing for another but on an affinity for the same thing.[21]

We would naturally assume that the one thing every player on a team wants is to come out ahead when the clock expires. But in order for that to happen, the players have to share many other common "loves." What separates a great coach from a good coach is the ability not only to use his players' individual talents well but also to build concord among them so they can bring out the best in each other. They all want to win, but they have to learn how to love the same things to emerge victorious.

"In my first season, I was less interested in individual performances, and more interested in building a team," explains Lou Holtz. "Teams win when everyone subjugates his own personal welfare for the benefit of the unit. A team is capable of accomplishing things that no individual can regardless of how multitalented he may be. The team player recognizes this fact, and does whatever it takes to make the team better."[22]

This might be the reason there are so many players in the Pro Football Hall of Fame and why it is so hard to select them. Of the many individual characteristics to consider, a key factor is also how well a player contributes to the overall good of the team through time.

The Love of the Game Is the Game of Love

British philosopher Bertrand Russell (1872–1970) once starkly contrasted competition in the political realm with competition on the sports field. He noted that whereas the former brings only hunger and despair to the world, the latter is the very raison d'être of athletic events. "If two hitherto rival football teams, under the influence of brotherly love, decided to co-operate in placing the football first beyond one goal and then beyond the other, no one's happiness would be increased."[23]

Russell's point is well taken, but he raises a further question. If healthy competition is the ultimate goal of sports, wouldn't it be safer to keep physical contact to a minimum? Should we not limit ourselves to baseball, basketball, soccer, and cricket? Is there room for "brotherly love"—or, to use Aristotle's terminology, philia—in a game that requires players to drag each other to the ground and permits them to slam into each other at breakneck speeds to do so? In the eyes of many, football is a violent sport. Indeed, it is. In the eyes of many, football is greedy business. Sadly, it is. But after all, it *is* still a game and not warfare. We play football and watch football to have fun, or we don't play it at all. Though it is a contact sport, it is more importantly a communal event. Before all else, it is based on friendship, not enmity. If you don't play it or watch it in that way, you probably won't play it or watch it for very long. If you play it or watch it for the sake of philia, you'll find it's almost impossible to give up.

No one knows this better than Penn State coach Joe Paterno. In the fall of 2007, he began his forty-first season at the helm of the Nittany Lions. Joe knows that friendship—indeed *love*—is at the heart of the game.

"People are surprised when I say that one of the things we talk about in a locker room is love," he writes. "I just cannot adequately describe the love that permeates a good football team." Paterno goes on to explain his team's pregame ritual of reciting the Lord's Prayer together: "To gather a team around you just before a big game . . . each one taking the hand of another on each side until every body and every soul in that room is connected, each pledging to give and to expect the best, each becoming a part of the others—if they can do it here, they will be able to do it anywhere."[24]

If only Aristotle were around to suit up.

Notes

1. Franco Harris's remarks are quoted from the Pro Football Hall of Fame Web site, http://www.profootballhof.com.

2. Aristotle, *Nicomachean Ethics,* trans. David Ross (Oxford: Oxford University Press, 1998), 246 (bk. 8, 10).

3. See Terry Bradshaw, with David Fisher, *It's Only a Game* (New York: Pocket Books, 2001).

4. Aristotle, *Nicomachean Ethics,* 192 (bk. 13, 1).

5. Aristotle, *Politics,* bk. 1, 2.

6. See Aristotle, *Politics,* bks. 5 and 6.

7. Aristotle, *Nicomachean Ethics,* 195 (bk. 8, 3).

8. Aristotle, *Nicomachean Ethics,* 203 (bk. 8, 7).

9. Aristotle, *Nicomachean Ethics,* 204 (bk. 8, 7).

10. Aristotle, *Nicomachean Ethics,* 196 (bk. 8, 3).

11. Bradshaw, *It's Only a Game,* 39–40.

12. Jerry Rice, with Brian Curtis, *Go Long! My Journey beyond the Game and the Fame* (New York: Ballantine Books, 2007), 36.

13. Aristotle, *Nicomachean Ethics,* 196 (bk. 8, 3).

14. Aristotle, *Nicomachean Ethics,* 197 (bk. 8, 3).

15. Bo Schembechler, with Mitch Albom, *Bo* (New York: Warner Books, 1989), 92–93.

16. Aristotle, *Nicomachean Ethics,* 198 (bk. 8, 4).

17. Aristotle, *Nicomachean Ethics,* 199 (bk. 8, 4).

18. See Aristotle, *Nicomachean Ethics,* 200–201 (bk. 8, 5).

19. Aristotle, *Nicomachean Ethics,* 221 (bk. 9, 1).

20. Walter Payton, with Don Yaeger, *Never Die Easy* (New York: Villard, 2000), 108.

21. See Aristotle, *Nicomachean Ethics,* 202 (bk. 8, 6).

22. Lou Holtz, *Wins, Losses, and Lessons* (New York: William Morrow, 2006), 215.

23. Bertrand Russell, *Authority and the Individual* (London: George Allen & Unwin), 72.

24. Joe Paterno, with Bernard Asbell, *By the Book* (New York: Random House, 1989), 130.

R. *Douglas Geivett*

INSIDE THE HELMET

What Do Football Players Know?

One of the great ironies of the sports world is that football players are believed to be more brawny than brainy—even though football is much more a head game than any other major team sport. You may be thinking, "Yeah, right, 'head game,' as in 'heads colliding with heads,' resulting in more concussions per capita than in baseball, basketball, or soccer . . . combined." Fair enough. Perhaps the only sport that tops football in serious head injuries is boxing, where *dementia pugilistica* is a sobering blight. But I'm talking about football as a *mental* game, where complex cognitive behavior plays a role equal to that of the size, strength, and speed of players' bodies.

Compare football with baseball. I'm an Angels fan myself. But let's face it: in baseball, mental alertness is mostly episodic. On-field players focus their acuity during that infinitesimal interval between windup and the swing of the bat. Most of the time, catching fly balls is pro forma. Ever notice the impassive nonchalance of an outfielder following a routine catch? His expression says, "I coulda' done that in my sleep." And I'm thinking, "Maybe he did." During any given play, offensive players in the dugout are sitting or standing around with their minds on who knows what. It probably isn't baseball. Baseball players set a good example for the fans at the ballpark, too. Mentally active spectators are more likely to be reading the *Wall Street Journal* or Kant's *Critique of Pure Reason* than watching the next pitch. If baseball is America's favorite pastime, it's probably because the pastoral atmosphere of the ballpark is so, well, relaxing. (Mike Scioscia, I hope you're not reading this.)[1]

What about basketball? Well, who is pro basketball's most famous fan? Did you say Jack Nicholson? I rest my case.[2]

Football is a game for thinkers, both on and off the field. There's a lot you have to know just to understand the game. But the thing is, many people don't know that. They pass the television set, see one play, and think, "I don't get it. It just looks like a bunch of guys bashing their heads together and piling on top of each other for no particular reason." It doesn't help that football icons like Vince Lombardi dole out dainty aphorisms like, "Football isn't a contact sport; it's a collision sport. Dancing is a contact sport."[3] Frank Gifford wrote in *Sports Illustrated* that "pro football is like nuclear warfare. There are no winners, only survivors."[4] There are a lot of women out there wondering, "Who wants to spend his weekend sitting in a La-Z-Boy, a Bud Lite in one hand and a bag of chips in the other, watching a nuclear war?"[5]

Novices have to understand the game. For that we have Howie Long's helpful book *Football for Dummies*.[6] The field has a mystifying arrangement of marks, obviously ordered and apparently for some purpose. At any given time there are usually twenty-two players on the field. And each team has an offensive unit of eleven players and a defensive unit of eleven other players.[7] Within each unit, individual players have specialized roles. The offensive unit includes a quarterback, a center, various running backs (halfbacks, fullbacks), guards and tackles, tight ends, and wide receivers; the defensive unit includes a nose tackle, defensive tackles, defensive ends, linebackers, cornerbacks, and safeties. Then there are the placekickers and punters. Each player has a job to do, and some have several responsibilities.

Today's game also requires seven officials who scrutinize aspects of each play and make immediate decisions about penalties, pass completions, turnovers, downs, and ball placement. These instantaneous decisions require intimate knowledge of an elaborate array of rules governing fair play.

I'm not making a serious argument that football is an intellectually superior sport. In what follows, my aim is to describe aspects of the game that illustrate a few principles from the field of epistemology. As we get under way, you need to know that epistemology is a branch of philosophy designated using the Greek word for "knowledge": *episteme*. Epistemology focuses on such issues as the nature of knowledge and the kinds of knowledge we have, sources of knowledge, and challenges to the conviction that we have knowledge.

What Do Running Backs Know?

More quarterbacks and running backs are awarded an MVP award than any other players, by a huge margin. Howie Long believes that running backs have "the toughest job on the football field." He writes, "No matter how fast an athlete is, or how big a brute he is, or how slippery or quick he is, he will not be able to play this position if he doesn't have a brain and can't think on his feet."[8] He goes on to list the sorts of things that a running back must *know:*

- The down for every play.
- The number of yards needed for a first down.
- Whether to go for a first down or coordinate a setup play.
- The time on the clock.
- When to go out of bounds to stop the clock and when to go for extra yardage.
- The defensive unit's assignments based on its lineup and individual player skills.
- The scheme planned for the quarterback's protection.
- All plays and their variations.
- Every pass route called.
- The precise distance he is to run for pass reception.
- Every hole number in the playbook, which may include between fifty and one hundred running plays.[9]

These are samples of what a running back must know. But that's not all. He must be able to act appropriately on the basis of what he knows—on every play. This is his responsibility.

Much of the knowledge a running back uses on game day is knowledge that he possesses prior to the game—plays, player stats, and so forth. But he must acquire additional knowledge as the game unfolds and be able to make immediate use of this new knowledge. The running back will acquire valuable new knowledge as offensive and defensive players settle into their positions on the line of scrimmage. He will acquire valuable new knowledge the instant the ball is snapped and all players begin to move. He will acquire valuable new knowledge if the defense reads the play the offense had planned. He will acquire valuable new knowledge as unexpected opportunities open up. All of this knowledge will be acquired in a matter of seconds and split seconds. And the running back, with precious little time to deliberate, will make use of this knowledge.

This illustrates a number of deep epistemological points. For starters, there are situations where we will not even be able to know some things if we do not first know certain other things. Our running back will not be able to make use of the data presented to him in his surrounding environment during a play if he doesn't already know the rules of the game, the playbook, his general responsibilities, the significance of various defensive line arrangements, and so on. He won't even *notice* most of the important stuff that's going on, much less be able to make sense of it.

This business of "making sense" of what is noticed is more than a matter of cognitive achievement, like understanding what is happening. It includes being prepared to move into appropriate action, given what has been noticed and apprehended. For this, what a running back knows about what's happening in the moment must be connected to what he knows should be done when that is what is happening. Since every play has unique features, he will have to combine knowledge of general principles with his new knowledge of the situation and apply all of this to act properly in a novel situation, one that never has arisen before and will never arise again.

Philosophers distinguish between factual knowledge and competence knowledge. Factual knowledge, also called "propositional knowledge," is knowledge that something is or is not the case. Competence knowledge is sometimes called "skill knowledge"; it's more a matter of knowing *how to do* something.[10]

The components of a running back's knowledge, as described above, seem to be a combination of factual and competence knowledge. And it appears that much factual knowledge is a prerequisite for competence knowledge. But there's another feature of responsible knowing that is worth considering at this point.

A person may have the knowledge required for acting appropriately in some situation but not act. The disposition to act on the basis of what one knows is different from being *in the know.* Armchair coaches and fantasy football players may have much of the same kind of knowledge that is used on the gridiron by actual players. But couch potatoes and computer geeks don't have the *opportunity* to act on the basis of what they know—at least, not in the real-world sense. And there's a huge difference between the knowledge used to second-guess a coach's decision, or the knowledge applied at a keyboard, and the knowledge that is *embodied* by being *enacted* in a real-world scenario, just the sort of scenario in which that kind of knowledge is most aptly deployed.

Knowledge is a key ingredient of responsible human behavior. Having the relevant *body* of knowledge, having the *opportunity* to make use of that knowledge in real-world situations, and having the *inclination* to act in that opportune moment all combine to explain the value of knowledge. There is a need for people in all walks of life to embrace this principle and go into the world prepared for responsible action, for their own sake and for the benefit of the larger world community (or "team") of which they are a part.

Let's turn now to the quarterback, where we see this indicated in other ways.

What Do Quarterbacks Know?

University of Nebraska physics professor Timothy Gay teaches "football physics" online and in his book *Football Physics: The Science of the Game.*[11] In one sixty-second online clip at his Football Physics Web site, he explains the concept of vectors and illustrates their significance when a quarterback throws a pass.[12] Gay is at the University of Nebraska, and I happen to be a fan of the University of Southern California Trojans (I earned my PhD in philosophy at USC). So I'll illustrate the key points of this section with reference to the most recent game between these two teams, which just happens to have been played yesterday.

During one play in the fourth quarter, USC quarterback John David Booty rolled out to his right, threw down the field, and hit his receiver, who caught the ball just in time to plant a foot before going out of bounds. In this scenario, three vectors were critical to the success of the pass.

First, there's the moving vector of the USC quarterback as he runs with the ball to avoid a sack and spot his receiver. Second is the moving vector of the ball, thrown on the run. This vector extends from Booty's gun arm to the arms of his receiver. Finally, there's the moving vector of the receiver's own dash across the field to meet the ball at the proper location. There are three moving objects: the quarterback as he scrambles sideways, the ball as it flies through the air, and the receiver as he runs. Think of each vector as an imaginary line that traces the pathway of each object as it moves. Completion of the pass depends on whether these vectors are properly coordinated. And this depends on the speed of each of the three objects.

Imagine a different scenario. The quarterback is stationary when he cocks his arm to pass the ball. His receiver is fifteen yards downfield, and he, too, is stationary. The ball is caught. From quarterback to receiver is a pathway that represents the moving vector of the ball. This is the only vector in the scenario. Suppose the vector just happens to parallel the sidelines.

Returning to the real-world scenario of September 15, 2007, there are three vectors. Booty rolls out and cocks his arm as if to throw straight downfield parallel to the sidelines. But because he's moving when he releases the ball, the moving vector of the ball isn't going to be parallel to the sidelines, as it was in the case involving a stationary quarterback and a stationary receiver. The vector traced by the ball will be several degrees off. The specific difference in degree between a rollout pass and a stationary pass will depend on the speed of the quarterback as he rolls out. The greater the speed, the greater the degree of angle between the vector of the ball when thrown from a stationary position and the vector of the ball when thrown on the run. So Booty has to be aware of his speed.

But it isn't enough for Booty to know his speed. He also needs to know the speed the ball will be traveling along its vector, since that also will determine the final destination of the ball. And, to complicate things even more, he needs to know the speed of his receiver, who is running to meet the ball. In the fourth-quarter rollout play of September 15, the receiver had not even cleared himself from the defensive protection that had been set up against him when Booty threw the ball. Booty had to count on his receiver to break out of the defensive jam, pick the proper course to run, and run with the right speed to meet the ball . . . before stepping out of bounds.

In his online video about vectors and the game of football, Gay plays a clip from a rollout pass. He stops the action just as the ball is about to be released, then asks, "Where will the ball go?" He explains that this depends on the speed of the quarterback as he runs with the ball and the speed of the ball once it's thrown. At this point, Gay playfully says, "So you see, it's very important for a quarterback to figure in his speed on a rollout pass"—as if the quarterback literally calculates the difference in degree between one vector and another given his speed, and then deliberately uses that information to select the ideal point at which to release the ball to complete his pass.

Of course, a quarterback doesn't actually make a precise calculation of this kind. But he does need to be aware of his own running speed, the speed at which the ball will likely fly when released, and the running speed of the receiver. A successful quarterback will get it right a decent percentage of the time.

Let's stop to consider what counts as a decent pass-completion percentage. As of this writing, with the 2007 season under way, NFL quarterback Kurt Warner has a career pass-completion percentage of around 65.6, the best in NFL history. During the 2001 season, he completed 375 passes out of 546 attempts, for a percentage of 68.7. Warner is the recipient of NFL MVP awards for 1999 and 2001 and the Super Bowl MVP Award for Super Bowl XXXIV (2000). To be considered "most valuable player"—not once, not twice, but three times—is doing pretty well. But get this: on average, Kurt Warner missed on more than one-third of his passes! Not to ruin the party, but, come to think of it, that's a lot of incompletions.

Does this mean that completing a pass is usually a matter of luck? Not at all. A quarterback has to really know his stuff to make 65.6 percent of his passes. But what stuff does he have to know? What kind of knowledge does he have? And how does he come to have that knowledge?

A good quarterback knows how fast he can run flat out. And he knows how fast he can run under various conditions. His running speeds can be recorded with a stopwatch during practice. He knows how fast he can throw a football. So if he also knows the math, he should be able to calculate vectors of a flying football, plugging in speed variables for different hypothetical situations.

Would this kind of knowledge do him any good in an actual game? It would seem not. During actual play, he won't know the actual values of speed variables. And he wouldn't have time to work out the vectors even if he did have precise knowledge of the speed variables. Real-world play doesn't allow for such mathematical wizardry.

And yet, by working out times and experimenting with vectors during practice, the quarterback acquires knowledge that improves his chances of completing a rollout pass on game day. In the midst of play, when he has only split seconds to react, he can recognize a match between the real-time scenario as it unfolds and patterns he has learned during practice. He may even get to the point where he sights the vector the ball must travel with something like a sense of the number of degrees off the vector of his scramble.

We sometimes speak of "muscle memory" to explain practically instinctual behavior that requires spontaneous motion of the body and its extremities to accomplish a specific task. But the patterns of movement required to achieve the task are not literally etched in the memory of one's muscles. The behavior is still the physical effect of a cognitive activity.

Unless a celebrated quarterback's pass-completion record is a matter of sheer luck, it does seem that knowledge plays a role during a rollout pass. Through trial and error, the quarterback gains experience that contributes to his success. He runs a play. If things go more or less as planned, this gets tucked away for future reference. If the play blows up, he still learns something that can be put to good use later on. We could say that he acquires information. But he has to be able to act on that information. And in the game of football, that means that he has to be able to adapt the information he has to the unfolding particulars of a given play. This information isn't useful unless it can be put to use in novel circumstances. And it isn't useful if it can't be put to use spontaneously and on the run.

The rest of life can be like that, too. We rely on memory to navigate our world. What is logged there had better be reliable information—true, or mostly true, beliefs. And our access to that information had better be reliable. Often, we must be able to count on both the information and our access to it without attending to these things in an explicit way. It is a tribute to our cognitive powers that we are able to act so successfully in the world when so much is at stake.

Knowledge and the Intangibles of Play

Yesterday, when the Trojans (ranked number 1) faced the Nebraska Cornhuskers at Memorial Stadium in Lincoln, it was game two for USC and game three for Nebraska. USC hadn't really been tested yet, since their only game had been against Idaho, an unranked opponent. At Idaho, two weeks before the Nebraska game, USC had won 38–10. The final score and the mixed quality of play left room for skeptics to rumble that USC was overrated.

On September 15, with several inexperienced freshmen playing key positions, USC would be confronted with an undefeated team ranked 14, a sea of red in the bleachers, and raucous noise from enthusiastic home-gamers. On game day, the *Orange County Register* reported that Memorial Stadium (a football shrine) was the home of 285 consecutive sellouts! Mark Saxon, of the *Register,* suggested that "if you see a close-up of the eyes of freshmen [players], see if they look freaked out. If not, USC shouldn't be too bothered by the venue."[13]

The venue. It's a potentially significant intangible on game day. For the home team, the atmosphere can energize. For the visiting team, it can confuse and demoralize. The visiting Trojans knew what to expect. They would have to let reason—a sober awareness of their actual knowledge of the game—prevail over emotion as the target of disturbing cacophony.

And so it is in ordinary experience. Our attention to what we know, when we most need to be focused on what we know, can be overwhelmed by the din of emotional turmoil in the circumstances of life. At such times it isn't enough to have a *fund of knowledge;* we must *be mindful of* the knowledge we have. Without mindfulness, our knowledge may be worthless. And we have an obligation, in the interest of cognitive fair play, to help each other toward the goal of acquiring true belief.

Epistemologists themselves can be guilty of diversion from this goal. A student enrolls in an introductory course in philosophy. She's required to read René Descartes' *Meditations on First Philosophy.* Aided by some diversionary in-class commentary on this classic work, the student becomes paralyzed with the thought, "Maybe we don't really know anything!" This is precisely the effect desired by the instructor, who probably isn't himself a skeptic at all. The student needs to be reminded that she has plenty of evidence that she has vast quantities of knowledge, and *no* evidence that she has no knowledge. Against the natural conviction that she knows things, all she's given is the mere *possibility*, tricked out with clever thought experiments (like the Brain in a Vat experiment), that she doesn't have knowledge.

A "thought experiment" is the kind of experiment a philosopher performs to test the coherence of a theoretical claim using imagination only. One of the most famous thought experiments is due to René Descartes, who reasoned that he could be mistaken about nearly every belief he had. He imagined that an evil genius (*malin génie*) could be the cause of his beliefs. If our beliefs are caused by an evil genius, then our beliefs may all be false, and we wouldn't know it. An updated version of Descartes' thought experiment suggests that I imagine the possibility that I am nothing more than a brain in a vat, and that a mad scientist has stuck electrodes into this brain to stimulate brain events that simulate what we take to be our ordinary set of experiences. Under these conditions, "I" (or rather, this brain in a vat) would have precisely the same sort of experiences with which I'm acquainted in the actual world. But is it the actual world that I'm acquainted with if I *could* be a brain in a vat? The evil genius scenario and the brain in a vat scenario are supposed to be genuine possibilities. So skepticism, some claim, can be induced in the basis of a mere logical possibility. However, possibility scenarios don't count as evidence that skepticism is true.

Philosopher Reinhardt Grossmann gives fair warning to those who defer too readily to the heroics of philosophers: "We must never underestimate the stubbornness of philosophers. In this respect, philosophers are not so different from the vulgar: Having finally, after much toil and trouble, arrived at their views, they are loath to give them up, no matter how silly they are. But in addition philosophers have a more perverse streak: They delight in shocking accepted opinion. Some philosophers, it seems, are only happy if they have arrived at absurd conclusions."[14]

The not-entirely-fictional professor we have envisioned, with all of his credentials and aura of authority, has "home team" advantage. But the noise he makes on behalf of skepticism is a disservice to students.

It is fitting to conclude with this wise counsel from Etienne Gilson: "Philosophy does not consist of encouraging others to continue in false beliefs, and the worst way of persuading others to abandon their error is to appear to share the same error. There is only one truth, the same for all, and the highest good for a rational being is to know the truth. When a philosopher sees the truth he can only submit himself to it, for that is true wisdom; and when he has discovered the truth, the best thing he can do for others is share it with them, for that is true charity."[15]

Notes

Sometimes a book title is worth the price of the book. In this case, the book wasn't even in print when I began writing this chapter. The main title of my chapter, "Inside the Helmet," is "borrowed," with due respect, from the book *Inside the Helmet: Life as a Sunday Afternoon Warrior* (New York: Gotham Books, 2007), by NFL Giants veteran Michael Strahan and NFL sideline reporter Jay Glazer.

1. What are the odds?

2. One of Nicholson's most famous movie lines is "You can't handle the truth!" exclaimed during courtroom testimony in the film *A Few Good Men*. Shortly after this outburst, he's heard muttering, "Hey, what's going on? I don't understand."

3. Quoted in James Michener, *Sports in America* (New York: Random House, 1976), 13; see Leonard Roy Frank, *Random House Webster's Quotationary* (New York: Random House, 2001), 287.

4. Frank Gifford, *Sports Illustrated*, 4 July 1960; see Frank, *Quotationary*, 287.

5. Humor columnist Dave Barry is credited with the remark, "I have seen women walk right past a TV set with a football game on and—this always amazes me—not stop to watch, even if the TV is showing replays of what we call a 'good hit,' which is a tackle that causes at least one major internal organ to actually fly out of a player's body." For this quote, see http://www.dontquoteme.com/search/quote_display.jsp?quoteID=11616&gameID=1.

6. See Howie Long, *Football for Dummies* (Foster City, CA: IDG Books, 1998).

7. Rarely has a player in college football or the NFL played in both units for a team.

8. Long, *Football for Dummies*, 96.

9. See Long, *Football for Dummies*, 96–97.

10. For a standard discussion of kinds of knowledge, see Keith Lehrer, *Theory of Knowledge* (Boulder, CO: Westview Press, 1990), 2–5.

11. Timothy Gay, *Football Physics: The Science of the Game* (New York: Rodale, 2004). Gay played football at Cal Tech and earned his PhD in atomic physics from the University of Chicago.

12. See University of Nebraska, Department of Physics and Astronomy, "Football Physics with Dr. Tim Gay," http://physics.unl.edu/outreach/football.html.

13. Mark Saxon, "Cornhuskers' Red Carpet," *Orange County Register,* 15 September 2007, Sports, p. 10.

14. Reinhardt Grossmann, *The Fourth Way: A Theory of Knowledge* (Bloomington: Indiana University Press, 1990), 23.

15. Etienne Gilson, *Thomist Realism and the Critique of Knowledge* (San Francisco: Ignatius, 1986), 215.

SECOND QUARTER

PLAYING WELL BETWEEN THE LINES

Scott F. Parker

THE BEAUTY OF FOOTBALL

The Setting

It's third and long in a tied game in the Georgia Dome. The Falcons are on their own 40 with two minutes left in the first half. They are out of timeouts and have to convert here or they'll be forced to punt and then try to hold the Ravens for the remainder of the half. The game has playoff implications and the fans have been invested in every play today. Mike Vick crouches behind his center, Todd McClure, and gives the count . . .

Ask most people for an example of something beautiful and they will respond by naming flowers, a natural landscape, a sunset, a child's eyes, maybe a favorite painting or piece of music, or a specific woman. What they will probably not respond with is football. Dictionary and colloquial definitions of beauty cluster around its function as a source of pleasure to our senses: beauty is what pleases us. Given this definition, it isn't surprising that few people name football when prompted to identify beauty. The pleasure derived from watching a football game doesn't come across to our senses in the same way that the beauty of a rose or a song does. In the case of the rose or the song, we are aware that what we're seeing or hearing is beautiful, if for no other reason than that we've been taught that these are principal occasions for beauty. In football, the sights and sounds (and smells) are not as apparently beautiful. That is, at most points in a game, a person would be hard-pressed to point out objects of beauty, even though most fans would believe they are there. After all, thousands of fans cram into stadiums to watch their favorite teams, and millions crowd around their TVs to watch from home every week. Their behavior reveals that something about football is pleasing for them. But what? And how can philosophy help us think about our interest in football?

The Snap

> *The Ravens are back in pass coverage, expecting Vick to throw. Michael Jenkins is in motion, settling into position just before McClure snaps the ball to Vick.*

The simple logic of watching football is that football fans watch football because it is pleasing for them. But this definition—*a football fan is someone who finds pleasure in watching football*—is tautological. That is, the definition replaces the term without adding to it. To say that a fan finds football pleasurable is to say very little. The more interesting question is what about football pleases him.

One answer we often give to this question is that we watch football because we care if our teams (however we decide which teams are "ours") win. By this thinking, we wouldn't watch if we didn't care who won the game; but this rarely holds in practice. It is a rare fan who is selective enough to watch only his or her team. Many fans will prefer to watch their particular teams and be more passionate about those games but, given the opportunity, will eagerly watch other games. As a simple but effective way to test this statement, ask a fan if he would rather watch a game (live or on TV) or read the box scores in the paper. If it were the case that what we cared about in football primarily was the result, there would actually be a preference for the box score, because we could get the same result by investing far less time. But we don't watch games to learn the final scores any more than we, as Alan Watts said, listen to music to get to the final notes, and no fan would choose the box score. I think that when we read box scores of games we haven't seen, it's to try to imagine what it would have been like to watch the game. Clearly, this shows that there is something in football, beyond winning, that holds our attention.

A better explanation of why we watch football instead of only reading the scores in the paper or watching *SportsCenter* is that we are drawn to the drama of the sport. There is something emotionally engaging about watching men struggle against each other so ferociously. The intensity at the line of scrimmage is palpable; the players act as if the next play is the only thing in the world. Yet, despite their focus, we know that the play's outcome is uncertain. Each play brings degrees of success and failure to each team that we can discover only in its unfolding.

But ask yourself if you would watch football if it were scripted the way that professional wrestling is. The games might be just as dramatic (they might be more dramatic), but few of us would watch. Football's authenticity depends on the uncertainty of its outcome, not just for us, but also for the players. Terrell Owens aside, football doesn't reduce to its players' personalities the way that professional wrestling does (essentially a male-oriented soap opera),[1] because we respect the reality of what the players are doing.

This aspect, the game's drama and uncertainty, though engaging and requisite for our viewing, fails to account in full for our watching football. The same drama, realness, and uncertainty of outcome that are present in an NFL playoff game are present in Pop Warner games, high school games, and even in games you play in the park with your friends. These are constituents of the game of football, but few people, except for some parents, want to watch at these lower levels of play.

I believe that what accounts for this difference is that at higher levels of play (college and professional), the level of skill brought to the game increases, and with it comes an increase in beauty. The skills of a player like Barry Sanders fascinate us. We are awed by his bodily control and timing as he bends the laws of physics (or at least our perception of those laws) with every unexpected lateral movement. Our thoughts are like defenders' flailing arms, failing to grasp his movements. The skill of his movements might be beautiful on their own, in the way that the movements of a dancer are beautiful, but the presence of some of the world's best athletes trying to stop him from doing just what he is doing underscores the difficulty of his task and enhances its beauty; it would not do to watch Barry Sanders make the same runs against a team of high schoolers.

Moving from the player to the team, there are teams in the NFL that are thought to be more beautiful than others, and generally the more beautiful teams tend to draw a lot of attention from fans. The St. Louis Rams teams of 1999–2001 are a telling example. "The Greatest Show on Turf," as they were known, set all kinds of offensive records as Kurt Warner, Marshall Faulk, Isaac Bruce, and Tory Holt picked apart defenses that at times didn't seem to be on the field. There was a beauty to their game that was absent from other teams of their era. The timing, precision, and balance of their offense were beautiful to watch. Other teams, like the New England Patriots, who have done the best job this decade of winning, don't have the same kind of beauty that those Rams had, or possibly that the current Colts have.[2] In saying so, I may be exposing an offensive bias in attributing beauty (whether it is mine or ours). Because the offensive team has the ball and is often the focus of our attention, it is easier to see what those players are doing and identify beauty in it. But that is not to say that defense can't also be beautiful. In order to know what can and cannot be beautiful, we need to get a better sense of what beauty is.

The Play Call

> *The play that Hue Jackson has called involves a play action fake to Warrick Dunn to give Michael Jenkins time to get downfield. The second option is Roddy White on a slant. Vick's third option is to dump the ball off to Warrick Dunn, who by now has had time to sneak out wide and should have room to run.*

Having identified a couple of instances of beauty in football, let's turn now to some more specific definitions of beauty. Immanuel Kant (1724–1804) gives a philosophically influential aesthetic theory in his *Critique of Judgment*. One of Kant's criteria for beauty that is pertinent to football is that its source be of disinterest to its viewers. That is, its viewers don't stand to make personal gains from the object of their affection. An investor, seeing the value of his stock double, is not justified in ascribing beauty to his gain. Likewise, the owner of a football team's opinion is compromised when he makes aesthetic judgments of his team. The beauty he sees on the field is dubiously tied in with his financial stake in the team. In contrast, fans, at least when they're not betting on the game, stand to gain little by their team's successes. Whatever pride they take in a win or excitement they gather from a great play fades with their memories of the game. It is only in the shortest of time frames that football fans have any personal interest in the game before them, and personal interest on a short time frame is little more than pleasure. The payoff for watching football comes in watching football. Except in rare cases, we don't watch football to get something else. We watch it because we like it. A situation might arise where a person watches a game, fakes interest even, to impress a boss, a client, or a girl, but generally watching football is an end in itself. And for Kant this is crucial for beauty. It cannot be instrumental. Beauty holds our attention and, at the time of perception, gives us no reason to look beyond it for some other end (including writing philosophy papers about it).

I, for one, am disinterested (in the Kantian sense) in football and can be absorbed in it during a game as an end in itself, as a source of beauty (even though, over the course of a game, there may be only a handful of instances I would call "beautiful"). But there are plenty of people who don't think football is beautiful. Who is right? Is there beauty in football, or isn't there? Kant thinks that aesthetic judgments are nonconceptual. I can't convince a football detractor that football is beautiful any more than he can convince me that it isn't. As we watch the same game, the beauty is apparent, or it isn't. While Kant leaves room for discrepancies regarding particular cases, he thinks that there is a universal claim behind all claims of beauty. When a person calls something beautiful, he is saying more than "I like it." He is also implying, "and you should too."[3] But beauty is nonconceptual; we can't argue it. So how can we expect universality? One possible answer comes through a kind of consensus. The more people who call something beautiful, the more beautiful that thing must be. This is helpful, but it makes beauty seem metaphysical, as if it's a thing in the world, which can be very difficult to defend to someone who disagrees with you about which things are beautiful. We have certain necessary conditions for beauty (from Kant: It must be an end in itself), but we don't have sufficient conditions. (We don't agree on which things are ends in themselves. My dad, for instance, would watch football only under very specific conditions, and then only as a means to something else.) Without sufficient conditions for beauty, its definition remains open. No one can *say* what beauty is. But this isn't really a problem because we all *know*, intuitively, what it is. And we know what beauty is because we know what is beautiful (even though we often disagree on this last part).

The Play

> *McClure snaps the ball to Vick. Vick takes a quick drop and extends the ball to a streaking Warrick Dunn. Dunn runs for two yards into the middle of a pile before the Ravens realize that Vick is holding the ball behind the line of scrimmage. He is looking for Michael Jenkins breaking down the right sideline, but he's tightly covered by Chris McCalister. Cutting across the center of the field, Roddy White is also tightly covered. Dunn is scrambling to get out wide for a quick dumpoff, but Ray Lewis has already broken the line. Vick sees him coming and tries to take off on his own, but as he makes his move, Lewis dives and gets a hand on Vick's leg, tripping him up. Vick loses his balance and hops on one leg to try to stay on his feet. As the play continues to fall apart, Terrell Suggs charges at Vick, diving at his legs. Vick, still hopping and trying to get back on two feet, leaps up over the diving Suggs and lands running to the outside. He makes it around the corner and breaks an open-field tackle.*

One of the compelling defenses of Kant's position is its irrelevance during its demonstration. The viewing subject, during the perception of the beautiful, is in no way concerned with the beauty of the object. Rather, he is consumed by it. The efficacy of the application of the theory is considered after the fact when we reflect on instances we already consider beautiful. Essentially, Kant is giving a rational defense of arational beauty and, if we follow him, restricting the discussion of which kinds of things can be beautiful to those that are ends in themselves. Given that restriction, the number of things fulfilling the definition remains innumerable. Football, as we've seen, is, by Kant's definition, a possible source of beauty and, judging from its popularity, an actual source as well. The question remains: What about football is beautiful?

Because I don't have access to any consensual arbiter of beauty, I have to make do with my senses and my judgments on football. To abstract a description of what I find beautiful in football, I would say that it comes primarily in the movements and spontaneity of certain plays and certain players. For instance, well-thrown passes, sharp cuts from runners that make would-be tacklers miss, poorly thrown passes that receivers turn into unlikely gains, and unexpected, successful, spontaneous reactions. That someone could watch Joe Montana throwing off his back foot under pressure and still find a double-covered Dwight Clark in the end zone (to win the game, no less) and not see beauty baffles me. The same goes for Jerry Rice catching balls all over the field, and Peyton Manning having the ball do anything he wants it to do. I don't think I'm alone in watching for these highlights. On every play I'm rooting for something special to happen, even though I know that it is because of the less spectacular plays that the great ones stand out. When Barry Sanders was playing, there was a chance on every play that he could end up spinning down the field, breaking tackles, and doing things that had never been seen before. But on most plays that didn't happen. Still, the chance of it happening was enough to compel me to watch games that otherwise might have been, well, boring.

Those are my proclivities. I'm biased toward offensively minded teams, preferably ones that throw more than run. And I would take that so far as to say I would rather watch a team lose with offense than win with defense. Heretical, perhaps, to prefer beauty to winning, but as a fan I know when my passions are engaged, and it's not when Tom Brady sets up a field goal.

For another fan, with another set of judgments, it would certainly be possible to appreciate and find beauty in other aspects of the game. All of my examples have come from the offensive side of the game, because this is the part of the game that draws me in. But I recognize the possibility of finding beauty in defense too. In fact, sometimes I do. My appreciation of a well-timed interception can be similar to the appreciation I would have for the receiver making the catch. I tend not to find beauty in a big hit (I react too strongly to the pain I imagine the player is feeling), though I know that to make a good hit requires skill in the forms of strength and exceptional timing. Though I don't find beauty there myself, it takes little effort to imagine someone else doing so. To contrast, I can't imagine anyone watching a player trip, clumsily, over his own feet and call that beautiful (even if the result of the play was "fortunate").

The philosopher Ted Cohen explains these differences in terms of circles of taste.[4] Every person has her own particular circle of taste, which she draws around those things that she appreciates. For some the circle includes football; for others it does not. Among the circles that include football, each will be drawn slightly differently to include different aspects of the game. Mine, as stated above, includes several kinds of offensive plays and a few defensive highlights. Someone else's circle (a former defensive player's?) might include more defensive plays and be more selective with regard to offense. Effectively, Cohen's circles say very little about the nature of beauty. After all, what do they say, other than that a person's circle of beauty includes those things he considers beautiful and excludes what he does not? This nominalism is very much the tautology we encountered earlier: beauty is in the beautiful, and the beautiful is what contains beauty. This circle is drawn around the subject, and beauty is in the subject's eye.

But Cohen draws another circle, this one around the object of beauty. Included in this circle are all those who find beauty in a particular object. All those who find football beautiful would be in the same circle. Dividing "football" into component parts, we could draw other circles around the aspects of the game that have been mentioned: passing, catching, running, tackling, and so on. What Cohen emphasizes in regard to these circles is that all we can know about the members of a particular circle is that they are in the circle. Because we do not know the reasons (if they can be called reasons) for someone's appreciation, we cannot postulate universal standards for beauty. Without the latter point, locating beauty in the eye of the beholder would not preclude a metaphysical basis to it. We could claim that divergent opinions of beauty reflect divergent abilities to identify beauty, *that thing*. Some are better at identifying it than others. With the object's circle drawn, beauty is seen strictly as a subjective valuation, without defense or justification. There is, as we say, no accounting for taste.

To test out these circles in an informal manner, I devised a short survey and sent it to three people who I thought would have very different football tastes. One, Brian, is an accomplished athlete and spirited football fan; another, John, my father, is not a fan; the third, Ally, is a Korean friend, unfamiliar with the rules of the game. I sent them links to videos of various plays and asked them two questions: (1) Was that beautiful? (2) Why or why not? I will briefly describe each video and give their reactions before trying to draw some conclusions.

Video 1 was Franco Harris's "Immaculate Reception." In it, Terry Bradshaw, throwing under pressure in a playoff game, has his pass broken by a defender. Luckily, the ball is deflected to Franco Harris, who makes a difficult catch and runs for a touchdown.[5]

> BRIAN: Thought it was not beautiful. Just a lucky play with no execution.
>
> JOHN: Found some beauty here, in Harris's ability to react to changing events with agility.
>
> ALLY: Thought it was messy and hard to follow; not beautiful.

Video 2 was Dwight Clark and Joe Montana's play "The Catch." Again, a quarterback, Montana, throws under pressure for a touchdown in a playoff game. This time the pass is completed to the intended receiver, Clark.[6]

> BRIAN: Beautiful throw. Beautiful catch.
>
> JOHN: Found some beauty in the excellent timing of the play.
>
> ALLY: Indifferent to this play. Not beautiful. But not not-beautiful, either.

Video 3 was a running play up the middle for a small gain.[7]

> BRIAN: Couldn't see any beauty in this play.
>
> JOHN: Found no beauty. Called it brute force against brute force.
>
> ALLY: Not beautiful.

Video 4 was a long touchdown pass from Joey Harrington to Sammie Parker (at the University of Oregon) that Parker caught in perfect stride.[8]

> BRIAN: Beautiful. The route was well run and the ball perfectly thrown.
>
> JOHN: The coordination and calculation were beautiful.
>
> ALLY: Beautiful because Harrington threw it so far and Parker ran so fast.

Video 5 was a highlight reel of some of Barry Sanders's best runs.[9]

BRIAN: Barry Sanders's runs were beautiful because of his speed, power, lateral quickness, creativity, agility, and balance.

JOHN: Found his movements to be beautiful in their agility and speed.

ALLY: Beautiful, because he moves everywhere.

Video 6 was of Reggie Bush getting hit hard by Sheldon Brown.[10]

BRIAN: It was a beautiful play by the defender because of his ability to read the play, then his quickness to the ball, and finally his power in the hit.

JOHN: Not beautiful, just brute force again.

ALLY: Very, very beautiful.

These responses might not tell us anything about beauty as such, and they do not hint at any objective beauty in football, but they are instructive in that they demonstrate various circles of taste. Brian's circle is the largest, with regard to football, as we would expect from a fan. His circle and comments indicate an interest in the more technical aspects of the game. John's circle appears to be drawn around plays similar to those in Brian's circle, with the exception of plays that emphasize the skill of force. But even on plays that both Brian and John called beautiful, Brian expressed more enthusiasm for the beauty, using definitive language, while John tended to qualify his responses, saying that plays had "some beauty," for example. This, I think, demonstrates that the attribute of beauty is assigned by degree, not in a dichotomous *yes* or *no*. Things are not *beautiful* and *not beautiful*; they are *more beautiful* and *less beautiful*. We could think of a person's most beautiful objects being found at his circle's center and the slightly beautiful falling around the perimeter.

Ally's circle is less consistent, suggesting that context matters to our judgments. Without knowing the rules of the game, she can only guess at the meanings of the actions she sees. Initially, after watching the unremarkable running play, she called it beautiful and commented that the guy who ran all the way into the end zone must be very good. When I explained that that guy wasn't directly involved with the play, that the ball carrier had been brought down upfield, she decided it was not beautiful. And with the hit on Reggie Bush, she told me that it would be more beautiful if it were legal and wondered what punishment Sheldon Brown received. When I told her it was legal and he didn't get in any trouble, she said it was the most beautiful of all the plays.

If there is a conclusion from this survey it is that, with regard to a specific object, such as football, whatever we understand of the context of the object impacts our judgments of beauty. Beauty is not only in the eye of the beholder but also in the mind behind that eye.[11]

The Outcome

Vick has room to run and it's only the safety between him and the end zone . . .

These questions of why we watch football and whether or not it is beautiful, who is asking them? The football fan isn't interested in such questions. He is, when in the role of fan, engaged with the game, attentively, emotionally, and aesthetically. The opportunity to ask these questions arises when this person shifts roles from fan to budding philosopher, either after the game or during some downtime in the game, but, critically, not simultaneously with beholding the game. These roles (beholding and reflecting) are distinct. Per the argument, the fan, as fan, has no time for the argument. It takes place on the philosopher's field in a different game, of which the particular football fan may or may not also be a fan. But whether or not the football fan is a recreational philosopher after the game, during the action he cannot be; the game transcends our conceptions of it.

But all games (football and philosophy) come to an end, and the questions have been asked, at least here. So, what do we learn by these inquiries? The definition of beauty is open. Its meaning depends on shifting circles of judgments that each of us makes. And while these judgments don't close the definition any tighter, they do give us an effective way to reflect on what it is that we mean when we call a rose, a child's eyes, or a touchdown pass beautiful. And although I said above that if all we say is that there is beauty in the beautiful and the beautiful is that which has beauty, then we say very little, perhaps there is nothing more to say.[12]

Notes

1. Thanks to Woodrow Pengelly for this point.
2. This was written long before the Patriots' beautiful 2007–2008 season.
3. The examples of beauty I've used in this paper have been presented as things

that "we" find beautiful, but, of course, you did not choose the examples and may disagree with my selections. What I am really saying is, "I think these examples are beautiful. And you do, too, don't you?"

4. Ted Cohen, "Liking What's Good: Why Should We?" in *Philosophy and Interpretation of Pop Culture,* ed. William Irwin and Jorge J. E. Gracia (Lanham, MD: Rowman & Littlefield, 2006).

5. http://www.youtube.com/watch?v=UnfbKKvUG9Q; accessed 6 January 2008.

6. http://www.youtube.com/watch?v=2PArRGCdJIA; accessed 6 January 2008.

7. http://www.youtube.com/watch?v=osItKwjOhKk; accessed 6 January 2008.

8. http://www.youtube.com/watch?v=gHwkQtxU-J4; accessed 6 January 2008.

9. http://www.youtube.com/watch?v=_6YQznRq0sM; accessed 9 March 2007.

10. http://www.youtube.com/watch?v=EiOSPYpxTDw; accessed 9 March 2007.

11. A compounding factor for these videos is the camera work for each play. The camera mediates our vision, and the disparity in the quality of the videos can disrupt the consistency of the eye. Bad camera work could make us misjudge a beautiful play. In a sense, then, we might not be talking about the beauty we see in football but about the beauty we see in the video of football. It's important to at least keep this in mind.

12. Thanks to my friend Mike Waite, who told me one day that the Falcons' new quarterback would change the way I watched and thought about football. I would also like to emphasize to readers that this chapter examines the aesthetics of Michael Vick as a football player and that ethical considerations are beyond its scope.

Scott A. Davison

VIRTUE AND VIOLENCE

Can a Good Football Player Be a Good Person?

We live in a violent culture. Just watch the news and you'll see that this is true. Some people argue that our violent culture is reflected in our love of violent sports, especially football. Is this true?

There is no doubt that football is a "savage ballet," involving a unique combination of beautiful athleticism and dangerous violence.[1] For instance, according to the National Center for Catastrophic Sport Injury Research, ninety-eight high school students died in the United States as a result of injuries directly attributable to participation in football from 1982 to 2005.[2] But is the violence in football symptomatic of a general societal trend that we should find troubling? Does the violence in football encourage more violence in society? Should we prohibit children from watching football, for example, in the way that many parents prohibit their children from watching boxing or ultimate fighting?

These are all good questions, but they are not the questions I will try to answer in this chapter. Instead, I want to ask a question about individual morality and the violence involved in football. We often think that, in general, people who engage in violent behavior are doing something morally wrong. Does this suggest that individual football players are doing something morally wrong by playing the game? I will argue in this chapter that the answer to this question is "Yes, sometimes." But first I need to clarify a number of things.

So Much Violence, So Little Time

First of all, in this chapter, I will talk only about violence that occurs as part of the game, when the ball is in play. This means that I will not discuss cases of violence that just happen to occur on the field of play, such as fights between players after the whistle has blown, or the infamous case involving Albert Haynesworth and Andre Gurode. In that incident, on October 1, 2006, Haynesworth stomped on Gurode's face as he walked past the line of scrimmage, long after the whistle had blown, leaving Gurode with multiple lacerations on his face that required thirty stitches.

Second, I will focus exclusively on violence that occurs within the rules of the game. Football includes a number of rules designed to protect players in vulnerable positions. For example, there are penalties for roughing the passer, roughing the kicker, and interfering with a player's opportunity to catch a punt. The idea seems to be that players should have a right to expect that they will not be harmed when performing certain activities that require them to be in especially vulnerable positions. These are good rules, and it is good that various football officials continually discuss them in order to find new ways of protecting players. But I will not discuss cases of violence that involve breaking these rules, because they do not indicate a problem with the game of football in itself.

Third, I will focus exclusively on violence that is intended, as opposed to accidental. Accidents happen in life, of course, and as long as people take reasonable precautions, what happens by accident is not morally wrong. Football players know that they can be injured accidentally, and presumably they undertake this risk voluntarily, in light of whatever benefits they receive in exchange for playing. Of course, it is not always easy to tell whether something that happens on the field of play is accidental or intentional; I will return to this point later.

Violence and Morality: Where Do We Draw the Line?

Before we can turn to our main question, we need to know something about what is morally right and morally wrong. Without going off the deep end into moral philosophy here, let me suggest a simple principle: if a person intentionally causes violent harm to another person, knowing that it is not necessary to the accomplishment of a greater good, then this person has done something morally wrong. Let's call this the Violence Principle for easy reference, and let's consider some examples to see how it works.[3]

Imagine that you walk across a bridge over a highway, and you ac-cidentally bump into a man and knock him down, causing him physical harm. Have you done something wrong here? Not according to the Vio-lence Principle, since it requires that you intentionally cause violent harm to a person, whereas in this case, you did not intend to harm the man.

Now imagine a different case. Suppose that you tackle the man on the bridge over the highway, causing violent harm intentionally. But imagine that you do this to prevent him from throwing a brick off of the bridge onto the traffic below. In this case, since you accomplish a greater good (namely, protecting the people driving below on the highway), and you have no other means at your disposal to accomplish this purpose, your action is not counted as morally wrong according to the Violence Principle.

Now imagine yet another case. Suppose that, as before, you are try-ing to prevent the man on the bridge from throwing a brick onto the highway below. But instead of tackling the man, you shoot him in the leg with a gun. Let's suppose that you decided to shoot him because you thought that he had a gun himself, so that you thought that trying to tackle him would involve serious risk to you. But suppose that he didn't have a gun after all, at least not a real one: he was carrying a realistic-looking toy, so shooting him turned out to be unnecessary for stopping him. Have you done something morally wrong here? Not according to the Violence Principle, since it requires that you must have known that shooting the man was not necessary to accomplish a greater good (and you did not know this, since he appeared to be carrying a gun).

Finally, imagine again that you are trying to prevent the man on the bridge from throwing a brick onto the highway below. You can tell that he's not very big or strong, and you know that you could stop him by tackling him. But since you would rather not get your clothes dirty, you decide to shoot him in the leg instead. This would count as excessive vio-lence. You did accomplish a greater good here, the protection of the in-nocent people driving on the highway below, but your pursuit of that end involved more violence than was necessary, and so you have done some-thing wrong, according to the Violence Principle.

The Violence Principle seems to be true. It gives us the right answers in the hypothetical cases just considered, answers that seem grounded in our common framework for morality. Also, I can't think of any cases in which the Violence Principle gives us the wrong answer. It isn't the only true principle concerning the relationship between violence and morality, of course, but it seems to be true as far as it goes.[4]

In what remains of this chapter, I will use the Violence Principle to argue that sometimes football players intentionally cause violent harm to players on the opposite team, knowing that it is not necessary to achieve a greater good, so that sometimes what they do is morally wrong.

The Violence Inherent in the System

Let's consider more carefully how the game of football works in order to see what role violence plays in it. Football is often defined as a "collision sport" because in order to prevent a team from scoring by advancing the ball, it is necessary to tackle the player with the ball.[5] Of course, there are limits to the methods that can be used in order to tackle opponents. It is against the rules to grab a player's face mask, for instance, or to trip, punch, kick, or spear a player by leading with one's helmet. There are also complicated rules that specify what methods can be used by offensive players in order to block defensive players.

Since tackling and blocking are essential parts of football, an element of violence is essential to the game. Without this element of violence, football would cease to be football. Just to be clear, I am not arguing in this chapter that all of the violence in football is morally wrong. I want to distinguish the "ordinary" violence that is essential to playing the game (and playing it well) from the excessive violence that sometimes occurs within the rules of the game and can result in serious harm. Let me explain.

To tackle or block a player, it is necessary to exert a certain amount of physical force. Of course, it is not always clear in a given situation how much physical force is necessary; a good running back has the ability to run through tackles, for example, so defensive players typically use as much force as possible when tackling. Also, sometimes players are unable to refrain from using excessive force because of the momentum of their bodies and the timing of the play. But there are many cases in which it is clear that players use excessive force that results in serious injury. And when that harm is intended, the player who causes it may be doing something morally wrong, as the Violence Principle suggests.

Some Notable Examples from the Field of Play

On August 12, 1978, in a preseason game, Darryl Stingley of the New England Patriots was attempting to catch a pass when he was hit by Jack Tatum of the Oakland Raiders. The hit injured Stingley's spine, permanently paralyzing him from the chest down and ending his football career. Tatum claimed that "it was one of those pass plays where I could have attempted to intercept, but because of what the owners expect of me when they give me my paycheck, I automatically reacted to the situation by going for an intimidating hit."[6]

Tatum, who was celebrated for his violent tackling, earned the nickname "the Assassin" and even participated in an informal contest with his teammate George Atkinson to see how many players they could injure by means of the now illegal "hook tackle."[7] With regard to Stingley's career-ending injury, Tatum later expressed regret: "When the reality of Stingley's injury hit me with its full impact, I was shattered. To think that my tackle broke another man's neck and killed his future . . . well, I know it hurts Darryl, but it hurts me, too."[8]

Some of Tatum's hits almost certainly satisfied the Violence Principle. "I like to believe that my best hits border on felonious assault," Tatum himself once said.[9] But in part because of the tragic results of tactics like Tatum's, the NFL introduced a series of rules designed to protect players by restricting the ways in which people can be tackled. For instance, today spearing is illegal, where this involves the use of "any part of a player's helmet (including the top/crown and forehead/'hairline' parts) or facemask to butt, spear, or ram an opponent violently or unnecessarily."[10] The rule also states that "game officials will give special attention in administering this rule to protecting those players who are in virtually defenseless postures," and it empowers referees to eject players guilty of especially flagrant spearing.[11] These are important improvements in the rules, and they are intended in part to make it clear that injuring opposing players should not be one's goal on the field of play.

Here is another case. On November 24, 2002, Brian Kelly of the Tampa Bay Buccaneers intercepted a pass from Green Bay Packer quarterback Brent Favre. As Kelly was running the ball upfield, Tampa Bay defensive tackle Warren Sapp leveled Green Bay's offensive tackle Chad Clifton, sending him flying to the turf with no feeling in his extremities.

He spent four days in a Tampa hospital with a sprained pelvis, a sprained back, and internal bleeding. According to Green Bay trainer Pepper Burruss, Clifton's career-threatening hip injury is often seen in auto accidents but had never been recorded on the football field.[12] Replays showed that Clifton never saw Sapp coming and that he probably had no play on the ball, either. There was no flag on the play, and NFL officials ruled that no fine would be levied against Sapp because the hit was legal.

Sapp claims not to have tried to injure Clifton, regardless of his celebration with teammates after the hit, and it's not my place to speculate about what Sapp's intentions were.[13] But suppose that we imagine a situation just like Sapp and Clifton's, except that it is clear that the player in Sapp's role deliberately injures the player in Clifton's role through excessive force. Although such a hit would be legal according to current rules, the Violence Principle implies that it would be morally wrong because the force employed would be unnecessary to accomplish any greater good. In the actual case of Sapp and Clifton, for instance, a much less violent block would have accomplished the legitimate purpose of removing Clifton from the play. Sapp's hit was unnecessarily violent, and it could very well have ended Clifton's career.

In another case, on September 10, 2006, the first game of the season, the Kansas City Chiefs' quarterback Trent Green ended a third-quarter scramble by hook sliding feetfirst near the sideline. But before the rest of Green's body made complete contact with the field, Cincinnati Bengals defensive end Robert Geathers hit Green's upper body, bouncing Green off the turf and rendering him completely unconscious. Green was unable to play for over two months, and the long-term effects of his severe concussion will become evident only with the passing of time. NFL officials ruled that Geathers's hit was legal, so no fine was levied against him, despite the fact that Green was sliding feetfirst (which is a standard way for quarterbacks to signal to defensive players that they are no longer attempting to advance the ball).

Commentators debated whether the Geathers hit on Green was intentional or whether it was unavoidable because of the speed with which the play developed (and because of the possibility that Geathers was pushed in Green's direction by Chiefs receiver Eddie Kennison). It is clear, though, that the Geathers hit involved unnecessary force, since Green was sliding already when it occurred.[14]

I have not argued here that Sapp's hit on Clifton or Geathers's hit on Green was morally wrong according to the Violence Principle, because it is not clear that all of the clauses of the principle apply in those cases. But because cases of excessive violence occur regularly in football, and some of those cases result in violent harm, it seems obvious that there are cases to which the Violence Principle does apply. Of course, it is not my purpose in this essay to point fingers at particular players. Instead, I want to draw attention to a general trend that highlights a moral danger involved both for those who play football and for those who watch it.

The general trend that I have tried to highlight by discussing these particular cases suggests that there is a moral danger involved in playing football and in watching it.[15] For players, the moral danger involves the very real possibility that they will compromise their own moral character by intentionally participating in violence that is unnecessary to achieve any greater good. Coaches share some of the responsibility here as well, especially if they communicate the expectation that maximum force is always appropriate. For fans, there is a moral danger in rejoicing in violence for its own sake, which is certainly morally wrong in itself and also contributes to dangerous levels of desensitization.[16]

The Role of Intimidation

Many fans will surely object to my application of the Violence Principle to football because of the well-known fact that a well-placed hit involving excessive force can make a big difference in terms of winning the game. For example, wide receivers who are hit while trying to catch a pass in the middle of the field are said to "hear footsteps" the next time they cross that part of the field, since it is impossible to forget what happened to them last time. Coaches routinely train players to make big hits to intimidate the opposing team and thereby gain a competitive edge. Does this mean that the Violence Principle does not apply here after all, since there is a greater good here (namely, winning the game) that is served by the violence in question, even if it isn't necessary to complete a given play?[17]

It all depends upon what counts as a greater good. On the one hand, there are those who emphasize the importance of winning at all costs. To quote Henry Russell "Red" Sanders: "Sure, winning isn't everything. It's the only thing."[18] On the other hand, we have Al McGuire's perspective that "winning is only important in major surgery and all-out war."[19] Surely the truth lies somewhere in the middle: winning is more important than some things but less important than others.

For example, what is more important, winning or playing by the rules of the game? Is cheating justified if it leads to victory? Clearly not; cheating is wrong, whether or not it leads to winning. More to the point, is winning the game more important than intentionally harming another person?

Suppose you are a defensive end playing in your first Super Bowl, and you have a clean shot at the quarterback, who is scrambling on third down. The outcome of the game is still undecided. The quarterback doesn't see you coming, so you have a clear shot at him. You can tell that you are going to stop him well short of the first down. Should you try to take him out of the game as well (without breaking any rules, of course)?

Those who emphasize the role of consequences in morality might say yes, because many good consequences could flow from taking the quarterback out of the game. Your team could win the game, for instance, and your teammates and coaches would celebrate your key play. Your career prospects might improve dramatically. But do all of these good consequences add up to a morally good reason for trying to injure the quarterback?

Not all by themselves, if morality is also about principles and intentions, in addition to consequences. It is common for philosophers to describe hypothetical situations in which a given action would lead to the best consequences overall but would still be wrong in virtue of violating some fundamental moral principle.[20] One famous moral principle along these lines involves the idea that persons should always be treated with respect.[21] Although football players consent implicitly to the possibility of injury when they play, they do not consent to be harmed intentionally.[22] Harming other people intentionally, to obtain some benefit for yourself, seems like a clear case of using people merely as means to your ends, without treating them with respect (as ends in themselves).[23] So even if the Super Bowl is on the line, it still would be morally wrong to try to injure the quarterback.

Of course, it is still possible to intimidate opposing players through big hits without intending to injure them. I have not argued that such intimidation is morally wrong, because the Violence Principle that I have defended only covers intentional harm. But there is a fine line between trying to injure and trying to intimidate, and players who do cause injuries to others should ask themselves whether they have become morally compromised by virtue of the role that they played in causing such harm, especially when it involved the use of excessive force relative to what was required in the play at hand.

Fans of Violence?

Of course, different people will react differently to my claim that there are important moral dangers associated with football. Some will not find this claim troublesome at all, whereas those who take seriously the Socratic examination of the soul should be given pause.[24]

Some people will point out that the celebration of violence for its own sake has a long and distinguished history in football (and in human history in most parts of the world, for that matter). Certainly the violence in football is part of its appeal. Media coverage of football, which tends to emphasize whatever might hold a casual viewer's attention in order to increase ratings and advertising revenue, contributes to this culture by emphasizing violence for its own sake. This is evident, for example, in the current *Monday Night Football* halftime segment entitled "Jacked Up," which celebrates especially violent hits from the previous week's games, whether or not such hits played important roles in the outcomes of the games in question. In this respect, one might suggest, the appeal of football is similar to the appeal of automotive racing, which is essentially connected to the inherent dangers of the activity.

In response to this kind of claim, I think we should distinguish different reasons for being a football fan, in the same way that we should distinguish different reasons for being a fan of racing. If people were to enjoy racing only because of the possibility of a crash, then they would be oblivious to the fine motor skills on display; in a sense, they would not be fans of racing in itself but fans of crashing. In the same way, if people were to enjoy football only because of the violence on display, then they would not really be fans of football in itself, since they would be oblivious to the many athletic skills on display.

In other words, the violence that is an essential part of football is essentially connected to the exercise of athletic skills. Making a great open-field tackle, for example, typically requires speed, strength, and quick reflexes. The pure football fan enjoys great tackles because of the skills that they display, whether or not they are especially violent; the fan who watches football in part because of the violence enjoys especially the violent tackles.

Consider what happened on January 6, 2002, when New York Giant Michael Strahan broke the record for the number of quarterback sacks in a single season. Strahan sacked Green Bay quarterback Brett Favre with 2:42 remaining in the final game of the regular season, erasing the previous record, which was set by Mark Gastineau's twenty-two sacks in the 1984 season. Fans were not happy about this, though, because it certainly appeared that Favre did not try especially hard to avoid Strahan, and Strahan did not tackle Favre with any force. The evident friendship between the two players encouraged the suspicion that Favre created the sack just so that Strahan could break the record.

We can distinguish at least two reasons for being unhappy with this play. On the one hand, the pure football fan would be disappointed because there was no skill on display, either in the person of Favre (who did not scramble with any earnestness) or Strahan (who did not overcome many obstacles on his way to Favre). On the other hand, the fan of violence in football would be disappointed because sacks are supposed to be dangerous and violent tackles, and this certainly was not one of those.

Of course, few (if any) of us are really pure football fans. We enjoy not just the athletic skills on display but also the violence that doesn't involve any particular skill. Perhaps this is a morally revealing fact about us, something that should give us pause, along with our apparent preoccupations with winning and domination in general.[25] Reflections such as these suggest that it is possible to be a football player or a football fan without falling prey to the moral danger outlined above. They also suggest that the morally cautious fan of football should celebrate those players who have the virtue of knowing how much violent contact is appropriate in a given situation. Such players would realize that it is morally important to treat other players with respect, not merely as means to the end of winning the game or boosting one's career. Although it might not be good for ratings, media coverage of football could emphasize the distinction between appropriate and excessive violence or intimidation, and the NFL and NCAA certainly could do more to emphasize this difference to players. In addition, it might be morally good to give referees more latitude in enforcing penalties for unnecessary roughness. All of these things would help players and fans alike to avoid the moral dangers posed by participation in football, that "savage ballet" of which many of us are so fond, although for different reasons.

Notes

Thanks to Glen Colburn, Layne Neeper, Thomas Flint, Mark Murphy, Jacob Mincey, Philip Krummrich, Grant Alden, Jack Weir, Josh Horn, and Mike Austin for helpful comments and questions concerning an earlier draft of this essay. I could not address all of their points to my complete satisfaction, but my efforts to do so certainly led to many improvements.

1. This is according to Lisa the Greek (see episode 14, season 3 of *The Simpsons*).

2. Direct injuries are defined as "those injuries which resulted directly from participation in the skills of the sport," whereas indirect injuries are defined as "those injuries which were caused by systemic failure as a result of exertion while participating in a sport activity or by a complication which was secondary to a non-fatal injury." During this same time period, there were 151 deaths resulting from indirect injuries. For more on this, see the National Center for Catastrophic Sport Injury Research's study, which is available at http://www.unc.edu/depts/nccsi/AllSport.htm.

3. It should be obvious from my comments concerning the Violence Principle that I believe that what is morally right and wrong is objective in some sense, not just a matter of a given person's beliefs or a given culture's norms (for example). I will not defend this view about the nature of morality here, but it is important to note that it is a highly controversial view among philosophers.

4. Just to be clear, I have not claimed that the contrapositive of the Violence Principle is true. The contrapositive of the Violence Principle is the claim "If a person has done something wrong, then that person has intentionally caused violent harm to another person, knowing that it was not necessary to accomplish any legitimate purpose." In fact, this principle is clearly false, since there are many other ways to do something that is morally wrong. So the "if" in the Violence Principle must be understood to be just an "if," not an "if and only if."

5. For example, see the definition offered at http://domainhelp.search.com /reference/American_football.

6. See Tatum's book, *They Call Me Assassin* (New York: Everest House, 1980), and "The Assassin," the review of Tatum's book in *Time* magazine, January 28, 1980, also available online at http://www.time.com.

7. The game was scored in this way: "knockouts" received two points, and "limp offs" received one point; see "The Assassin."

8. "The Assassin."

9. "The Assassin."

10. Rule 12, sec. 2, art. 8(g) in the NFL's official rulebook.

11. Rule 12, sec. 2, art. 8(g).

12. For more on this story, see "Clifton Happy That Sherman Confronted Sapp," available in the archives of ESPN at http://espn.go.com/nfl/news/2003/0306/1519492 .html.

13. I am not arguing here that Sapp's block was morally wrong, according to the Violence Principle, since it is not clear that Sapp's case satisfied the clause concerning intention. But it is a good example for purposes of discussion because it clearly involved unnecessary force.

14. It is not clear, however, whether Geathers would have known this in time to make a split-second decision not to hit Green's upper body; Geathers himself claims to have tried not to hit Green with full force. So as before, in connection with the Sapp case, I am not arguing here that the Violence Principle implies that Geathers's hit was morally wrong. But it is a useful case to consider, again, because of the excessive violence that it involves.

15. This is not to say that other activities and professions have no moral dangers, but rather to highlight a moral danger that is especially acute in the case of football (and other violent sports, like hockey).

16. These same moral dangers arise more acutely in connection with sports in which winning is closely connected to harming one's opponent, such as boxing, and in which there are few restrictions on the kinds of techniques that can be used to achieve victory, such as so-called ultimate fighting. The popularity of these sports (along with many other signs) suggests that future generations will certainly look back upon our culture as an extremely violent one.

17. Thanks to Mark Murphy, Tom Flint, Grant Alden, Jake Mincey, Mike Austin, and Glen Colburn for pressing this line of objection in response to an earlier draft of this essay.

18. *Sports Illustrated,* December 26, 1955, 48. See also Steven J. Overman, "'Winning Isn't Everything. It's the Only Thing': The Origin, Attributions, and Influence of a Famous Football Quote," *Football Studies* 2, no. 2 (October 1999): 77–99.

19. Tom Kertscher, *Cracked Sidewalks and French Pastry: The Wit and Wisdom of Al McGuire* (Madison: University of Wisconsin Press, 2002).

20. For example, see the discussion of utilitarianism in Nils Ch. Rauhut, *Ultimate Questions: Thinking about Philosophy,* 2nd ed. (Upper Saddle River, NJ: Prentice Hall, 2006).

21. The most famous philosopher to develop this approach to ethics is Immanuel Kant (1724–1804); see his *Groundwork for the Metaphysics of Morals* (1785), trans. H. J. Paton (New York: Harper & Row, 1964), 4:429. For a thorough and helpful discussion of the notion of respect, see Robin S. Dillon's article in the *Stanford Encyclopedia of Philosophy,* http://plato.stanford.edu/entries/respect/.

22. Thanks to Jack Weir for helping me to gain clarity on this point.

23. This is the way that Kant talks about these things.

24. "The unexamined life is not worth living for man" (attributed to Socrates by Plato; see *Apology* 38a).

25. Thanks to Glen Colburn and Jake Mincey for making this point in correspondence (and making it more eloquently than I could have).

Sharon Ryan

WHAT'S SO BAD ABOUT PERFORMANCE-ENHANCING DRUGS?

The use of performance-enhancing drugs (PEDs) in sports has sparked serious ethical debate.[1] Although this book is about philosophy and football, the arguments discussed in this chapter apply to every sport.

A recent investigation revealed that six players on the Carolina Panthers 2004 Super Bowl team were filling prescriptions for steroids. Barry Bonds, the former San Francisco Giants' slugger and Golden Glove Award winner, broke Hank Aaron's career home run record during the 2007 Major League Baseball season. Although Bonds denies ever knowingly using steroids and has never tested positive for steroid use, many people believe that he has been using steroids and other PEDs for years. In fact, in November 2007 a federal grand jury indicted Bonds for perjury and obstruction of justice, claiming that he lied when he testified that he never knowingly used PEDs when questioned by a grand jury in the Bay Area Laboratory Co-operative investigation. Because of the suspicion of PED use, many people discredit Bonds's baseball accomplishments. In 1998, Mark McGwire broke Roger Maris's record for most home runs hit in a single season. Despite his record-breaking hitting performance, many people are vehemently opposed to McGwire's ever being inducted into the Hall of Fame because they believe his incredible hitting power was fueled by PEDs. Lance Armstrong, the American cyclist and seven-time winner of the Tour de France, has been repeatedly accused of using performance-enhancing drugs and blood doping. If these accusations are ever proven to be true, Armstrong will be regarded no longer as an American hero but as a despised cheater.

Many people believe that the use of PEDs is morally wrong and ought to be banned from sports. Is there a good argument for this conclusion? This chapter will explain and evaluate carefully three main arguments for the view that using PEDs in athletic competition is morally wrong. The first argument is based on the idea that the use of PEDs, such as anabolic steroids, is currently against the rules. The second argument focuses on the unfair advantage PED users have, regardless of what the current rules happen to restrict. The third argument is based on the health risks of PEDs to athletes.

The Against the Rules Objection

The first argument is very simple and straightforward. Many PEDs are banned. Currently, players can be fined and suspended for using PEDs such as steroids. Athletes are tested for steroid use, and if they test positive, they can be punished and prevented from competing. Shawne Merriman, a San Diego Chargers linebacker, was suspended for four games in 2006 after testing positive for steroids. Athletes who use banned PEDs, and who either are not tested or find a way to disguise their steroid use and trick the test, are cheating.[2] Cheating is wrong. Here is the first of the three arguments in a nutshell.

1. Athletes who use PEDs gain a competitive advantage by knowingly violating the rules.

2. Any activity that gives an athlete a competitive advantage by knowingly violating the rules is morally wrong.

3. It is morally wrong for athletes to use PEDs.

When thinking about this argument, one could compare athletes using PEDs to a marathoner jumping on the subway for ten miles to relax and speed ahead of the other runners. The rules of the marathon require that runners stay on the course and that they run the entire race without assistance from subways, cars, rollerblades, bicycles, helicopters, or the like. To do otherwise would break the rules, and that is wrong. Using PEDs is a violation of the rules of the game, and thus using them is obviously morally wrong.

While this argument is very strong and it captures the reaction many people have to Barry Bonds's "beating" Hank Aaron's record and Mark McGwire's "beating" Roger Maris's record, it does not show as much as some opponents of PED use might want it to show. The problem with this line of reasoning is that it would show only that using PEDs is wrong given the current rules. That is, the argument shows that using PEDs is wrong because it is against the current rules, but it does not show that using PEDs *should* be against the rules because using PEDs is fundamentally wrong. *Should* the use of performance-enhancing drugs be banned?

This deeper question, which is not answered by the Against the Rules Objection, is whether the rules are morally justified. Perhaps the rules are unjust. An athlete with a headache or inflammation in a joint could legally and morally take some ibuprofen before competition. The use of ibuprofen in such a case might very well enhance an athlete's performance. An athlete suffering from depression might take an antidepressant and that might enhance his or her performance. Is that morally wrong? What, if anything, makes athletes' use of anabolic steroids and other banned substances morally wrong? Suppose that sports did not ban the use of steroids. Would using steroids be wrong then? This argument does not address this deeper question. The second argument does address this question, and it attempts to provide reason to think that using PEDs is wrong, not just because of the current rules, but because of the inherent unfairness PED use brings to athletic competition.

The Unfairness Objection

The second argument, which is a popular argument in the PED debate,[3] is stated as follows:

1. Athletes who use PEDs have an unfair advantage over athletes who do not use PEDs.

2. Anything that gives some athletes an unfair advantage over other athletes is wrong.

3. It is wrong for athletes to use PEDs.

This argument is much more complicated than the previous argument, but it addresses the question of whether there is something inherently wrong with athletes' using PEDs for their competitive advantage. The rationale for premise 1 is based on the fact that PEDs such as anabolic steroids, amphetamines, and human growth hormone can help athletes get stronger, run faster, jump higher, hit harder, reduce body fat, and recover faster than athletes who do not use PEDs. Athletes who use PEDs, according to this premise, are cheating against their drug-free opponents. Would Ben Johnson have been able to beat Carl Lewis in the hundred-meter sprint without the help of steroids? Is any steroid-free athlete capable of beating the home run records of Roger Maris, Babe Ruth, and Hank Aaron? Have some outstanding athletes missed the cut for Olympic competition and lost out on a dream because they were competing against athletes who had the advantage of taking PEDs? Have some players missed out on multimillion-dollar contracts because someone taking PEDs ran a fade route a little faster or made a few more tackles behind the line of scrimmage?

Premise 2 is based on the idea that athletic contests, by their very nature, should be fair and square. Violations of fairness are wrong.

Although the Unfairness Objection is popular and plausible on its face, careful reflection will reveal important questions and problems for this argument. What makes a situation or event unfair? That is a giant philosophical question that cannot be answered adequately in this short chapter. For the purposes of this chapter, I will use the term "unfair" to capture the basic idea that an unfair situation is one in which everyone does not get the same opportunities, treatment, and resources.[4] On this basic interpretation of "unfair," it is clear that there is an enormous amount of unfairness in the world and in the lives of athletes. Because of economic circumstances or even luck, some athletes have better nutrition, "natural" supplements,[5] coaches, trainers, nutritionists, information, lawyers, and equipment than others do. Some athletes have more free time to train than others do. Some athletes are naturally smarter, faster, and stronger than others are. All athletes, whether or not they use PEDs, are not "playing on a level playing field," and that is, in the sense of "unfair" used here, unfair.

Given this interpretation of "unfair," premise 1 is plausible but not obviously true. If PEDs were legal and available to every athlete, then it would seem that PED users would not have an unfair advantage. Realistically, though, PEDs are not legal or readily available. Moreover, even if PEDs were legal and readily available, they would come at a cost. There is no reason to suppose that all athletes would have the same opportunity to purchase and correctly use PEDs. Thus, premise 1 will be accepted for the sake of this argument.

Premise 2 raises some extremely interesting and important questions. The main issue is whether all forms of unfairness (given the sense of unfairness assumed here) are wrong. Is it always morally wrong for an athlete to exploit an unfair advantage? Even if it is unfair that one player has better equipment than another, is it morally wrong for that player to use that equipment? Even if it is true that some athletes are better coached, better fed, more intellectually gifted, and better equipped than others, is it morally wrong for an athlete to take advantage of the unfairness? Even if it is unfair that Jim Thorpe did not have the advantages available to current athletes, such as knowledge of biomechanics, sports medicine, nutrition, and highly breathable fabrics, is it morally wrong for current players to take advantage of this unfairness?[6] It seems that a proponent of the Unfairness Objection is forced to accept that it is morally wrong. But if a proponent of the Unfairness Objection is forced to accept this much, then it seems that an advocate of the Unfairness Objection will be forced to conclude that the world of athletics (and beyond) is full of immoral activity. After all, it is certainly clear that in football and throughout the sports world there is unfairness of the sort identified here. Since most people who are morally opposed to PEDs are not willing to endorse this extreme conclusion, it is clear that the Unfairness Objection is not an argument that is available to most opponents of PEDs.

The Harm and Pressure Objection

The third argument is based on worries about the health risks banned PEDs pose to athletes and the pressure that athletes are under to engage in this risky behavior. Here is the third argument that we will consider:

1. Using PEDs is harmful to athletes, and athletes are under enormous pressure to take PEDs.

2. All things that are harmful to athletes and that athletes are under enormous pressure to do are morally wrong and should be banned from sports.

3. Using PEDs is morally wrong and should be banned from sports.

The rationale for premise 1 is that PEDs pose serious health risks to users. Among the risks are cardiovascular problems, liver problems, adverse effects on blood lipids, fertility problems, vision problems, extreme acne, baldness, and anger and other behavior problems.[7] Lyle Alzado, an outstanding defensive end for the Denver Broncos, Cleveland Browns, and Los Angeles Raiders, was diagnosed with brain cancer just before he wrote a *Sports Illustrated* article in which he admitted to using steroids throughout his NFL career. Not only did he confess to steroid use, but according to Mike Puma, an ESPN reporter, "Alzado was certain the drugs were responsible for his cancer. He became a symbol of the dangers of steroid use."[8]

Premise 1 is also backed by an acknowledgment of the pressure that athletes, even very young athletes, are under to take PEDs if they want to compete at the highest levels possible. Some of the athletes questioned in the recent investigation of the Bay Area Laboratory Co-operative (a laboratory that supplied illegal PEDs to many well-known athletes such as Marion Jones, Jason Giambi, Gary Sheffield, Bill Romanowski, and Tim Montgomery) said that they saw dramatic improvements in their performance during the period in which they were suspected of having used steroids.[9] For example, sprinter Tim Montgomery confessed under oath that he was using human growth hormone and "the clear" when he ran one hundred meters in 9.78 seconds to set the world record. In the *Sports Illustrated* article, Lyle Alzado admitted that steroids were his ticket to the NFL.[10] Alzado explained that he was a mediocre junior college player, with no hope for a spot in the NFL, until he started using steroids. Although many of the world's greatest athletes are under no suspicion of using banned PEDs, many athletes are suspected of, and perhaps guilty of, using banned PEDs. The world of sports is highly competitive and can be very lucrative and fun. The slightest edge can mean the difference between being merely a great high school athlete and being an Olympic champion. It can mean the difference between a job working in a coal mine and the job of being linebacker for the Pittsburgh Steelers. It can mean the difference between coaching a high school baseball team and pitching for the New York Mets. If PEDs work, great athletes have a very strong incentive to take them.

Premise 2 is based on the claim that if something is very harmful, and if people are under a lot of pressure to do if it is not banned, then it ought to be banned. Many people would argue that this is an excellent reason to keep heroin, for example, illegal. Heroin is very dangerous, highly enjoyable, beneficial in the short term for some people, and highly addictive, and so we have a moral obligation to keep it illegal.

The Harm and Pressure Objection is full of controversy. Premise 1 is a completely empirical premise, and its evaluation is better left to the experts in sports medicine and sports psychology. Some very important facts would be helpful in an evaluation of premise 1. It would be important, for example, to know how serious the risks are for athletes using PEDs for their relatively short competitive careers. Many athletes would be willing to put up with some of the short-term side effects such as acne, baldness, anger, and temporary fertility problems in exchange for the benefits of being a professional athlete and a winner.[11] Moreover, it would be interesting to know how much PEDs actually help a typical athlete. Cal Ripken Jr. has never been suspected of using steroids, and he was one of the greatest baseball players of all time. Would he have been even better on steroids, or was he the best that he could be even without them? Barry Bonds was an outstanding baseball player when he was a young and lean Pittsburgh Pirate under no suspicion of drug use. Would he have had a great career without whatever made his body transform into what it is today? Would Barry Sanders, Jim Brown, and Dick Butkus have been better players if they were hopped up on steroids? Finally, it would be interesting to know the effects of PEDs under legalized and carefully monitored conditions. Athletes are buying drugs from people like Victor Conte, who has no pharmaceutical or sports medicine credentials, and they are shooting up in locker room stalls. If PEDs were used properly and developed in reputable labs by top scientists, perhaps their risks would be much lower. Perhaps PEDs could be developed that have very little risk and enormous benefits.[12] These are serious questions for the scientists to figure out. Knowing these empirical facts is essential before we can know what to think about the first premise of the Harm and Pressure Objection to PEDs. Premise 1 cannot be decided from the philosopher's armchair.

Premise 2 is the premise for philosophers. It raises a very important controversy that is much too large to resolve once and for all here, but we can at least lay out the basic debate for reflection and discussion. Some philosophers would prefer to leave the decision of whether to use a risky substance up to the individual athletes. Driving a race car, boxing, skiing, and playing football, for example, are dangerous activities. Although we require helmets and other safety gear, we do not ban these sports. Many philosophers would deny premise 2 and claim that even if the use of PEDs is dangerous and athletes are under pressure to use them, using them is not morally wrong and they should not be banned from sports. The athletes themselves should decide whether to take the risk of using PEDs.

Other philosophers would disagree and paternalistically contend that the harm is so great, and the pressure is so great, that allowing the use of PEDs is morally wrong and these drugs ought to be banned. Such philosophers would argue that if athletes believe they substantially lower their chances of winning—or of competing at all—by not taking steroids, and if they are dangerous, athletes are, in a sense, coerced to harm themselves.

Some other philosophers might be willing to allow adult athletes the autonomy to use PEDs but would want the use of such drugs to be illegal for children. Clearly, this serious philosophical debate must be worked out before we can accept premise 2.

Testing

Another serious issue is testing for steroid use. There are many masking agents that athletes can use to beat the tests. Moreover, in some sports, tests are not performed frequently or randomly and athletes know about the tests well in advance, giving them ample time to prepare. Some PEDs, such as amphetamines, will show up only if an athlete is tested within approximately one day of ingestion. Proponents of legalization might argue that since we cannot accurately test for PEDs, we should not ban the drugs even if they lead to massive advantages for users. Others would say that we ought to ban PEDs but urge much better and tougher testing procedures.

Conclusion: Should There Be a Ban?

So, is it morally wrong for athletes to use PEDs? The strongest argument against their use is the Against the Rules Objection. However, that objection shows only that it is wrong because it is against the actual rules. It does not support the conclusion that the rules are good rules or that

PEDs ought to be banned. Over the years, new fabrics have been developed, new running shoes have been designed, new helmets have been created, new supplements have been concocted. Which ones should be allowed by sports and which ones should not? The Against the Rules Objection does not answer this question. The second argument we considered, the Unfairness Objection, is faced with serious questions and problems. Defenders of the Harm and Pressure Objection still have a lot of work to do. The harms of PEDs, if developed and used under legalized conditions, need to be clearly demonstrated by science. In addition, it needs to be shown that we ought not leave to individual athletes the decision of whether or not to take the risks of using PEDs. Until such work is accomplished, the jury is still out on the Harm and Pressure Objection to performance-enhancing drugs. After considering three interesting arguments, we have found a strong argument against using PEDs given the current rules, but we have not found a strong argument for the general conclusion that using PEDs ought to be against the rules. The Harm and Pressure Objection may well turn out to be an excellent argument. At this point, however, it raises many questions that must be answered before we can rationally conclude that PEDs ought to be banned from sports.

Notes

I am grateful to Mike Austin, Kenneth Enoch, Kristin Kuntz, David Roth, Mark Ryan, Russell Ryan, Amy Steinberg, and Kimberly Zaph for help on this chapter.

1. Some PEDs are banned and some are not. Unless it is stated otherwise, this chapter will focus on the controversial PEDs that are banned, such as anabolic steroids, growth hormone, amphetamines, and the like, and not the innocent performance-enhancing drugs such as ibuprofen.

2. I do not have space here to take up the very serious issue of testing. How do we know who is using steroids? If there is a good argument against PEDs, then a lot more work needs to be done on developing accurate tests as well as random and frequent testing.

3. For an excellent discussion of this argument, see Roger Gardner, "On Performance Enhancing Substances and the Unfair Advantage Argument," in *Philosophy of Sport: Critical Readings, Crucial Issues,* ed. M. Andrew Holowchak (Upper Saddle River, NJ: Prentice Hall, 2002).

4. There are other legitimate senses of 'unfair,' but I believe none of the most obvious senses will do a better job of getting this argument off the ground. I stick with this interpretation for the sake of clarity and simplicity.

5. An important issue that cannot be addressed here involves clarifying the differences among natural supplements, foods, drugs, acceptable PEDs, and unacceptable PEDs and what the distinctions mean for this debate.

6. If it is not morally acceptable, what should an advantaged athlete do? How should a smarter or better-coached and morally sensitive athlete behave? How should sports morally handle the unfairness?

7. National Strength and Conditioning Association Performance-Enhancing Drug Summit handout, 14 April 2007 meeting, Baltimore.

8. Mike Puma, "Not the Size of the Dog in the Fight," ESPN Classic, http://espn.go.com/classic/biography/s/Alzado_Lyle.html.

9. For an interesting discussion of this investigation and the use of PEDs among top athletes, see Mark Fainaru-Wada and Lance Williams, *Game of Shadows: Barry Bonds, BALCO, and the Steroids Scandal That Rocked Professional Sports* (New York: Gotham Books, 2006).

10. Lyle Alzado, "I Lied," *Sports Illustrated,* 8 July 1991.

11. It is worth noting that every day, ordinary patients are willing to take medications with serious side effects for problems that are not life threatening.

12. Similar issues come up in some discussions about the legalization of prostitution and currently illegal drugs such as marijuana.

Marshall Swain and Myles Brand

THE TRUE NATURE OF CHEATING

It is the game of the century. Two powerhouse college football programs, both undefeated the entire year, will meet in the BCS Championship game. Each year, the Bowl Championship Series has matched two excellent teams in the season's final game, but never has the game brought together two more accomplished and successful teams with two such different philosophies.

State University has had the leadership of Coach Smith for almost two decades. He has created a program that not only wins on the field but also graduates its student-athletes. State takes great pride in always being in compliance with all NCAA rules—not an easy task, given the enormous multitude of rules—and doing everything in the right way. State has produced a half-dozen Heisman winners in this period, as well as many student-athletes who have gone on to be prominent physicians, lawyers, and businessmen.

In contrast, Coach Jones was hired by Central University just a few years ago. Central has aggressively pursued football dominance. Coach Jones is known to be tireless in his recruiting, tough with his players, and relentless in his desire to win. While others sometimes think that Central goes too far, its fans love the maverick approach of their coach and the "take no prisoners" attitude on the field. These fans are not upset that Central is on NCAA probation or that the school's graduation rate is poor, to say the least.

Game day arrives. Students from both universities have been drinking since Wednesday. Even State's and Central's faculty members, many of whom normally cannot find the football stadiums on their campuses, are excited about the game. Literally thousands of members of the media are on site. Everyone expects a great game—though the nagging feeling that Central will cheat persists.

State kicks off; Central runs it back to the 25. The two teams face each other at the line. Then it starts.

Central's linemen start trash-talking. "I've got a pet turtle that's faster than you," "You look cute in those tight pants," and other such demeaning remarks.

The media have the field covered with new, powerful microphones. To give the television audience the sense of what it is like to be part of the game, they pick up the sounds on the field—including these remarks by Central's players. Viewers are stunned. Calls come into the network from State's fans demanding the referees assess a penalty to Central. In the stands, a chorus erupts yelling that Central is cheating.

Are they cheating? Have the referees missed a penalty call? The NCAA football rules prohibit unsportsmanlike conduct. But is this mild trash-talking by linemen included? Central's players do not seem to be overly aggressive in their comments. They have, in fact, been effectively coached in the matter of trash-talking—they have strict orders to keep their comments at the level of harmless needling, designed to irritate without really being offensive.

But then several State linemen lose it. Their comments in reply to Central's comments are far more offensive, including angry racial slurs and other personal insults. They have stepped over the line as to what is acceptable within the guidelines. The referees penalize State. Its fans are outraged by the idea that their team has been penalized for actions that were clearly provoked by Central's trash-talking.

After a third down, Central must kick the ball away. State begins its drive and quickly marches down the field. State's quarterback is on top of his game. It looks to be a long day for Central's defense.

Coach Jones grabs his backup middle linebacker off the bench and tells him to get into the game and take out State's quarterback. "We need to get that guy out of the game. Take him down!" The linebacker enters the game, and he does what he is told. He blindsides State's quarterback on a late hit, wrecking his knee; he is carried off the field, ending his season.

With that, State's fans go wild! The entire side of the stadium is screaming "Cheaters!" (among other things). The television announcers look at each other and simultaneously mouth the word "cheaters." But Central's fans merely smile and say that's only hardnosed football.

Who is right? Did Coach Jones cheat by sending in a "hit man"? Coach Jones and his linebacker broke the rules, which clearly say that it is not permitted to intentionally harm another player or for a coach to instruct a player to do so. It is wrong, but is it cheating? If the linebacker is caught and thrown out of the game, is it cheating then? In fact, he was caught and thrown out of the game, and no doubt he will be severely punished, as will Coach Jones. But did either of them cheat?

What is cheating, after all?

Let's roll up our sleeves and do some philosophy. We will return to the big game later.

What Is Cheating?

One good way to articulate the nature of cheating is to develop a definition of cheating. We start with some examples from which to generalize, including the story we have been telling about the big game, and then test and revise the definition. The goal is to develop a definition that captures our intuitions, or commonly held and widely shared beliefs, about cheating. We strive to find a definition that withstands test cases (counterexamples) and explains the key concept in a way that makes clear its underlying meaning.

The central idea to be captured is that cheating is a reflection of the intentions and attitudes of the participants—the players, coaches, and fans—in the context of rule-governed sports. We are principally concerned with organized sporting events, such as high school, college, and professional sports. In these contests, the rules are formally stated, promulgated, and understood by the participants. To obtain a general definition of cheating, it must also fit, though perhaps loosely, less-organized gaming contexts, such as a touch football game, a weekend game of golf, and even a Saturday night poker game. Whenever there is a sports contest or competition governed by rules that the participants are expected to know and understand, there is the potential for cheating.

What are the rules themselves that govern a game? Organized sports are actually played under two kinds of rules. First, there are the *formal,* or *constitutive, rules* of the game. These are usually written rules adopted and endorsed, and subject to revision, by appropriately authorized governing bodies. These rules specify what is permitted or not in the game itself, what kind of equipment is used, the requirements for the field of play, and so forth. Second, there are the *informal rules,* or *conventions,* that are associated with the game. These are usually not written, and they are typically not subject to review or revision by a governing body. Conventions can be different for different locales and groups, and they can change over time. It is an informal rule of most college sports, for example, that the players will shake hands after the event. If they fail to do this, there is no penalty, but it is bad form. The participants in a game, especially at the highly organized level, understand both the formal and the informal rules of the game.

Cheating involves intentionally breaking the rules in an effort to gain an unfair advantage over your opponent. Indeed, this is at the core of the concept of cheating. At first appearance, moreover, it seems that only breaking the formal rules of a game could count as cheating. If you intentionally refuse to shake your opponent's hand after a game, you are breaking an informal rule of the game and being rude, but you are not cheating. Further, a player who does not understand a rule might fail to act in accordance with that rule (thus breaking it) but not be guilty of cheating. Such a player would still be assessed a penalty. Cheating, that is, is purposeful. It is natural, then, to think of a cheater as someone who intentionally breaks a formal rule of the game for the purpose of gaining an unfair advantage in the contest. Let us express all this as a formal definition:

(C) A person, P, cheats with regard to a game if and only if:

(1) P is a participant in that game as a player or coach; and

(2) P intentionally breaks a formal rule of the game with the purpose of gaining an unfair advantage over P's opponents in the game.

Before considering the adequacy of this definition, we want to clarify one point. Although we have formulated the definition for players and coaches, we believe that there may be cases in which officials, and even fans, are guilty of cheating. To capture such possibilities, we could formulate a definition parallel to (C) applying to officials that would replace condition (2) by something like

(2*) P intentionally judges that a formal rule of the game was broken when it was not, or was not broken when it was, with the purpose of enabling one participant (or group of participants) to gain an unfair advantage over the other (or others) in the game.

Fans or others associated with the sporting event may be guilty of cheating when they intentionally assist a participant (or group of participants) in breaking the formal rules of the game with the purpose of providing an unfair advantage to that participant (or the group of participants). We could capture this in yet another auxiliary definition. However, let us focus on the core of the concept of cheating, which involves participants in the game, namely, the players and coaches. The resultant definition can be expanded to cover these additional categories of cheaters in the manner we have suggested.

The situations that have arisen so far in the game between State and Central can be used to illustrate this definition. Both Coach Jones and his linebacker have chosen to intentionally harm State's quarterback, which is against the formal rules of the game, in order to gain an unfair advantage. The actions of Coach Jones and his linebacker satisfy conditions (1) and (2) of the definition (C), and thus each is guilty of cheating in this game. That is as it should be and provides confirmation of our definition.

In the examples of trash-talking, the answer is more complicated. The formal rules in college football make it clear that abusive and provocative language is not permitted, since it is unsportsmanlike conduct, and it is subject to a penalty. When the State linemen began making extremely derogatory comments about Central's players, they were breaking this rule. But they were not breaking the rule to gain an unfair advantage. They were doing so because they were angry at the Central players; they lost it, as it were. So, the State players were properly penalized for breaking the rule, but they were not cheating. Not all rule breaking is cheating.

The Central players were smarter. Their comments were provocative, but they did not cross the line. Their comments were meant to anger the State players, which they did, but without breaking the sportsmanship rule as judged by the officials on the field. Since they did not break a formal rule of the game, they were not cheating. Rather, the Central players were exercising gamesmanship, which is not cheating. The officials correctly did not penalize the Central players, despite what State's fans wanted.

Cheating and Performance-Enhancing Drugs

So far, so good. Our definition seems to get the right results in the examples considered. Unfortunately, there are counterexamples. To see this, let's turn for a moment to a case from another sport, professional baseball. This one is based on the real-life superstar Barry Bonds. As of this writing, Bonds is just a couple of home runs away from breaking Hank Aaron's hallowed, all-time home run record.

Bonds is accused of using performance-enhancing drugs at an earlier time in his career. At this time, he remains under investigation, but there has been no proof that can stand legal scrutiny that he intentionally used performance-enhancing drugs.

For our purposes, the interesting part of this case is that Major League Baseball (MLB) only recently passed a formal rule prohibiting the use of performance-enhancing drugs (steroids, for example). Prior to this time, there was no such rule in professional baseball. Bonds is under investigation for using those drugs prior to the passage of the rule. That is, when he presumably was using those drugs, it was not contrary to the formal rules of baseball. Their use and the ways in which he obtained the drugs may have been illegal at this earlier time, but at that time Bonds broke a different rule, namely, that one obey the law, not a rule within baseball against using these drugs—since, again, there was no such rule at the time.

Imagine now, strictly hypothetically and for philosophic purposes only, that Bonds did use performance-enhancing drugs, but only at times before the passage of MLB's antidoping rules. Imagine also that he obtained these drugs legally. Thus, he did not break any formal rule during any of the games in which he played.

Under these imagined, hypothetical conditions, did Bonds cheat? According to definition (C), he did not. To cheat, in accordance with (C), you have to break a formal rule of the sport, and he did not do so at the time he was using performance-enhancing drugs.

But that conclusion appears to us to be incorrect. Using performance-enhancing drugs gave him an unfair advantage, even if MLB failed at that time to have a rule against it. Part of the issue is whether Bonds had an unfair advantage, not whether the politics within MLB prevented a rule from being passed. But another part of this issue is whether there was an informal rule or convention against the use of such drugs at the time. We believe that there is now, and always has been, such a conventional stricture against these drugs.

To capture this point, a straightforward revision of the definition is necessary:

> (C.1) A person, P, cheats with regard to a game if and only if:
>
>> (1) P is a participant in the game as a player or coach; and
>>
>> (2) P intentionally breaks a formal rule or informal rule or convention of the game with the purpose of gaining an unfair advantage over P's opponents in the game.

That is, condition (2) is broadened to include informal rules and conventions. We have claimed that there is a strong convention in baseball, as there is in all sports, against using performance-enhancing drugs, even at times when there is no formal rule against it. This revised definition (C.1) gives the right answer, under the hypothetical conditions, that Bonds cheated.

Bonds's supporters might object, even in this hypothetical case, by rejecting our claim about the conventional rules. They might argue that there is no convention in baseball, or for that matter in any professional sport, against using performance-enhancing drugs. In the case of professional sports, the players are adults and they may choose to take whatever steps they want to enhance performance. Steroids may have unfortunate health consequences, but an adult may choose to take the risk. It is only those with some vague ideal of "pure" sports, the supporters may say, who hold that there is a convention against the use of performance-enhancing drugs. Using drugs to enhance your strength is no different in principle than lifting weights for that purpose, and there certainly is no convention against the latter.

There is a difference between defining cheating in terms of informal conventions and being able to tell, in any individual case, whether there is such a convention. In the case of formal rules, there is not a similar problem; formal rules are written, and all we have to do is check the official rulebook. But when we add informal rules and conventions to the definition, there can be cases in which it is difficult to know whether the definition applies.

In this hypothetical case, however, we believe there is good evidence for an informal convention or rule against the use of performance-enhancing drugs. Bonds and others accused of using these drugs, even in the absence of formal rules, go to great lengths to deny that they used them. If there were no informal prohibition against using performance-enhancing drugs, then no one would protest strongly. It simply would not matter whether these drugs were used. Similarly, if there were no informal convention or rule against the use of these drugs, then there would not be investigations as to whether they were being used. The investigations are occurring, in part, because there is a convention, known to the public and the players, against using performance-enhancing drugs. Notice that there are no investigations, denials, or cover-ups in connection with weight lifting.

Incidentally, adults cannot do whatever they want to enhance athletic performance. In baseball, they cannot secretly pay off the opposing pitcher or the home plate umpire to assist them when at bat. Such approaches give an unfair advantage to some athletes over others. Similarly, they cannot enhance performance by taking drugs.

Cheating to Win

Back to college football. Consider now another case, a rather fanciful one. Suppose Coach Smith learns that several of Central's best players are academically ineligible but are playing anyway because Coach Jones has hidden the fact. Rather than report Coach Jones to the authorities, Coach Smith puts several of his own student-athletes into the game despite their being academically ineligible. Coach Smith rationalizes his action by saying to himself that he needs to do so to create a "level playing field." Central's Coach Jones would have an unfair advantage unless Coach Smith too played his academically ineligible stars. As Coach Smith sees it, neither team has an unfair advantage as a result.

Both Coach Jones and Coach Smith are cheating. It is clearly against the rules in college football for a player to be academically ineligible. Definition (C.1) gives the right answer in the case of Central's Coach Jones. He broke this rule in order to gain an unfair advantage. But the definition gives the wrong answer in the case of State's Coach Smith. He broke this rule not to gain an unfair advantage but rather to level the playing field, to remove his opponent's unfair advantage. This wrong answer constitutes a counterexample to definition (C.1).

To correct for this problem, motives other than gaining an unfair advantage should be recognized for cases of cheating. In the case at hand, Coach Smith is breaking the rules in an effort *to enhance his team's chances of winning;* he is not attempting to gain an unfair advantage. Ironically, he wants to eliminate all unfair advantages in the game. The goal of enhancing one's chances is broader than, and includes, the goal of attempting to gain unfair advantage. If someone intentionally breaks the rules in the effort to achieve this broad goal, then he or she cheated. With that in mind, definition (C.1) should be modified:

> (C.2) A person, P, cheats with regard to a game if and only if:
>
> (1) P is a participant in that game as a player or coach; and
>
> (2) P intentionally breaks a formal rule or an informal rule or convention of the game with the purpose of enhancing P's chances of winning the game.

This revised definition yields the right results in the case of Coach Smith's actions, as well as Coach Jones's, while preserving the correct answers in the earlier cases.

The latest example raises considerations having to do with the goals that might motivate one to cheat. It is natural to think of winning the game, or enhancing one's chances of winning, and the like as the primary motivations for purposeful breaking of the rules. While we think this is so, we also find that other goals might motivate cheating behavior. For example, we can imagine a superstar in some sport who is so much superior to his or her opponents that winning a contest is hardly ever in question. Rather, what motivates this individual to cheat in a particular event is the desire to achieve a new world record, or to gain notoriety as the first to win five such events in a row, or something of that sort. We could also imagine a player who has gambled on the outcome of the game and puposefully drops a pass, or overthrows one, in order to influence the outcome of the game in favor of his bet. Breaking the rules for any of these purposes would certainly count as cheating even if the primary motivation is not just winning the game. We think that such motives can be incorporated into our basic definition in a straightforward manner, but we will not attempt to make that revision here.

Unfortunately, there are further counterexamples even to our revised definition of cheating, and these examples lead to a significant complicating factor. Consider a situation that often arises in football games, but also in any game where there are clear time limits. Suppose the score is State 14 and Central 12, and there are twenty-five seconds left on the game clock. State has the ball, and it is third down. To avoid allowing Central to have any chance of getting the ball and scoring, State's Coach Smith instructs his team to purposefully let the play clock run down, thereby assuring that they win the game. This kind of strategy is very common; indeed it is expected by players, coaches, referees, and fans, and it is considered to be acceptable, if frustrating, behavior in an organized game of football. And yet it would count as cheating in accordance with our definition (C.2). State's coach intentionally breaks a rule with the goal of enhancing the chances of winning the game. Although State must take its penalty, and perhaps a few boos from Central's fans, no one would consider it to be a case of cheating.

To fix this problem, let us turn to the field of ethics for an analogy. It often happens that conflicts develop between different sets of ethical, moral, or legal prescriptions, and a decision must be made concerning the dominant rule. For example, if a person owes money to a bank for a mortgage loan, then that person prima facie has an obligation to pay the loan in a timely fashion. However, if unforeseen circumstances beyond that person's control force bankruptcy, then the obligation to pay the loan is overridden (at least temporarily) by these unforeseen developments. The prima facie obligation to pay the mortgage is *defeated* by the circumstances that drove the individual into bankruptcy. In the case at hand, the informal rules of a game can sometimes override the formal rules, and when this is so, a prima facie case of cheating might be nullified. In the case of running out the clock, there is an informal rule or convention, accepted by everyone involved in the game of football, that judicious use of the game and play clocks as a strategy to win is acceptable. When a coach uses this strategy, the informal rule nullifies the charge of cheating, although it does not nullify the play clock rule. So, in this case, there is an intentional rule violation with the goal of enhancing the team's chance of winning, but the prima facie charge of cheating is defeated by the informal rule concerning strategy.

To account for these types of cases, a further revision of the definition is required:

(C.3) A person, P, cheats with regard to a game if and only if:

(1) P is a participant in that game as a player or coach; and

(2) P intentionally breaks a formal rule or informal rule or convention of the game with the purpose of enhancing P's chances of winning the game; and

(3) There is no generally accepted informal rule or convention of the game that allows P to intentionally break this rule for the purpose of enhancing P's chances of winning the game.

This revision gives the right answer. There is a generally accepted convention that allows coaches to use the play clock to their advantage.

The End of the Game

Well, State wins. The fans leave the stadium in anticipation of next year's game of the century, the students sleep off their hangovers, and the faculty go back to their classrooms. And now we know what cheating is.

M. Andrew Holowchak

"THEY DON'T PAY NOBODY TO BE HUMBLE!"

Football's Ego Problem

November 18, 2003, was a turning point in professional American football—perhaps in professional sport. Tampa Bay Buccaneer wide receiver Keyshawn Johnson was officially deactivated. Johnson had stated openly to his teammates during the year that he did not plan to be with the team at the end of the season. He felt that he was being underutilized and that the team was suffering because of that. There were many instances, in front of players and fans alike, where he let the coach know how he felt. Spokespersons for the team stated that Johnson was let go because he was a distraction to the team. He had been missing training sessions and team meetings and was not shy about showing his disgust for his coach, Jon Gruden.

Why was this event such a turning point in professional football? What is so significant about Johnson's deactivation? Players, fans, and owners are coming belatedly to learn what the best coaches have always known: self-absorbed or ego-puffed players, however talented, are in the long haul a detriment to their team. Johnson's deactivation was a signal to the rest of the league and to all of sport that at least one team thinks it is easier to win consistently without such players, however gifted. The underlying premise is this: A team of talented players—who are committed to their coach, their fellow players, a system of team play, their sport, and their fans—will generally outperform a team of superstars, each of whom is chiefly committed to himself.

This argument against self-absorption is forceful, yet it does not go far enough. Players do not harm their team merely through fewer wins and more losses over time. Some players also harm their sport, their society, and even, perhaps unknowingly, themselves. To aid in seeing the weight of this problem, in what follows I phrase the difficulty not just in terms of self-absorption but also in terms of other-concern: Why is it that so many athletes have such a barefaced disregard for others—players, coaches, and fans—in professional football today?

Ego-Puffing

Perhaps a large contributing cause of this problem is the manner in which players are marketed before they make it to the professional ranks. They are scouted and assessed principally as individuals, not so much as members of a team. Too often we assume that raw talent and athletic potential will make a player a factor at the next level. When players turn professional, the lure of a multimillion-dollar salary entices them to market themselves as individuals, not as members of a team. A talented wide receiver like Johnson is attractive to a contending team in need of receivers. Unfortunately, those fishing for talent seem seldom to consider whether such players will be an asset or a distraction to the team in the long haul.

Playing on and for a team is important, but increasingly players strive to make themselves visible in team sports through ego-puffed displays: self-promoting exceptional play, showboating, taunting, and even fighting opponents, coaches, or teammates. What is most unsettling is that players are generally praised, even rewarded, by fans for drawing attention to themselves at the expense of their opponents and even their teammates and coaches. When things are going well for the team, ego-puffed players are the first to let everyone know just how their play has led to such success. When things are going badly, it is, of course, not they who are to blame. Football analyst and former player Merril Hoge had this to say about Johnson, before his deactivation from Tampa Bay: "Oftentimes, it's during adversity that you find out what a person is truly made of. And, true to character, when something doesn't go right, Keyshawn Johnson has repeatedly been the first guy to beat his chest and say, 'What about me?' In the midst of a three-game skid, what the Bucs players should be saying is, 'What about the team?'" [1]

The narcissistic antics of self-absorbed athletes in football exist because we not only tolerate them but also encourage them. As football fans and fans of competitive sport, we eat up ego-puffed athletes.

Sensationalism and Other-Concern

What of Terrell Owens, perhaps today's most celebrated ego-puffed athlete not only in football, but in American sports? Owens seems to love football, and his showy displays suggest that he has a certain amount of fun competing. Still, after a series of episodes that were deemed harmful to the team, he was released in 2006 from the Philadelphia Eagles, only to be picked up by Dallas the following year.

Ego-puffing may be fun for athletes like Owens, and it may have a great deal of fan appeal; nonetheless it is wrong for competitive sport. First, ego-puffing always undermines the efforts of teammates and the rest of the supporting cast (from owners and coaches to trainers and boosters). For instance, after being sidelined with a broken leg toward the end of the 2005 season, Owens made these comments about the Philadelphia Eagles' chances of making it to the Super Bowl without him:

> It hurts bad just to hear how now people are walking around town saying, "We're done." or "Without T.O., they can't get it done." Everybody knows they have to step up. There's no ifs, ands or buts about it. What I brought to this team—on and off the field—through 13, 14 games . . . that's enough to take them, to get over the hump. That will take them to the NFC Championship. I honestly believe this team will win the NFC Championship once we get there. There's no doubt in my mind. I feel like I've done what I had to do. I've set the table. Now all they have to do is go eat.[2]

The implication of the last sentence is plain: Owens has done the dirty work for the team through some thirteen or fourteen games; now it is "their" turn to do the rest, and the rest is easy. Just sit and eat. Owens has set the table. The contrast between his use of "I" and "they" throughout suggests that he has set himself apart from, or is above, the team. Only once does he use the word "we."

Second, self-promotion makes light of the efforts of opponents. One has only to consider the 2002 episode of Owens's autographing the ball after a touchdown against the Seattle Seahawks. Seattle's coach Mike Holmgren said afterward, "I think it's shameful. There's no place for anything like that in our game. It's too great of a game." Holmgren then added that one of his ballplayers should have confronted Owens. "I think certain times players cross the line, and you've got to take care of business."[3] The incident shows that self-promotion and other-deprecation are related issues. It is virtually impossible to puff yourself up without deflating opponents.

On the self-absorption of Owens, Paul Willistein writes: "While we enjoy Terrell Owens' athletic acumen, do we really need post-game analysis of his sideline [antics] and *Desperate Housewives* TV commercial antics? Based on the amount of newspaper ink and commentators' air time, Owens symbolizes the triumph of team member over team."[4] Owens's "triumph" is difficult to swallow, since he has not done for football what, say, Babe Ruth did for baseball or Ali did for boxing. As the implications of his career unfold, both for himself and his sport, his triumph may very well turn out to be Pyrrhic.

Why do sports fans, coaches, players, and owners not only tolerate, but also encourage, ego-puffing in athletes? Part of the answer is the sensationalism of competitive sport and the natural human tendency to be drawn toward sensational events. According to philosopher John Dewey (1859–1952), a sensationalist attitude is oversimplified and anti-intellectual —one that takes episodes out of their proper context and fails to see them in relation to other things. Writes he: "One effect [of sensationalism] . . . has been to create in a large number of persons an appetite for the momentary 'thrills' caused by impacts that stimulate nerve endings but whose connections with cerebral functions are broken. Then stimulation and excitation are not so ordered that intelligence is produced. At the same time the habit of using judgment is weakened by the habit of depending on external stimuli. Upon the whole it is probably a tribute to the powers of endurance of human nature that the consequences are not more serious than they are."[5]

The effect of sensationalism is the abandonment of what Dewey calls an "intellectual" approach to events—here competitive sporting events—for a momentary, thrill-seeking approach to them. People prefer the sudden jolt of episodic thrills that sporting events offer—being unexpectedly blown away by a gargantuan home run or by a basketball slam-dunk—to a fuller and richer grasp of athletic competitions, within the larger context of other events. We are moved more by Owens's 2002 ego-puffed signing of the football after a touchdown than by the concerted effort of his team that allowed the catch to happen (the strong play by the defense that enabled the offense to get the ball, the solid blocking by the offensive line, the quarterback's precise throw, the other receivers who blocked or acted as decoys, etc.). Ego-puffing is the bastard child of sensationalism, because it promotes further sensationalism at the expense of a fuller grasp of what is going on in a contest. One puffs up oneself and, at the same time, deflates others.

After Owens was released from the Eagles at the end of the 2005–2006 season, former teammate N. D. Kalu had this to say: "What did I learn from it? That the chemistry thing is real. I never was one to believe in chemistry, but you had to notice that we'd always brought in the same kind of guys, guys who didn't care about the spotlight or about stats, guys that just wanted to win. You bring in one guy who doesn't feed into that thinking and it disrupts the whole team."[6]

Individual Statistics and the Lack of Genuine Concern for Others

Another reason why ego-puffing and lack of other-concern are such problems in contemporary competitive sport is our modern-day preoccupation with statistical analysis in all aspects of competitive sport—a concern that is especially evident in fantasy football. Today there is not just victory, but categories of victory, where statistical components come into play. For example, many sports fans know that Texas beat Michigan in the 2005 Rose Bowl, 38–37, in a drama-filled game, but the more enlightened mavens know that sixteen Rose Bowl records were tied or broken in the process. Of these, some of the more noteworthy are as follows:

- Texas quarterback Vince Young was responsible for five touchdowns (four rushing, one passing; ties record)
- Young also rushed for 192 yards and four touchdowns (new record, quarterback)
- Michigan receiver and kick returner Steve Breaston had 315 all-purpose yards (new record)
- Breaston also had 221 kickoff return yards (a record for all bowl games)

- Michigan quarterback Chad Henne passed for four touchdown passes (ties record)

- Michigan All-American receiver Braylon Edwards caught three touchdown passes (new record)

- Michigan scored the most points scored in a losing effort (ties record)

In short, an after-the-game statistical analysis of the 2005 Rose Bowl reveals that there are numerous contests within a single contest and even the losing team can claim its share of victories. Henne, Breaston, and Edwards, in a losing effort, did what they did in front of a national audience and a multitude of NFL scouts. With great individual performances, they also became part of college football history. The Wolverines may have lost the war, but they won a good number of battles along the way.

Why is there such an obsession with numbers in competitive sport today? Bero Rigauer says that numbers give sport objectivity.

> Athletic achievements now take place in the "objective framework" of the c-g-s (centimeter, gram, second) system or in point scores which rely either upon objectively measurable achievements (as in the pentathlon and decathlon) or in referees' calls and subjective judgments (as in team games, gymnastics, boxing, etc.). The application of a socially sanctioned system of measurements allows the objective comparison of all athletic achievements—exactly like the achievements of labor productivity. They are all rationalized into universally understandable measurements of value. With such quantified, abstract forms, it is possible to compete even against opponents who are not present. One may race, for example, against a world record.[7]

Statistical analysis allows us to rank athletic performance on an absolute scale, and absolutism gives athletic competition legitimacy. Michigan's Steve Breaston's 315 all-purpose yards beat the former record of O. J. Simpson (276 yards in 1969), and that put him "on the map." That is legitimacy.

Of course, numbers related to competition are themselves neither good nor bad. Some seem interesting for their own sake. Michigan and Texas were deserving of their Rose Bowl matchup, among other things, because they are two of the most winning programs in college football—with 842 and 787 wins respectively at the time. This shows that both schools have football programs, steeped in tradition, with commitments to winning football games. Other statistics, like Michigan's tying the record for most points scored in a losing effort, seem insipid. Nonetheless, the 2005 Rose Bowl is an illustration of today's frenzied application of numbers to competitive sport. There are various games we can play with numbers before, during, or after a contest for self-amusement. There are various games within a game.

This application of numbers to competitive sport has one ugly consequence. Far too often players are evaluated by statistical data that function to pull them outside the framework of the team or the sport they play. Statistical data focus on players as individuals, and that has a marked impact on their team or their sport. Certain players, usually the most insecure, become ego-puffed because of the numbers that "prove" their superiority. Like leeches on flesh, ego-puffed players feed off numerical analysis to the extent that they care more for their own numbers than for their team or sport.

One of the most notorious present-day examples of ego-puffing is football star "Neon" Deion Sanders (a.k.a. "Prime Time").[8] One of the most talented defensive backs ever to play in the NFL, Sanders is also one of the showiest. As a senior at Florida State, he arrived at FSU's stadium for a game against the University of Florida in a limousine, dressed in a tuxedo. Exiting the limousine, he said, "How do you think defensive backs get attention? They don't pay nobody to be humble!" This ostentation he took to Major League Baseball and to the NFL, where he has had unquestioned success as a defensive back and kick and punt returner. Sanders has never been shy about letting others know about his greatness.

Over time, the flashy jewelry and clothes, fine cars, and other by-products of his competitive successes took a toll on Sanders. Despite Super Bowl victories with Dallas and San Francisco, difficulties in his personal life led him to attempt suicide in 1997. He then found meaning, as he tells the story, by turning away from Deion toward Christ. "I'll have to be honest. I never liked Deion Sanders. Too much of a showboat for me. Now I'm going to spend eternity with him because he is trusting in Christ."[9]

Why do coaches, owners, players, and fans tolerate such self-centered arrogance? One has merely to look as Sanders's numbers over his career as a defensive back and punt and kick returner. Those numbers, it seems, justify the self-absorption and give Sanders, whether his team wins or loses, legitimacy.

Aretism: An Ideal for Competitive Sport

In several sport-related publications, I have sketched a normative and integrative account of competitive sport called "Aretism."[10] I have argued that Aretism commits athletes to threefold excellence: (1) excellence through personal integration; (2) excellence through civic integration; and (3) excellence through a type of global integration.

Personal integration involves athletes' own autonomous striving for a greater sense of self through competitive sport. Through integrative participation, athletes come to see sport as a vehicle for both physical and even moral self-improvement.

Civic integration implies that athletes are citizens of a competitive community in which they treat sport as a social institution and they recognize and respect others while competing.[11] While competitively and creatively distinguishing themselves from others in a particular sport, athletes acknowledge the contributions of other athletes, who also accept sport as a social institution. Civically integrated athletes agree to conduct themselves in a manner respectful and appreciative of the efforts of other competitors. In short, following the dictum of the philosopher Immanuel Kant (1724–1804), others are to be treated as ends and not means.

Finally, global integration entails deliberately engaging in competitive sport in a manner consistent with the set of relatively stable values that define its practice over time, such as friendliness, patience, perseverance, and commitment.[12] Athletes come to understand that their own athletic expression in sport, as a celebration of human perseverance and creativity, takes on meaning because of these global values. Thus, through global integration, individual competition merges with moral responsibility, and individual autonomy is thereby suitably nurtured. In a word, global integration requires that athletes are answerable to, not freed from, the dictates of justice.

In short, because of its regard for people as social animals and sport as a social institution, Aretism places normative constraints on athletic competitors.

How is Aretic integration best grasped? It is helpful to think of concentric circles. Beginning with personal integration in the centermost position, there follows civic integration and, finally, global integration. The overall system owes much to Stoic philosophy, a school of thought that thrived in Greco-Roman antiquity.[13]

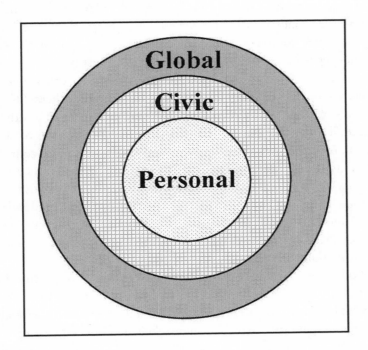

In what follows, I attempt to flesh out Aretism as a modified version of Stoic ethics. The idea here is to give not just an ethics of sport, but an ethics of life that is respectful of competitive sport as a valued social practice.

Stoic Balance: Ethics for Sport and Life

The Stoic philosopher Chrysippus (280–207 B.C.) speaks of virtuous activity in life as a competitive footrace: "When a man enters the footrace . . . it is his duty to put forth all his strength and strive with all his might to win, but he ought never with his foot to trip or with his hand to foul a competitor. Thus, in the stadium of life, it is not unfair for anyone to seek to obtain what is needful for his own advantage, but he has no right to wrest it from his neighbor."[14] For Chrysippus, virtue entails that one may compete for the first prize in life, so long as one does not trip or shove competitors along the way. This is, in effect, the Stoic notion of *oikeiosis*.

Oikeiosis for the Stoics was a matter of achieving a balance between self- and other-concern in life.[15] One strives to help others but does not need to sacrifice completely one's own interest to do so. In all actions, even other-regarding actions, one's own interest must be considered too, because one is as much a part of the cosmos as is any other person. In other words, one's own interest impacts the interests of others. One must not, however, secure one's own interest to the detriment of another. Cicero states it thus: "For one person to deprive another in order to increase their welfare at the cost of the other person's welfare is more contrary to Nature than death, poverty, pain, or any other thing that can happen to one's body or one's external possessions. To begin, it destroys human communal living and human society. If we are each about to plunder and carry off another's goods for the sake of our own, then that will necessarily destroy the thing that is in fact most according to Nature—namely the social life of human beings."[16]

Yet oikeiosis for Stoics is more than just a matter of respectful competition with others, where "respect" is cashed out as refusal to harm another while competing. It embraces Stoic egalitarianism, other-concern, and global culpability. Virtue through oikeiosis implies that one knows fully well what is one's own and what is not one's own—that is, what is another's—and that seems a clear statement not only of self- and other-knowing but also of self- and other-concern. The virtuous athlete competes to the best of his ability, but he does so with full respect for himself, other competitors, and the sport that he plays.

"In the Moral Zone"

How would an athlete who is committed to respectful, Aretic competition behave? He would behave no differently than one who is committed to respectful living. Again, I return to the ancient Stoics to explain.

The ancient Stoics thought not only that a person could progress toward virtue but also that a person could attain *perfect* virtue—a stable state of soul that lent itself to flawless living. The best way to understand this perfection of soul, Stoic sagacity, is by analogy with an athlete in the zone.

Athletes who have experienced being in the zone typically speak of complete immersion in the game, things slowing down, effortless play, freedom from distractions, extreme confidence in their capacities, and lack of deliberation while competing. Similarly, what Stoics describe when they describe a sage seems to be a type of being in a moral zone. The chief difference is this. Most consider athletic zoning to be a phenomenon that may last from a few minutes to a few days. Stoic sagacity is considered to be a lasting state of soul—a way of life. Once a sage, a Stoic is "in the moral zone," as it were, if not for life, then for a lengthy period of time.[17] This would be comparable to the impossible scenario of an athlete finding his zone one day and then not leaving it.

What I have sketched above is a model of moral zoning that is characteristic of Stoic sagacity. Yet this model also applies well to Aretic activity in competitive sport. The following rules characterize the model during competition (whether inside or outside competitive sport):

1. Harm no one.

2. Preserve the common utility.

3. Hold what is one's own as one's own and let others do the same.

4. Strive only for advantageous things within one's reach and outside the reach of others.

5. Fulfill oneself to the best of one's capacity, through knowledge of self and others.

This model, when fully fleshed out as a child of Stoic ethical thinking, has one startling feature that may not be obvious. Unlike sporting contests, like football games, where ultimately only one team can win, in the contest of life there is no such constraint. If anything, Stoic sagacity entails that the contest will be better the more winners it produces. So according to the rules of the contest, mutual assistance is morally desirable, and that is a strange sort of contest!

How do we make sense of life as a contest where as many people win as is possible? Such a contest begins with self-understanding—that is, *knowledge of what is one's own and what is not one's own.* The right sort of upbringing will help a youth to learn about himself, what he can and cannot do, in spite of his desires. It will also help him to hone his reasoning skills, so that he will know how to adapt himself uniquely to ever-changing circumstances each day. With careful nurture, he will develop discernment of his circumstances and a clear grasp of his capacities, and he will not strive for what is beyond his reach. The Stoic Epictetus gives a helpful analogy in his *Handbook*. At a banquet, a virtuous person does not call out or stretch out his hand for food. Instead, he waits for it to come to him, and, when it does, he takes what he wants and passes it immediately to the next person, so that he too may have his share.[18] In the analogy, one merely acts to the best of one's capacities in circumstances, and, when one cannot help others, one allows sufficient space for others to act to the best of their capacities. That is accepting one's role in life. That is oikeiosis. That is what it means to play by the rules of the game of life.

There are, of course, limits to this moral-zoning model. Perfection in life, like perfection in sport, is an unreachable ideal. Aretism, grasped as a tripartite ethical theory, rejects Stoic perfectionism in favor of progressivism. If the perfectionist ideal of canonical Stoicism is continued peak performance through always performing right acts, the Aretic progressivist ideal is peak performance as often as possible through the greatest possible proportion of right acts to non-right acts. A "competitor" in life is rewarded most not only for immersing himself in the contest of life but also for helping to immerse all other competitors in the contest of life as much as he can. Fullest immersion in the contest of life is striving to one's fullest ability to hit the target at which one, striving to live virtuously, aims. Consistent with canonical Stoicism, winning the contest is not a matter of hitting the target but of right-intended action aimed at hitting the target.[19] Right-intended action is winning. In a similar fashion, what is true of right living is equally true of good athletic competition.

Conclusion: Aretism and American Football

How then does Aretism attempt to solve the problems of ego-puffing and lack of other-concern in competitive sports—most notably American football? First, it is important to call attention to them not only as genuine problems in today's competitive sports but also as problems of significant moral weight. Next, I have tried to show that competition itself is not the cause of these problems, though *excessive* competitiveness and sensationalism are certainly causal factors. Finally, I have argued that Aretism—understood as a progressivist ideal for competitive sport that is modeled after early Stoic ethical thinking—allows for a virtue-based way of dealing with ego-puffing and other-concern in a manner that is true to the spirit of competition and respectful of competitive sport as a valued social practice.

Notes

1. "Johnson's Time in Tampa Appears Over," ESPN.com, 20 November 2003; http://sports.espn.go.com/nfl/news/story?id=1664796.

2. This quote was formerly on Terrell Owens's Web site and is no longer available.

3. The incident was widely commented upon in the press; the quotes here were found at http://findarticles.com/p/articles/mi_qn4155/is_20021020/ai_n12488126.

4. Paul Willistein, "'Basketbrawl' Epitomizes Pro Sports' 'Slam Dunk' Non-Team-Player Mentality," *East Penn Press* (Allentown, PA), 8 December 2004, 18.

5. John Dewey, *Freedom and Culture* (Amherst, NY: Prometheus Books, 1989), 39–40.

6. Dana Pennett O'Neil, "At Season's End, Several Eagles Come Clean about Terrell Owens," *Philadelphia Daily News,* 5 January 2005.

7. Bero Rigauer, *Sport and Work,* trans. Allan Guttman (New York: Columbia University Press, 1984), 57–58.

8. Sanders often notes with pride that he gave himself both nicknames.

9. "Where Sanders Goes, Teams Win," ESPN.com, http://espn.go.com/sportscentury/features/00016459.html; accessed 10 January 2008.

10. M. Andrew Holowchak, "Excellence as Athletic Ideal: Autonomy, Morality, and Competitive Sport," *International Journal of Applied Philosophy* 15, no. 1 (2001): 153–64; "'Aretism' and Pharmacological Ergogenic Aids in Sport: Taking a Shot at Steroids," *Journal of the Philosophy of Sport* 27, no. 1 (October 2000): 35–50.

11. "Political" in "Excellence as Athletic Ideal."

12. "Cosmic" in "Excellence as Athletic Ideal."

13. The model I propose is Stoic and resembles that of Hierokles' ten concentric circles. Hierokles writes: "The first and closest circle is the one that a person has drawn as though around a center, his own mind. This circle encloses the body and anything taken for the sake of the body. It is virtually the smallest circle and it almost touches the center itself. Next, the second one, further removed from the center but enclosing the first circle, contains parents, siblings, wife, and children. The third one has in it uncles and aunts, grandparents, nephews, nieces, and cousins. The next circle (4) includes the other relatives, and this is followed by (5) the circle of local residents, then (6) the circle of fellow-demes-men, next (7) that of fellow-citizens, and then (8) in the same way the circle of people from neighboring towns, and (9) the circle of

fellow-countrymen. The outermost and largest circle (10), which encompasses all the rest, is that of the whole human race." Stobaeus, *Florilegium*, vol. 4, ed. C. Wachsmuth and O. Hense (Berlin: Weidmannos, 1884–1912), 671.

14. Cicero, *Duties*, 3.10.42. My translations throughout.

15. Literally, the process by which things are rendered familiar to oneself or one's own. Humans have a natural impulse to pursue what is appropriate to their own nature and shun what is not. When I refer to oikeiosis here, I am referring to what is most rightly one's own as a fully rational, adult human being.

16. Cicero, *Duties*, 3.5.21.

17. Allowing for the possibility that virtue can be lost, once gained. The Stoic Cleanthes believed that virtue, once secured, could not be lost. And so, wisdom, once secured, was the continual exercise of virtue. Chrysippus thought that even a sage had to be on guard, as drunkenness or forlornness could cause one to slip from virtue. Diogenes Laertius, *Lives, Teachings, and Sayings of Famous Philosophers*, 7.127–8.

18. Epictetus, *Handbook*, 15.

19. Cicero, *Ends*, 3.6.22.

THIRD QUARTER

PHILOSOPHICAL ARMCHAIR QUARTERBACKING

Michael W. Austin

CROWNING A TRUE CHAMPION

The Case for a College Football Playoff

The 2007 Fiesta Bowl was arguably one of the greatest college football games ever played. Incredibly, Boise State and Oklahoma combined to score twenty-two points in the last 1:26 of the fourth quarter. With the ball at midfield, fourth and 18, Boise State ran a hook-and-ladder play. Drisan James caught Jared Zabransky's pass at the 35-yard line and then pitched the ball to teammate Jerard Rabb, who took it into the end zone. The extra point forced the game into overtime. In OT, Boise State scored a touchdown on fourth down and then decided to go for the win with a two-point conversion. They succeeded, defeating the Oklahoma Sooners by one point, 43–42. Though the Broncos of Boise State finished the season a perfect 13–0, they didn't get a shot at the national title. That opportunity was reserved for the then undefeated Ohio State Buckeyes and the 12–1 Florida Gators. The Gators beat the Buckeyes in a 41–14 rout. The only undefeated team in NCAA Division I-A college football finished the season ranked fifth in the final Associated Press poll and sixth in *USA Today*'s final rankings.[1] In each of these polls, two teams with *two* losses each—the University of Southern California and Louisiana State University—were ranked ahead of the undefeated Boise State Broncos. The 2007–2008 season underscored the need for a playoff in the minds of many, as in the Associated Press's final rankings the top six teams each had *two* losses, while Kansas finished seventh at 12–1 after defeating Virginia Tech in the Orange Bowl. LSU is the first team ever to have two losses and finish atop the AP's final poll. Something is wrong with the current system.

Justice and the BCS

Why isn't the champion of NCAA Division I-A football decided on the field? Keith Dunnavant chronicles the relationship between television and college football in his explanation of the creation of the Bowl Championship Series (BCS).[2] The tradition of the bowl games is a long and storied one, and the excitement, importance, and profitability of those games have grown as television and college football have grown together. The whole story would take too long to cover here, and it is well chronicled by Dunnavant. However, it is important to point out that the changes undergone by college football in the past have been wrought by (among other things) money, television, and a desire to get the top two teams facing off in postseason play. And it is this last factor that is important for my argument.

I would now like to offer a philosophical case for why the NCAA championship should be decided on the field. In so doing, I will claim that this is in fact a moral issue. As such, it belongs to the field of ethics, which is the area of philosophy that studies how we ought to live, principles of right and wrong, and what it is to live a fulfilled human life. Now there are certainly more important moral issues in our world than whether we should scrap the BCS for a playoff system. The war in Iraq, genocide in Darfur, the AIDS crisis in Africa, and global poverty jump to mind. As *Sports Illustrated*'s Tim Layden puts it: "Bowls, polls, and computers will often burn some deserving team while rewarding another, and . . . there will often not be closure at the end of the season. . . . The true national champion was in dispute in '90 (Colorado or Georgia Tech?), '91 (Miami or Washington?), '93 (Florida State or Notre Dame?), '94 (Nebraska or Penn State?) and '97 (Michigan or Nebraska?). On none of these occasions did the earth open up and swallow civilization."[3] Civilization has survived the frequent failures of "bowls, polls, and computers." And yet a significant part of the attraction of sport, and college football in particular, is that it provides an opportunity to display both athletic and moral greatness. We can all recall times when, either as a fan or as an athlete, we have seen both the best and worst in human nature. Sports also teach us about fairness, competition, and what it takes to excel in life. However, the current system in college football runs counter to these values. Given this, I would like to argue that the issue of crowning a true champion in college football should not be thought of as primarily a matter of money for the schools involved or entertainment for those of us who are fans. Rather, one of the primary issues at the heart of this matter is the issue of justice.

Justice has been a topic of perennial concern for philosophers, as they have focused on issues of political justice, global justice, legal justice, and justice as a personal virtue. In this section, I'll focus on applying the idea of *distributive justice* to the question of whether or not we should implement a college football playoff.[4] To do this I'll make use of a particular principle of distributive justice. A principle of distributive justice is a principle that focuses on a particular good or benefit to be distributed, such as income, wealth, jobs, or opportunities. There are numerous such principles, though I will focus on and make use of a *merit-based* principle of distributive justice in an argument for the claim that all Division I-A college football teams should have the opportunity to win the national championship on the field of play.

A merit-based principle of distributive justice with respect to economic benefits holds that people deserve economic benefits because of the actions that they've performed. On this type of principle, a doctor, an electrician, and a teacher all deserve certain economic benefits because of the socially productive work that they do. Different philosophers have offered different views with respect to what it is that gives rise to deserving these benefits, including the value of the contribution made to society, the effort expended in socially productive work, and the costs incurred by people as they engage in such work. None of these versions of a merit-based principle of distributive justice will suit our purposes, because while sport, including college football, offers a distinct context that certainly has economic ramifications, those ramifications are not intrinsic to the sport itself. We wouldn't want to give a team the chance to play in the national championship game because it made a valuable contribution to society, or tried really hard, or made great sacrifices in order to play the game. So we need a different basis of merit here. If we focus on the *opportunity* to win a national championship as the benefit that a merit-based principle of distributive justice allocates when applied to college football, then we're on our way to having a basis for a philosophical argument in favor of a playoff.

After the 2007 Fiesta Bowl, Boise State quarterback Jared Zabransky said, "We went 13–0 and beat everyone on our schedule. We deserve a chance at the national title."[5] If we apply a merit-based principle of distributive justice to sport, we can see that Zabransky is right. We've already seen that the main categories that such principles fall under in the economic realm don't work in the realm of sport. There must be something different that gives rise to a team's deserving a shot at the national title, but what is it? One of the primary aims of athletic competition is winning. This is one of the main rewards athletes seek as they develop and display their athletic skills.[6] The ultimate goal with respect to winning is to win the championship. Moreover, given the nature of sport, champions should be determined by wins and losses, rather than opinion polls. I propose that for the purpose of deciding who has the opportunity to play for a national title, we should employ *victory on the field* as the criterion of a merit-based principle of justice that is appropriate for sport, including college football. The best way to do this, as I discuss in more detail below, is to institute a sixteen-team playoff in which all eleven conference champions receive an automatic bid, with room for five additional teams to receive at-large bids. This would give every team the opportunity to win the national championship. Win your conference, and you get your shot.

That victory on the field is the best criterion for a merit-based principle of justice for sport might seem like a trivial or fairly obvious point. And that's the point! It *should* be obvious that in competitive sports, we ought to determine who the champion is by allowing teams to play for and win the championship on the field. But a team like Boise State is denied the opportunity to win a national championship. This is wrong because the players certainly deserved this opportunity, in view of the fact that they went undefeated. A team that goes undefeated deserves the opportunity to win (or lose) the national championship on the field of play, rather than in a poll of sportswriters or coaches.

The Nature of Athletic Competition

How should we think about the nature of athletic competition? Philosopher of sport Robert Simon states that the proper way to think of athletic competition is as "a mutual quest for excellence through challenge."[7] Under this ideal of competitive sports, athletes are obligated to work hard to excel on the field of play not only for the sake of victory but also to present a challenge to their opponents that requires that they excel as well. Applying this ideal to college football, opposing teams not only compete against each other to win the game, but they also compete against one another to bring out the best in themselves and their opponents. And as fans of college football, we know that nothing is better than seeing two teams play at their very best for four quarters in a hard-fought, well-played game.

Adopting this ideal of athletic competition doesn't mean that we need a playoff in order for excellence to be demonstrated on the football field, as the Boise State–Oklahoma game made clear. However, not allowing those who demonstrate such excellence a chance to win the championship is problematic, not only because of considerations of distributive justice, but also because this denial is in tension with the ideal of athletic competition as a mutual quest for excellence through challenge. Allowing athletes the opportunity to bring out the best in themselves and their competitors *on the field* in pursuit of a championship provides a better context for this quest for excellence. The national champion should be decided through a playoff system where athletes can challenge each other on the field of play, not by the collective judgment of a group of voters. College football is not ballroom dancing, after all.

Bull Rushing the Backers of the BCS

The current bowl system and Bowl Championship Series do have their defenders. John Brasier argues that the current system has many benefits, which help to offset its deficiencies.[8] For example, the players get gifts, travel money, and a great week of fun. Coaches get more practice time and the opportunity to finish the season with a win. Fans can plan a vacation around a bowl game. Cities take in large amounts of revenue as fans come for bowl week. The BCS and bowl system provide benefits to players, coaches, fans, and the host cities, and usually competitive games as well. Brasier suggests that this is worth the trade-off of crowning a true national champion on the field.

While the foregoing points are important, especially from a social perspective, I would think that fans, players, and coaches, at least, would give up many of these benefits in order to have a genuine chance to win or lose the championship on the field of play. Whether it is undefeated Penn State in 1994, Auburn in 2004, or Boise State in 2006, this would seem to be the case. Moreover, justifying the current system in this way runs counter to both of the arguments previously made in favor of a play-off, from a merit-based principle of distributive justice and from the nature of athletic competition.

Others have defended the BCS for different reasons. John Tamny points out that NFL teams who have secured their playoff spots can take a week or two off in December to rest and protect their starters as they gear up for the games that matter, the playoffs. And those who are out of playoff contention in the NFL are thought by some to tank games to secure a higher pick in the draft. But college football is superior in that every game is a must-win game, because one loss can knock a team out of contention for a national title. This brings playoff excitement and intensity to the entire season. Tamny states that the best argument for a playoff system is that things should be settled on the field, but he questions whether a playoff would truly lead to a clear-cut champion. Using NCAA basketball as an example, he states that "while many (including this writer) reveled in Georgetown's loss to Villanova in the 1985 NCAA basketball championship, does anyone truly believe Villanova was college basketball's best team that year?"[9]

These two arguments can be faced head-on. First, while it is true that the current system allows for a playoff atmosphere during the regular season, a properly built playoff system could do the same thing.[10] The playoff could be set up so that all the conference champions would receive automatic playoff berths. A sixteen-team playoff would include the eleven conference champions and five teams receiving at-large bids. This would leave spots open for any deserving independent teams (read "Notre Dame"). It would also give teams who are among the nation's best but didn't win their conference a chance to compete for the title. One might object that this would still leave room for controversy. It is likely that a strong runner-up from a conference like the Big 12 or the Atlantic Coast Conference could be left out, while the champion from a weaker conference like the Mid-American or Sun Belt obtains an automatic bid. However, in such a case, a strong runner-up would have had the chance to make the playoffs by winning its conference's championship. The team's postseason destiny was in its hands, and it failed to accomplish what would have guaranteed it a shot. This is more than one can say for Boise State under the current system.

Like Tamny, John Brasier also questions whether a playoff system would produce a true champion: "Let's look at what an eight-team playoff might have looked like this year: In the first round, top-seeded Ohio State draws Wake Forest, No. 2 Florida plays No. 7 Oklahoma, No. 3 Michigan gets No. 6 Southern Cal and No. 4 Louisville plays No. 5 LSU. If lucky enough to be included, Boise likely would have been crushed by Ohio State, Michigan, or Florida."[11]

Perhaps Brasier is right that Boise State would have been soundly defeated by one of these teams, but perhaps not. Consider what Oklahoma linebacker Zach Latimer said after the Fiesta Bowl loss to Boise State: "They should be up there playing for a national championship—12–0, finish the season 13–0—and hopefully they get some more looks in the future. At least a chance. That's all you ask for is a chance. You never know what can happen."[12] Latimer is right. College football is unpredictable. You never know what might happen. In fact, the very same year that Latimer's Oklahoma Sooners lost to the Broncos of Boise State, the University of Florida soundly defeated a favored Ohio State team to win the title. Few people thought the Gators would win, much less win by nearly thirty points. The year before, Texas upset USC to win the national championship. The point is that football teams and football games are unpredictable. Our judgments of the talent and quality of football teams are hampered by the limits of our knowledge. This is what wrongly keeps a team like Boise State from contending for a national championship. These limitations provide us with a further reason for instituting a playoff.

Perhaps Tamny is right that Villanova was not the *best* team in college basketball the year they beat Georgetown in the finals in some sense of the term, but they were the true NCAA champion that year because they won when the title was on the line. This is a mark of a true champion, and teams like Boise State deserve the chance to show whether or not they have what it takes when it counts the most.

An Academic Worry

There is a different sort of concern about implementing a college football playoff. In the 2007 annual meeting of the Southeastern Conference, University of Florida president Bernie Machen discussed his playoff plan, which included setting up a corporation independent from both the NCAA and the BCS to run a playoff.[13] However, while at the meeting, he decided to work within the framework of the BCS, seeking to improve it. Vanderbilt chancellor Gordon Gee was opposed to Machen's proposal, stating, "We've been consistent all along that we're trying to bring some semblance of integrity and some semblance of balance back into what we're doing, and this moves in exactly the wrong direction. This is a slippery slope toward us finally just throwing in the towel and saying what we're about is fielding football teams and we have a university on the side, and I'm just not in favor of that."[14] Gee's concern here is both valid and laudable. As a university professor, I'm concerned about the negative effects of big-time college athletics on the education of both student-athletes and student-fans.

Several points should be considered as we reflect on the tension between academics and athletics. First, all of the other major college sports have playoffs in place, including Division I-AA football. Therefore it does not seem as if having a playoff in Division I-A football is uniquely problematic.

Second, in its proper context sport can be a powerful educational tool for both athletes and fans, if we're intentional about drawing out the important lessons that it can provide.[15] If this were done, athletics could *enhance* the mission of the university in the lives of students.

Third, on the sixteen-team playoff proposal, the season would be extended by only one week, or not at all if the regular season were shortened by one week to accommodate the additional postseason week that such a playoff would require. Even if we did end up extending the season, a one-week extension is not especially problematic given that football players miss much less class time than other student-athletes.

Fourth, a factor that determines to a large extent whether the academic mission of a university is properly emphasized and given the priority it deserves in the lives of its football players is the coach's approach to academics. The attitude and actions of a coach can have a profound impact. Joe Paterno is one clear example of a coach who has had great success with his teams both on the field and in the classroom, proving that one can play at a championship level without devaluing or ignoring academics. Paterno's approach, in which he seeks to educate players about much more than football, has led to his teams' having among the best graduation rates in Division I-A. A necessary trait of any coach should be a commitment to academics for athletes that goes beyond mere lip service. We should seek to hire only coaches who fulfill this requirement.

Fifth, there are also institutional and organizational ways to support the academic success of student-athletes. A recent effort by the University of Georgia deserves mentioning because of its initial success. The school's athletic director, Damon Evans, instituted a plan in which athletes who fail to show up for class or academic appointments without a valid excuse are fined $10 or suspended from games. The policy states that students who miss more than two classes of the same course without a valid excuse will then be suspended for 10 percent of the games they can play for every missed class thereafter. Since this strategy was put into place, for the first time ever over half of Georgia's student-athletes had a grade point average of at least 3.0. Additionally, there was a 90 percent drop in student-athletes' missing class or academic appointments, fewer dropped classes, and more credit hours earned. At the Southeastern Conference meetings in which Gee was quoted above, legislation requiring every school to put an attendance policy into place was passed, which is another step in the right direction.

In sum, I propose that we begin to address the tension between college athletics and college education in these and other ways in order to allow sport to serve a more socially and educationally productive role at the university, and to give athletes a better chance to complete their degrees during their time on campus. If this were done, student-athletes would receive more support in their educational endeavors, and the integrity of the university would also be maintained. We should focus our energies on devising effective strategies to accomplish these goals, rather than worry that a playoff will exacerbate the current problems.

Sudden Death

We have good reasons for letting the BCS expire and implementing a playoff system in college football. But will this ever happen? University of Tennessee coach Phillip Fulmer says, "I don't really hear very many presidents or commissioners in the meetings I'm in really talking about a playoff. I don't think that you can get a consensus with our head coaches.

But will it eventually happen? I'm sure it will, because of the television and the dollars it can create."[16] In the end, Fulmer may be right. It might be television money that kills off the BCS and replaces it with a playoff system, or at least modifies the BCS to include a playoff of some sort. Fortunately, this same course of action can also be taken for moral reasons. Instituting a playoff would be just and fair to the athletes who compete, and true to the ideal of athletic competition as a "mutual quest for excellence through challenge." In light of this, we should go ahead and give the athletes in the NCAA's premier game the opportunity to win the championship on the field, regardless of whether they take their trophy back to South Bend, Indiana; Gainesville, Florida; or even Boise, Idaho.

Notes

Thanks to Greg Bassham for his helpful comments on a previous version of this chapter.

1. NCAA Division I-A football is now called Division I FBS (Football Bowl Subdivision), though I retain the more familiar I-A title in this chapter. Interestingly, Division I-AA, which uses a playoff system, is now called Division I FCS (Football Championship Subdivision).

2. See Keith Dunnavant, *The Fifty-Year Seduction: How Television Manipulated College Football, from the Birth of the Modern NCAA to the Creation of the BCS* (New York: Thomas Dunne Books, St. Martin's Press, 2004).

3. Tim Layden, "Pros and Cons of a Playoff," from http://sportsillustrated.cnn.com/inside_game/tim_layden/news/2000/11/22/layden_viewpoint. Accessed 29 March 2007.

4. The following discussion draws from Julian Lamont and Christi Favor, "Distributive Justice," in *The Stanford Encyclopedia of Philosophy* (Spring 2007), ed. Edward N. Zalta, from http://plato.stanford.edu/archives/spr2007/entries/justice-distributive. Lamont and Favor focus on economic activity in their explanation of this topic.

5. Andrew Bagnato, "Broncos Stun Sooners with Two-Point Conversion in OT," Associated Press, 2 January 2007.

6. There are other important motivations for pursuing athletic excellence, such as the development of moral virtue.

7. Robert L. Simon, "Good Competition and Drug-Enhanced Performance," in *Sports Ethics: An Anthology,* ed. Jan Boxill (Malden, MA: Blackwell, 2003), 179.

8. John Brasier, "Boise Victory Shows Good in Bowl System," from http://www.bcsfootball.org/. Accessed 15 May 2007.

9. John Tamny, "Playoffs and College Football, Imperfect Together," from http://www.nationalreview.com/. Accessed 29 March 2007.

10. A cursory Google search will bring up numerous proposals for how to structure a college playoff, including the one I discuss. The notion that there are structural
barriers to implementing a playoff that cannot be overcome is false.

11. Brasier, "Boise Victory Shows Good in Bowl System."

12. Bagnato, "Broncos Stun Sooners."

13. "Florida President to Push Playoff Plan at SEC Meetings," from http://sports.
espn.go.com/ncf/news/story?id=2885646. Accessed May 30, 2007.

14. "Florida President Backs Off Playoff Plan at SEC Meetings," from http://
sports.espn.go.com/ncf/news/story?id=2889798. Accessed 4 June 2007.

15. For more on this, see Heather L. Reid, *The Philosophical Athlete* (Durham,
NC: Carolina Academic Press, 2002).

16. "Florida President to Push Playoff Plan at SEC Meetings."

Heather L. Reid

HEROES OF THE COLISEUM

The sun shines brightly over the Coliseum, illuminating masses of rowdy spectators, who strain to catch glimpses of their favorites. The air is thick with excitement just moments before the event. Music plays and a colorful procession of costumed performers draws the attention of the crowd, but it is all just a prelude to the real contest everyone came to see. Athletes, finely trained and ritually armored for competition, wait nervously in the wings as the announcer's voice booms. All at once they burst into the arena and the crowd erupts into applause, shouting the names of their favorites and hurling insults at their rivals.

This scene could just as easily describe a USC Trojan game in twenty-first-century Los Angeles as a festival featuring gladiatorial games in first-century Rome. The modern American phenomenon of big-time college football has much in common with the gladiatorial spectacles of ancient Rome—too much in common, some might say. Like Rome's gladiatorial bouts, or *munera,* college football's contests are followed with interest by masses of passionate spectators who regard the athletes' performance as an inspiring representation of their community's competitive virtues and noble fighting spirit. And, as in Rome, there is a certain irony to this because the players themselves aren't usually representative of their college communities.

Like the ancient gladiators, college athletes at NCAA Division I "football schools" often differ from the mainstream population in terms of race, socioeconomic class, and geographic origin. The difference is compounded in both settings by legal and social marginalization. On campus, athletes are unlikely to study or socialize with ordinary students, and their sports commitments leave them with fewer liberties.[1] Neverthe-less, they are expected to face grave physical risks for those same stu-dents' entertainment. The phenomenon of the burned-out and used-up college star, abandoned with little more than memories and scarred knees at age twenty-five, is a dirty little secret of our college sports machine. Furthermore, some universities exploit players economically; as in Rome, the athletes toil and perform at a near-professional level for little or no pay while others reap both profit and power from their exploits.

What's most fascinating about college football players and Roman gladiators, however, is not their daily hardships or social marginalization. Rather, it is that so many transcend these things to distinguish themselves as revered symbols of excellence or virtue, *virtus* in Latin, *aretē* in Greek. Roman society and modern universities both focus on producing excellent citizens. Should we be surprised that gladiators and football players, oth-erwise considered social outcasts, so often end up as examples of virtue?

Not according to the philosophy of Roman Stoicism, a school of thought that disdained strong emotions, accepted inevitable fate, rejected common values, and prized virtue above all else. For the Stoics, college football players and gladiators can achieve virtue despite—and maybe because of—their difficult situations. Virtue in the Stoic sense does not depend on external circumstances; rather, it requires independence from them. In fact, college football players' general lack of personal wealth, social privilege, and political power is precisely what makes them such inspiring symbols of Stoic freedom from worldly concerns. Considered from the perspective of such Stoic philosophers as Seneca (ca. 1 B.C.E.–65 C.E.), Epictetus (ca. 50–130 C.E.), and Cicero (106–43 B.C.E.), big-time college athletes may achieve virtue and happiness despite their predica-ment. Following the Stoic emperor Marcus Aurelius (121–180 C.E.), however, those with the power to improve players' situations have a mor-al obligation to do so. We may admiringly call college football players "gladiators," but we should do what we can to prevent their situation from too closely resembling that of their ancient Roman counterparts.

Students of a Lesser Good

Unlike the vast majority of student athletes who deftly combine sport and study at colleges and universities all across the United States, there is an enduring perception that college football players in Bowl Championship Series (BCS) programs are something less than full-fledged students. People believe that players are on campus not to study but to play a dangerous and sometimes brutal game that provides inspiration and entertainment for those at the university who do the "serious" work. Roman gladiators were also considered entertainers and counted accordingly as part of a lowly class of moral outcasts called *infamia*. Romans conventionally regarded a gladiator as "crude, loathsome, doomed, lost . . . utterly debased by fortune, a slave, a man altogether without worth and dignity, almost without humanity."[2] As a matter of fact, gladiators generally were slaves or criminals condemned *ad ludum*—to the life of the arena. Although some free men and women, including members of the nobility, did elect to fight in the arena, they were rare exceptions who nevertheless swore the gladiator's oath *(sacramentum gladiatorium)* to be "burned by fire, bound in chains, to be beaten, to die by the sword."[3] This oath amounted to a renunciation of one's rights as a Roman citizen.[4]

College football players may not be foreign slaves or convicted criminals, but many do come from neighborhoods and upbringings that are worlds away from those of their typical classmates. In fact the large number of African American students recruited to play football at predominantly white schools may improve those universities' diversity statistics, but rarely are these athletes fully integrated into the college community. Studies show that on most campuses, recruited athletes differ markedly from students at large in terms of academic credentials, academic outcomes, and the way they live and socialize at college—a phenomenon dubbed "the academic-athletic divide."[5] It turns out that those students who so warmly cheer their classmates on Saturday are unlikely to study, party, or even eat lunch with them during the week. Although many colleges and universities use "representativeness" of the larger student body as a criterion in recruiting athletes, it is rarely achieved. In any case, there is a social stigma attached to athletic participation that marginalizes even those athletes who do reflect the college population.[6] Student-athletes may not formally be denied basic rights and privileges, as were Roman gladiators, but the time required for practice and travel to games, as well as strict amateur regulations in the NCAA, result in their having fewer practical liberties than their classmates.

Despite their daunting power and celebrity in the arena, football players and gladiators turn out to be relatively powerless within their respective societies. Far from autonomous, they are controlled and manipulated by the elites of their communities. In Rome this was illustrated by the etiquette of the arena. Fights generally ended when one gladiator signaled concession or was brought to the ground by an opponent. At this point, the victorious gladiator was to look to the presiding dignitary, or *editor,* for the signal to kill or spare the loser. The editor decided who lived or died; he could even grant a gladiator freedom, a prize symbolized by a wooden sword, or *rudis.* Of course the crowd offered their vociferous advice on these decisions. If a loser had fought valiantly, they would call out "*Mitte!*" ("Let him go!"); if they thought he lacked valor, they would call for his death. Given the editor's political ambitions, he usually indulged their wishes, so in effect the power remained with the people in the stands. The gladiator himself was more or less a pawn in this political game.

The Roman crowd's influence was not unlike that of modern college fans and boosters. Nor is the modern coach's control over action on the field much unlike the editor's control of the arena. Indeed, college football teams are generally guided by a whole cadre of coaches, who gain obedience from their players not through slavery but through the all-important power to decide who does and doesn't play. Independent strategy decisions made by players on the field are quickly becoming a rarity. Most quarterbacks call plays that come prepackaged from coaches on the sidelines. The University of Florida's offensive success in the 1990s was regularly attributed to the strategic decisions and play-calling of their coach, Steve Spurrier. The football player who executes a brilliant play today is often regarded as unthinking brawn serving brainy skybox masters. Just as in Rome's Coliseum, the strongest guys in the stadium turn out to be political weaklings.

Free to Be Brave

So how can they be heroes? Most theories of virtue, including the Roman ideal of *virtus,* seem to require free agency (of the philosophical, rather than economic, type). As slaves, gladiators were compelled to fight, if not by their masters, then by their oath, or by the fact that someone was charging at them with a knife. Participation in college sports, by contrast, is voluntary almost by definition. Nevertheless it would be hard to deny that many college players compete out of financial necessity. Faced with the challenges of poverty and poor schooling, many perceive football to be one of precious few avenues toward a better life. It is a venerable species of the American dream: the impoverished and academically challenged child from the ghetto or cornfields combines his native strength with motivation from the promise of financial patronage to beat the odds, attend college, and perhaps reap riches and fame as a professional athlete. It is a path with a high statistical chance of failure, but for many football players it can seem like the only path available.

The situation was not so different for Roman gladiators. Those captured as slaves or condemned as criminals had an opportunity to earn their freedom and readmission to Roman society by demonstrating their valor (and social worth) in the arena. Those who volunteered, the *autocrati,* were usually freed gladiators who returned to their craft less out of free will than the cold reality that they could find no better means to support themselves. Volunteers of independent means were rare, and emperors who took to the arena, as Commodus does in the movie *Gladiator,* seem to have been indulging in fantasy rather than subjecting themselves to its real risks and dangers. The real emperor Commodus apparently won all his gladiatorial "fights"; his movie death at the hands of Maximus in the Coliseum is Hollywood fiction, not historical fact.[7] In any event, the fact that some gladiators and all college athletes can be said to have chosen their lives does not erase the worry about voluntary participation and its connection to concepts of virtue and heroism.

For the Stoic idea of virtue, however, free choice to participate is hardly an issue. Stoics believe that external circumstances are determined; therefore moral worth derives from internal events, especially the adoption of certain attitudes. "Ask not that events happen as you will," counsels Epictetus, "but let your will be that events should happen as they do, and you shall have peace."[8] One reason Stoics were willing to consider even enslaved gladiators as symbols of virtue is that their enslavement was only a more explicit version of the slavery we all face under the common master of fate. Making the point that slaves are human beings who share the same roof as their owners and should be regarded as friends,

Seneca reminds his fellow citizens that "strictly speaking they're our *fellow* slaves, if you once reflect that fortune has as much power over us as over them."[9] No doubt college football fans also see some reflection of their own social struggles in the hard-luck players' improbable success. The goddess of the Roman arena was Nemesis, who represents the unexplainable effects of mysterious, uncontrollable forces. The same sorts of forces often seem present in college football. For Stoic gladiators and football players alike, virtue is revealed in response to adversity.

Of course the Stoic ideas of determinism, slavery, and their effect on virtue were more sophisticated than popular beliefs about fate and fortune. The slavery condemned by Stoicism was self-imposed, caused by desires for things outside a person's control. Says the erstwhile slave Epictetus, "Let him . . . who wishes to be free not wish for anything or avoid anything that depends on others; or else he is bound to be a slave."[10] Enslaved gladiators are cut off from the things most people desire (wealth, status, power), and self-reliance is necessary for their survival. The gladiator who wishes only for what he or she can control is, in the Stoic sense, completely free. Therefore those gladiators who accept their role and choose to fight achieve liberty, while those who lust for escape are trapped by their own desires.

Perhaps this is why we are so puzzled by and admiring of the star college athlete who resists the temptation of a multimillion-dollar professional debut in favor of another year of frequenting the coin laundry, cramming for exams, and eating mystery meat from the dining hall. His heroism is displayed not in athletic indifference to pain but in Stoic indifference to the prizes and pleasures we're all conditioned to covet. Gladiators earned cash and glory too, but it was their freedom from society's corrupting distractions that Stoicism finds more valuable. Stoics such as Seneca believe that it is our attachment to scarce goods and the resulting fights over them that cause disturbance and unhappiness in our souls.[11] We should admire the player who opts to stay in school for his apparent freedom from those desires.

So the freedom of the Stoics is a paradoxical sort of freedom, but if determinism is true and all things are fated to happen as they do, it is the only sort available to any of us. The appropriate attitude is extremely difficult to achieve, and the Stoics believed that it would take extensive philosophical training. But in the end it is a matter of facing up to the truth about fate and striving for virtue within the prescribed limits of self-sufficient activity. In a sense, the Stoics see fate as something we accept, just as players accept the rules of a game. And we all have a particular fate, whether it is to be a slave like Epictetus or an emperor like Marcus Aurelius. Says Epictetus, "Remember you are an actor in a play, and the Playwright chooses the manner of it: if he wants it short, it is short; if long, it is long. If he wants you to act a poor man you must act the part with all your powers; [likewise] if your part be a cripple or a magistrate or a plain man. For your business is to act the character that is given you and act it well; the choice of the cast is Another's."[12]

The Stoic athlete's virtue, then, depends not upon the freedom to choose football rather than medicine but rather upon the choice to excel in whatever activity he finds himself in. It is not unlike the situation of a soldier involuntarily drafted into a war. He may fight valiantly and virtuously while regarding his presence on the battlefield as a morally neutral matter of fate. Of course our common fate as human beings is death, and that fate is not just something to be accepted but something potentially within our power. Just as the voluntary participant always has the option to quit playing, the Stoic sage always has the option to quit living. Says Seneca, "No one has power over us when death is within our power."[13] Indeed, suicidal gladiators are Seneca's favorite examples of courageous expressions of virtue and freedom; not just facing but actually choosing one's death to preserve one's dignity could be the ultimate act of bravery and autonomy.[14]

Risk and Violence

Considered against the idealized backdrop of college sports, however, suicide seems rather an extreme option for expressing a person's freedom. For that matter, the comparison between college football and gladiatorial combat may seem invalidated by the extreme violence of the latter. For many, the risk of death and dismemberment pushes gladiator fights outside the realm of sport altogether. How can killing cultivate virtue? Survival is simply too serious a concern to be made into a game. Michael Poliakoff excludes gladiators from his book *Combat Sports in the Ancient World* on the grounds that criteria for sporting success should be "different from those that mark success in everyday life." Since war was part of everyday life in antiquity, he decides that "a gladiator fighting to kill or disable his opponent and save himself in any manner possible is not participating in a sport, but in a form of warfare for spectators."[15] Does the risk of serious injury prevent football from being a sport?

However brutal and violent college football may be, comparison to warfare is a stretch. One may interpret the game as opposing armies assembling lines and attacks in order to gain territory from each other, but deaths are uninvited, unexpected, and relatively rare. College football players can and do express their excellence on the field with medical assistance close at hand and the threat of death far in the distance. In the historical and cultural context of ancient Rome, the risk of death was necessary to test a gladiator's virtue. Unlike the gruesome public executions that pitted weakened convicts against hungry lions, gladiator fights were evenly matched precisely because this was a precondition for the display of Roman virtue and the achievement of personal glory.[16] Says Seneca, "A gladiator reckons it ignominious to be paired with his inferior in skill and considers him to have conquered without glory who has conquered without peril."[17] The threat of career-ending injury is an analogous risk in college football, not least because it often represents the end of that dream path toward fame so many players are following. The pain and fear we see on an injured player's face are only partially physical, and our empathy for him often recognizes the compound fracture of body and dream. Safer versions of the game certainly exist, but it seems that the kind of virtue we admire in college football players cannot be had without the risk of injury any more than the Roman virtue attributed to gladiators could have been had without the risk of death.

Death, of course, was not a required outcome in gladiatorial fights; at first it wasn't even a frequent outcome. A gladiator's statistical risk of death changed along with cultural expectations over the years. In the first century of the Common Era, typical gladiators survived fewer than ten contests, although some survived more than one hundred and others were successful enough to earn their freedom.[18] In succeeding centuries the odds got worse. Contests fought to the death became more popular as the political stakes rose and the public experienced what some contemporary philosophers called a "degeneration of taste."[19] Historian Carlin

Barton has speculated that the Roman demand for brutal and bloody spectacles ironically grew as a result of increasingly posh living conditions and ease of life among Roman gentry.[20]

Perhaps it is America's relative wealth and ease of life that drive our passion for the violent game of football, but there may be something more serious at stake. It has been alleged that the Roman public's bloodthirstiness stemmed from a disregard for anything like universal human rights.[21] Gladiators were members of a kind of disposable class whose health and lives were brazenly risked and destroyed for the entertainment of more important people. According to modern sport philosophers, violence in athletics stems from disrespect for persons.[22] Could it be that our tolerance for violence in college football is based on socioeconomic class difference and the so-called athletic-academic divide? Was the system that forced gladiators to risk their lives in the arena really so different from the system that forces some athletes to risk their health in the stadium today? These may be questions worth pondering.

To the Stoic mind, however, risk is a fact of life, and death is a common human reality that must be confronted consciously. Says Seneca, "Death is not an evil. What is it then? The one law mankind has that is free of all discrimination."[23] Being forced to kill and facing death oneself are, for the Stoic, prime occasions to demonstrate human dignity. Gladiators exhibited their readiness to die by baring their torsos in the arena.[24] The gladiatorial fight, according to historian Thomas Wiedemann, is a ritualization of the encounter with death designed to put "death in its place."[25] Gladiators enter the arena through the gate of life and face the opposite gate of death; the battle takes place, symbolically, in the space between life and death.[26]

The gladiators' status as "socially dead" renders more dramatic the struggle to redeem themselves through valor. Explains scholar Roland Auguet, Romans did not regard the confrontation with death as undignified or even an act of "exceptional heroism; it was the normal way of proving oneself a Roman."[27] Likewise, modern Americans may see nothing undignified in an underprivileged youth's using the gridiron as a social ladder. Neither need we interpret his physical play as disrespectful toward opponents (trash-talking and egotistical end zone antics notwithstanding). The risk and brutality of college football seem to be part of what validates its function as a revealer of virtue, just as the risk of death validated gladiators' social redemption and public glory.

Virtue without Status

Even as big-time college football exploits its servile gladiators for the benefit of the rich, even as it strips student-athletes of liberties and (more seriously) social equality on campus, even as players risk pain, injury, and public humiliation, there is one thing that cannot be taken from a right-minded college athlete: virtue. What kind of prize is that? To put a Stoic spin on the old phrase about winning, virtue isn't everything; it's the only thing. At least it is the only thing that matters to a Stoic. "Each man has a character of his own choosing," says Seneca; "it is chance or fate that decides his choice of job."[28] The Roman audience clearly recognized and appreciated virtue in these outcasts of the arena. The idea that slaves could have virtue entered the Roman psyche as early as 216 B.C.E. after the defeat at Cannae in which oath-bound slaves had fought more effectively than free men.[29] Not unlike the college sports adage that "there is no 'I' in 'team,'" the Roman idea of military virtue was grounded in obedience to one's general and service to one's state. As Seneca observes, a gladiator's subjection to the will of the presiding official, or editor, actually enhances his status as an example of Roman virtue.[30] Cicero's description of true courage seems tailor-made for gladiators or even college athletes:

> The soul that is altogether courageous and great is marked above all by two characteristics: one of these is indifference to outward circumstances; for such a person cherishes the conviction that nothing but moral goodness and propriety deserves to be either admired or wished for or striven after, and that he ought not to be subject to any man or any passion or any accident of fortune. The second characteristic is that, when the soul is disciplined in the way above mentioned, one should do deeds not only great and in the highest degree useful, but extremely arduous and laborious and fraught with danger both to life and to many things that make life worth living.[31]

What makes Stoicism work for victims of exploitation and social injustice like gladiators and college football players is that it assumes external conditions, such as worldly wealth and power, to be unreliable as indicators of virtue. In fact, Stoic writers came to regard gladiators as evidence that social conventions about human worth and inequality were unsound. This was a therapeutic idea for struggling Roman citizens.[32] As Wiedemann sums it up, "The criminal condemned [to the arena] was a socially 'dead man' who had a chance of coming alive again."[33] In a world where, as Epictetus observes, climbing the social ladder meant bending down to kiss someone's feet, the gladiator emerges as a paradoxical hero whose lack of autonomy and social status comes to symbolize freedom, opportunity, and old-fashioned Roman values.[34] Perhaps this explains why college football players are regarded as all-American heroes despite their social marginalization. They embody the rags-to-riches American dream symbolized by our beloved Statue of Liberty. Football becomes the social meritocracy so elusive off the playing field—a place where individuals can transcend their humble origins and reach heroic heights through talent, hard work, and the ancient ideal of virtue.

Conclusion: The Challenge of Justice for Gladiators and Left Tackles

Of course American society is *not* a perfectly level playing field, and neither is college football. There is reason for serious concern about players' exploitation, lack of autonomy, and physical risk. Although Stoicism teaches us to find and cultivate virtue even if fortune lands us in such hostile conditions as the Roman arena, those who have a choice would be unlikely to participate in or promote the Roman games. The Stoic emperor Marcus Aurelius's distaste for the gladiatorial fights was well known, and he attempted to limit their scale, if not to eliminate them.[35] Big-time college sports' own emperors should consider diluting the resemblance between their premier game and that of Rome's ancient Coliseum. To what extent do entertainment concerns dictate the management of college sports today? Is the amateur student-athlete a worthy ideal, or an excuse for the economic exploitation of talented young men? How do the phenomena of financial need and athletic recruiting affect the ideal of voluntary participation? What is the worth of a college scholarship when poor academic preparation and extensive demands on time and energy keep student-athletes' graduation rates low? At what point do the risks of sport outstrip the benefits to athletes and society at large? Stoicism helps individuals to transcend unjust circumstances, but it also compels us to labor for justice. Let us meet our challenge with the courage of Roman gladiators.

Notes

I wish to acknowledge assistance and resources provided by the American Academy at Rome, the Ver Steeg Faculty Development Fund at Morningside College, Nigel Crowther, Mark Holowchak, Sam Clovis, Robert Reid, Stephen Ryan, and Michael Austin. Parts of this paper were previously published as "Was the Roman Gladiator an Athlete?" *Journal of the Philosophy of Sport* 33, no. 1 (2006): 37–49.

1. William G. Bowen and Sarah A. Levin, *Reclaiming the Game: College Sports and Educational Values* (Princeton, NJ: Princeton University Press, 2003), 5.

2. Carlin Barton, *The Sorrows of the Ancient Romans* (Princeton, NJ: Princeton University Press, 1993), 12.

3. Donald G. Kyle, *Spectacles of Death in Ancient Rome* (New York: Routledge, 1998), 87.

4. Thomas Wiedemann, *Emperors and Gladiators* (London: Routledge, 1992), 113.

5. Bowen and Levin, *Reclaiming the Game*, 5.

6. Bowen and Levin, *Reclaiming the Game*, 196.

7. Ludwig Friedlander, "The Spectacles," in *Roman Life and Manners under the Early Empire*, trans. J. H. Freese and L. A. Magnus (London: Routledge & Kegan Paul, 1908), 2:50.

8. Epictetus, *Discourses and Manual,* trans. P. E. Matheson, 2 vols. (Oxford: Clarendon Press, 1916); Epictetus, *The Handbook (The Encheiridion)*, trans. N. P. White (Indianapolis: Hackett, 1983), 8.

9. Lucius Annaeus Seneca, *Letters from a Stoic (Epistulae Morales ad Lucilium)*, trans. R. Campbell (London: Penguin, 1969), Epistle 47.

10. Epictetus, *Encheiridion*, 14.

11. Martha C. Nussbaum, *The Therapy of Desire: Theory and Practice in Hellenistic Ethics* (Princeton, NJ: Princeton University Press, 1994), 421.

12. Epictetus, *Encheiridion*, 17.

13. Seneca, *Letters from a Stoic,* Epistle 91.

14. Seneca, *Letters from a Stoic,* Epistle 70.

15. Michael B. Poliakoff, *Combat Sports in the Ancient World* (New Haven, CT: Yale University Press, 1978), 7.

16. Barton, *Sorrows of the Ancient Romans*, 28.

17. Seneca, *On Providence*, 3.4, quoted in Barton, *Sorrows of the Ancient Romans*, 31.

18. Kyle, *Spectacles of Death,* 86.

19. Friedlander, "The Spectacles," 85.

20. Barton, *Sorrows of the Ancient Romans,* 46.

21. Friedlander, "The Spectacles," 78.

22. Robert L. Simon, *Fair Play: Sports, Values, and Society* (Boulder, CO: West-view, 1991), 108; Jim Parry, "Violence and Aggression in Contemporary Sport," *Ethics and Sport,* ed. M. McNamee and J. Parry (London: E & FN Spon, 1998), 204–24.

23. Seneca, *Letters from a Stoic,* Epistle 123.

24. Marcus Junkelmann, "*Familia Gladiatoria:* The Heroes of the Ampitheatre," in *Gladiators and Caesars,* ed. Eckart Köhne and Cornelia Ewigleben (Berkeley: University of California Press), 31–74.

25. Wiedemann, *Emperors and Gladiators,* 97.

26. Amy Zoll, *Gladiatrix* (New York: Penguin, 2002).

27. Roland Auguet, *Cruelty and Civilization: The Roman Games* (London: George Allen & Unwin, 1972), 198.

28. Seneca, *Letters from a Stoic,* Epistle 94.

29. Kyle, *Spectacles of Death,* 48–49.

30. Seneca, *De providentia,* 4.4–16.

31. Cicero, *De officiis,* trans. Walter Miller (New York: Macmillan [Loeb], 1913), 66.

32. Auguet, *Cruelty and Civilization,* 197.

33. Wiedemann, *Emperors and Gladiators,* 105.

34. Epictetus, *Encheiridion,* 25.

35. Wiedemann, *Emperors and Gladiators,* 134–39.

Stephen Kershnar

A TRUE MVP

How should we value football team members as players? In this chapter, I argue that we should judge a player's value to his team by comparing how well his team does when he plays and when he doesn't. The notion of a player's value is relevant to various tasks that professional teams engage in, such as drafting, paying, and trading players.

An Illustration: The Most Valuable Player

One area where player value is important is the award for the most valuable player, since the award compares players on the basis of their value. In the NFL, the Associated Press selects the MVP. A nationwide panel of sportswriters and broadcasters who cover the NFL choose the winner. There are other MVP awards, but this one is the most widely recognized and the most prestigious award given to an individual player.

Most of the winners have been running backs and quarterbacks. Players from these positions won the last twenty awards, and forty-six out of fifty since 1957, when the Associate Press MVP award was first given. The winner is usually the statistical leader in an important offensive category such as touchdowns (rushing or passing), yardage (rushing), or effectiveness (passing). Fifteen of the last twenty winners have led in one of these categories. Although the MVP focuses on regular-season performance, the winners are almost always from winning teams. Thirteen out of the last twenty winners were from teams that were in the Super Bowl. The remaining winners came from teams that won 77 percent of their regular season games.

MVP Awards (Associated Press)

Year	Name	Statistical Leader[a]	Team Success[b]
2006	LaDainian Tomlinson	Touchdowns, Rushing	14–2
2005	Shaun Alexander	Touchdowns, Rushing	Super Bowl
2004	Peyton Manning	Passing Touchdowns, Passing	12–4
2003	Peyton Manning Steve McNair	Passing (McNair)	12–4 (Manning) 12–4 (McNair)
2002	Rich Gannon		Super Bowl
2001	Kurt Warner	Passing Touchdowns, Passing	Super Bowl
2000	Marshall Faulk	Touchdowns	10–6
1999	Kurt Warner	Passing Touchdowns, Passing	Super Bowl
1998	Terrell Davis	Touchdowns, Rushing	Super Bowl
1997	Brett Favre Barry Sanders	Passing Touchdowns (Favre) Rushing (Sanders)	Super Bowl (Favre), 9–7 (Sanders)
1996	Brett Favre	Passing Touchdowns	Super Bowl
1995	Brett Favre	Passing Touchdowns	11–5
1994	Steve Young	Passing Touchdowns, Passing	Super Bowl
1993	Emmitt Smith	Rushing	Super Bowl
1992	Steve Young	Passing Touchdowns, Passing	14–2
1991	Thurman Thomas		Super Bowl
1990	Joe Montana		14–2
1989	Joe Montana	Passing	Super Bowl
1988	Boomer Esiason	Passing	Super Bowl
1987	John Elway		Super Bowl

a. The "statistical leader in touchdowns" refers to the number of touchdowns a player ran for. The "statistical leader in rushing" refers to the number of yards the player ran for. The "statistical leader in passing touchdowns" refers to the number of touchdowns the player threw for. The "statistical leader in passing" refers to the player's quarterback rating. This rating is a function of the following factors: completions, touchdowns, yards, attempts, and interceptions.

b. The win-loss record involves the team's regular-season performance. "Super Bowl" refers to the team's presence in the Super Bowl.

There are probably three main reasons that the award has so often been given to these positions. First, how players in these positions perform probably has a greater effect on team success than does the performance of other players. Second, it is easier to measure and compare the statistical performance of players in these positions than in other positions. Third, the viewer's attention naturally tends to focus on these positions so they receive more attention. One reason the MVP is often given to players on a winning team is that a player can be more easily seen to contribute to his team's success when the team actually succeeds.

What Makes a Player Valuable?

This section attempts to provide an analysis of the value of a player. I will adopt parts of an earlier analysis of player value by Neil Feit and myself.[1] On this account, player value is concerned with what a player contributes to his team, rather than what he contributes to the average team or the league in general.[2] More specifically, one player has more value than a second if and only if he contributes more to his team than other players do to their teams. The underlying idea is that a player can have value to another team (e.g., he keeps on fumbling the ball) or to the league (e.g., he attracts fans), but neither counts as a positive contribution as a player.

Competitive Success as the Ultimate Goal of Competitive Athletics

Since player value to a team exists only in the context of competitive athletics, we need to identify what is valuable in this context. The value to be identified with an activity is a goal that is central to successful participation in it; that is, in virtue of that feature, one achieves excellence with regard to that activity. This goal must be something that acts as the litmus test, so to speak, for excellence in any form that this activity takes.

The distinctive goal of competitive activities, including competitive athletics, is winning. There are other valuable goals—for example, showing respect for others and developing moral character—that can be realized in an athletic context, but there is nothing about these goals that is unique to the athletic realm. They might form a reason for participating in competitive athletics, but they are not the goal of the athletic contest itself. Winning also can occur in nonathletic contexts—for example, war—but only in competitive athletics does it seem to be the central purpose for which persons engage in the activity.

Role- and Team-Based Value

In addition to the analysis of player value in terms of what he contributes to his team's success (that is, winning), a further tightening up of the concept of player value is necessary. Specifically, a player's value comes about via his role as a player. This is opposed to the other roles in which he might serve (e.g., coach, general manager, or owner). That is, the same person might make several kinds of contributions to a team's success, only some of which are relevant to his team's success. On this account, the player-based value might include not only the particular plays he makes but also his role as a mentor, role model, leader, spiritual adviser, or the like, depending on the tasks that constitute being a player. This role specificity rules out contributions such as that of Hall of Fame linebacker Lawrence Taylor, who used to pay prostitutes to keep opposing running backs up all night, thereby reducing their effectiveness.[3]

Depending on how broadly a player's role is construed, this player-based value might take into account not only a player's performance on the field but also such factors as the player's draft number and pay, since these probably affect who the likely backup is and hence the differential contribution. For example, a player taken at the beginning of the draft restricts his team's ability to obtain other high-quality players in the draft more than if he were picked later in the draft. The same is true with regard to his pay in leagues that cap the overall amount that a team can pay its players. Similar problems arise with regard to team members who both play and make innovative contributions to strategy. For example, Tony Dungy was one of the persons who introduced the modern version of a common NFL defense, the cover two. His formation of the defense came in part when he played in the NFL and in part when he coached in it.[4] If Dungy had made his contributions while still playing, then we would have a good test case for what counts as a player-based contribution. Other factors are even less clear, for example, the positive effects a player has on his teammates through humor or friendship. Here we need a theory of whether a player's role includes his effects as a teammate, draftee, collector of salary, strategist, and friend.

Since a role is a set of descriptive conditions that result from the way in which society thinks about the role and since this way of thinking might be indeterminate, role indeterminacy threatens to make player value indeterminate. I think that society views a person's contribution as a player as solely a function of what he does on the field. For example, we might say of a player like Terrell Owens that his media comments so damage team chemistry that they eclipse his tremendous worth as a wide receiver. If this is correct, then the other factors (e.g., draft number, salary, and friendship) are not relevant to a person's contribution as a player. In addition, if on-the-field contribution is determinate, then so is player value.

If this account is correct, then winning is the central goal of competitive athletics and a player's value is a function of the degree to which he contributes to that goal via his on-the-field play. Another way to say this is to say that a player's value is the net benefit that his on-the-field play brings to his team.

Net Benefit to a Team

The net benefit is the difference between a player's benefit and cost to his team. The net benefit is measured by comparing the team's performance with the player against some other state in which the player is not present. The latter state is called the "baseline state." At issue is the nature of the baseline state.

There are three different states that might serve as the relevant baseline state.[5] For example, consider the states I might compare to Joe Montana's playing quarterback for the San Francisco 49ers. First, the state might be compared to one in which no one occupies that position (e.g., no one plays quarterback for the 49ers). Second, the state might be compared to one in which a counterfactual player occupies that position. The counterfactual player might be the mean (or perhaps median) backup quarterback. Alternatively, it might be a reasonable backup quarterback. Third, the state might be compared to one in which the actual backup player occupies that position. So, for example, Montana's playing quarterback might be compared to the state in which his actual backup leads the 49er offense. In determining which of these comparative states is relevant to determining a player's value, I shall argue that we will gain a greater understanding of player value.

Model 1: No-Substitute State

The notion behind this model is that it tracks the way in which contribution is normally considered in economics. For example, the marginal benefit of a type of input into production is the additional benefit gained from the last unit of input.[6] That is, the marginal benefit of a unit of input involves the comparison of output with the unit and without it. Hence, on this account, to measure a player's net benefit to a team, we compare his team's success when he played and when no one played that position.

One idea that might be seen to motivate this approach is that it measures causal contribution of a thing to an outcome. For example, the causal contribution of an additional acre on which a farmer grows wheat is the comparison of wheat the farmer produces with and without the acre.

The problem with this baseline state is that it fails to track the value of a player because it results in a baseline state involving a game that is very different from the game in which the player in question plays. For example, consider a case in which Drew Bledsoe's net benefit to the New England Patriots is determined by comparing the team's success when he is at quarterback and when no one plays that position. The latter state consists of either the scenario in which the Patriots alone have no quarterback or one in which no team has a quarterback. In the former case, given the centrality of the quarterback to the offense, the Patriots would probably have lost every game. However, even if Drew Bledsoe's play at quarterback contributed to every Patriot win in 2001, this approach overestimates his contribution to his team. This is because the Patriots would likely have won many of the same games were Bledsoe not to play. This is particularly true if he had a particularly talented backup. For example, in the 2001–2002 season, Tom Brady replaced Drew Bledsoe. Brady led the Patriots to three Super Bowls in four years, and during the 2004–2005 season, Brady helped the Patriots set an NFL record with twenty-one straight wins (including the previous year).[7] The same is true if we consider other players in the Patriots' lineup. This results in the team's being unable to win without a number of particular players, because it would be one player short, and this isn't the case. If instead we consider the baseline state to be the one in which no one has a quarterback, the comparative state is so different from the actual state that comparing the two tells us nothing.

In conclusion, the no-substitute baseline fails to provide a proper estimate of player value. It likely tracks causal contribution, and this is not the correct baseline for determining player value.

Model 2: Average-Substitute State

On a second account, the baseline state is one in which a counterfactual player occupies a position. The idea here is that if the player in question (e.g., Drew Bledsoe) doesn't play quarterback, we imagine that some player who might not even be on the Patriots occupies that position, and we compare the Patriots' success with Bledsoe and the counterfactual player. The counterfactual in this case might vary depending on the particular account.

The counterfactual player might be the average backup player in the league at the time.[8] This baseline state is used to measure a player's contribution against a uniform standard across teams. Alternatively, the counterfactual player might be a reasonable backup player in the league at the time. If there is too much talent in the backup for one position (e.g., quarterback) and too little at another (e.g., fullback), the reasonable standard corrects for this maldistribution of talent and thus allows for a better comparison of value across positions. The reasonable backup might vary depending on whether we are comparing players from the same era or from different eras.

This model is useful in measuring the caliber of past performance. For example, in judging a person's performance as a quarterback, this model looks at how well he does in a range of relevant cases. This would allow us to compare performance by screening out the effects of skill differences in backup players and between positions. In principle, we might further tweak the average- or reasonable-player baseline to screen out interteam differences that might come about from factors such as whether the team plays outdoors and the caliber of the surrounding lineup.[9] For example, a running back might be more effective when playing with a stellar cast than he would otherwise be. This is because he runs better when given big holes and when the defense has to respect the pass. In measuring past performance, this model likely also gives us a better estimation of future ability than the other two models, at least once we discount age, injury, rule changes, and so on.

An example of a running back with such a stellar cast was Emmitt Smith. Smith, the NFL's leading rusher, gained many of his yards behind arguably the best line ever in the NFL. It included Larry Allen (ten Pro Bowls), Nate Newton (six Pro Bowls), Mark Stepnoski (five Pro Bowls), and Erik Williams (four Pro Bowls). Smith also played with an all-pro quarterback (Troy Aikman, six Pro Bowls), wide receiver (Michael Irvin, five Pro Bowls), and tight end (Jay Novacek, five Pro Bowls) on the team.[10] It is unlikely that he would have been as productive surrounded by an ordinary cast.

One problem with this account is that it is not a measure of a player's actual value to his team but his hypothetical value to a range of teams. For example, a player's value to his own team might be negligible, given an unusually talented backup, but for other teams it might be considerable.

A second problem is that the choice of counterfactual player seems arbitrary. The average backup player gets us closer to a player's value to the average team but handicaps comparisons across positions by failing to correct for a maldistribution of talent. In contrast, looking at a reasonable backup player involves the choice of the features of an efficient market that are present in the baseline state. For example, it is not clear if we should take the current crop of players and redistribute them across positions or take into account how more complete information might provide an incentive for other great athletes to enter or leave football. There doesn't seem to be any principled way in which these conditions can be determined. Also, in determining what a reasonable backup player would be like, we would have to determine how much information players, managers, and owners have, the degree to which these persons have rational preferences, and the degree to which there is free entry into and exit from the market. The more we deviate from actual conditions, the less this model measures a player's performance rather than his value to his team.

A third problem concerns the notion of an *average* backup. Since we are trying to model contribution, it would beg the question to invoke the average contribution to model the backup player. The notion might be filled out in terms of some statistical measure. However, we would need a theory to explain which measure is relevant. To the extent that we cannot find a plausible way to fill out the average backup player, we should reject this model.

In summary, the average-substitution model might be a good measure of a person's past performance but not of a player's value to his own team. Even the former claim isn't obvious, since the notion of an average or reasonable backup player appears to be problematic.

Model 3: Actual-Substitute State

This model focuses on the team's performance with the player in question when compared to its performance when an actual or likely backup plays. On probabilistic accounts, it focuses on the team's performance with the actual player and with each potential backup multiplied by the likelihood of that backup substituting in. It is worth noting that this model takes a perspective similar to that of the team's owner.

This model has an advantage over the first model in that it takes into account the intuition that a player who has the best statistics but who has competitive advantages (e.g., a running back who plays with the best offensive line and an all-pro quarterback) might be less competitive for the MVP than he initially appears. This makes sense on the actual-substitution model, since his replacement would likely have greater success than would replacements on other teams. The actual-substitution model also explains why a great player from a team with a losing record might also be less competitive than he initially appears. His team's lack of effectiveness might lead to less focused and less motivated play from opposing teams, thus making it more likely that his backup would also have greater than average success. The average-substitution model, however, also has these advantages.

There are a number of problems with this approach. First, if a player has a very talented backup, he could have the best statistics and cause the most wins yet fail to have much value. This is because the team would have done nearly as well with his backup. For example, in the late 1980s, Joe Montana was an all-pro quarterback for the San Francisco 49ers. Despite his superb play, he might not have great positive value since his backup was Steve Young, who had the second-highest career passing rating ever and the highest single-season passing rating (Montana was third and second respectively).[11] This is counterintuitive.

Second, a player's net benefit to a team is team specific since the comparative states are tied to the performance of a particular team. Thus, it is possible that the same player with the same statistics could have more value than a second player on one team and less on another. Again, this is counterintuitive.

Third, a player whose team doesn't win with him doesn't have much actual value no matter what he contributes. This is because he doesn't bring success to his team.

These problems are not fatal. Consider the first two problems. It is true that a player with the same statistics might be less valuable on one team than another, but this is merely to point out that the contribution a player makes is context dependent. This is no different from the notion that a mediocre doctor in a region of the Congo without any other doctors might make a bigger difference than a superb cardiac surgeon in a large Boston hospital. Statistical measures of performance are also affected by context. For example, a running back's surrounding cast will likely affect his statistics.

Consider the notion that a player didn't bring success to a team that had none. He might make such success more likely, shoulder more than his share of the burden, or be praiseworthy for his efforts, but he doesn't make the team more successful, and, if the above assumptions are true, that is a measure of his value as a player. Here we are interested in actual value, not expected value. The former looks to the past; the latter looks to the future (e.g., it tells us whom to draft and pursue as a free agent).

There is a real-world indicator of a player's net value. On some accounts, the flow of money tends to track contribution to welfare. The assumptions here are that persons spend money in a way that tracks their preferences and that their preferences track contribution to their welfare. If this is correct and if owners pay players to help their team win, players' salaries will tend to track their net value to their teams. The two will deviate in some cases because economic valuation focuses on expected rather than actual net value.

An objector might note that this view could yield the result that a mediocre player with a terrible backup has more value than any other player. The objector would then assert that this is a knockdown counter-example to the theory. There are two problems with this objection. First, the example is a little hard to imagine, and this may contribute to the oddness of having a mediocre player have the most value. It seems far more likely that a player from another position would be used as a back-up or that a decent backup would be obtained via trade or free agency. Second, if the odd scenario obtains, then the player does help his own team more than any other player in the league does, and thus the notion that he has the most value is not so counterintuitive. The mediocre player would also likely be paid the most.

Fitting *Actual Value* into the Traditional Categories of Value

The table below is a summary of my findings with regard to the three models. In this chapter, I have argued that in the context of team sports the value picked out by the actual-substitute model measures a football player's net value to his team. This claim is based on the assumption that these are the three most plausible models of a player's net value and that the two competitor models fail.

	Nature of Baseline State?	This Model Measures?	Correct Account of Player Value?	Good Indicator of Future Value?
Model 1: No Substitute	Team success when no one occupies a player's position	Causal Contribution	No	No
Model 2: Average Substitute	Team success when an average (or reasonable) substitute occupies a player's position.	Past Performance across a Range of Teams	No	Yes, if past performance indicates future performance
Model 3: Actual Substitute	Team success when the actual (or likely) substitute occupies a player's position	Actual Value	Yes	No

The analysis in this chapter can be applied to issues outside football. It can be used to compare the contributions of different persons to an organization—for example, those of a surgeon and an anesthesiologist to a particular hospital. It is even relevant to broader inquiries such as whether a particular person contributes more to others' welfare and to making the world a better place when, for example, she becomes a stay-at-home mother rather than an investment banker.

Notes

1. See Stephen Kershnar and Neil Feit, "The Most Valuable Player," *Journal of the Philosophy of Sport* 28 (2001): 193–206.

2. The total value of something is the sum of its intrinsic and extrinsic values. Intrinsic value is value that depends on a thing's intrinsic properties. Extrinsic value is value that depends on a thing's extrinsic properties. There is an issue as to whether things are extrinsically valuable only after the intrinsically valuable state has obtained. The idea for this point comes from Toni Ronnow-Rasmussen, "Instrumental Values—Strong and Weak," *Ethical Theory and Moral Practice* 5 (2002): 29–32. One concern here is that something might be conducive to bringing about intrinsic value but not actually do so. This concern might be connected to issues regarding whether things exist only in the present and when the future is open. I shall sidestep this issue since my analysis is independent of it. There are two types of extrinsic value: instrumental value (the means to an intrinsically valuable end) and contributory value (the part of an intrinsically valuable whole). In this chapter, I explore different notions that are related to extrinsic value.

3. This comes from an interview of Lawrence Taylor on *60 Minutes,* 30 November 2003.

4. Tim Layden, "Two Tough," *Sports Illustrated,* 27 November 2006, 48–52, esp. 51.

5. One way to view the choice of baselines is as a way of picking out a thing's extrinsic value. For an account that analyzes extrinsic value in terms of the difference between its total value and its intrinsic value, see Earl Conee, "Pleasure and Intrinsic Goodness" (PhD diss., University of Massachusetts at Amherst 1980), 111, cited in Ben Bradley, "Extrinsic Value," *Philosophical Studies* 91 (1998): 113. However, this account doesn't specify the way in which we pick out the baseline account. Ben Bradley argues that the baseline state is context specific. Bradley, "Extrinsic Value," 109–26. This chapter differs from Bradley's analysis in that it is not trying to analyze extrinsic value but merely trying to identify the type of extrinsic value that we should care about.

6. This definition comes from Steven Landsburg, *Price Theory and Applications,* 5th ed. (Cincinnati: South-Western, 2002), 120.

7. "Tom Brady," http://en.wikipedia.org/wiki/Tom_Brady.

8. In baseball, one firm that provides a statistical analysis of baseball analyzes a player's value in term of his value over replacement player (VORP). "VORP" is defined as "the number of runs contributed beyond what a replacement level player would contribute if given the same percentage of team plate appearances." Stathead. com defines a "replacement level player" as "one who hits far below the league positional average as the league backups do relative to league average, who plays average defense for the position, and is a breakeven base-stealer and baserunner." Keith Woolner, "Introduction to VORP: Value Over Replacement Player," http://www. stathead.com/bbeng/woolner/vopdescnew.htm; accessed 13 July 2001.

9. In baseball, for example, one statistic, equivalent average (EqA), is a measure of total offensive value per out. The statistic makes corrections for league offensive level, home park, and team pitching. Baseball Prospectus, "EqA," http://www. baseballprospectus.com/glossary/index.php?search=EqA; accessed 22 September 2006.

10. "Pro Bowl Index," http://www.pro-football-reference.com/misc/pbindex. htm; accessed 24 May 2007.

11. "Record and Fact Book: Individual Records—Passing," NFL.com, http:// www.nfl.com/randf/indiv_passing.html; accessed 24 May 2007. A similar thing would likely have been true of Trent Green had he played in 1999. He had a very strong year in 1998 but was in injured in 1999 and replaced by Kurt Warner, who went on to win two MVP awards and is the third-highest-rated quarterback in NFL history. "Kurt Warner," http://en.wikipedia.org/wiki/Kurt_Warner.

Joshua A. Smith

UPON FURTHER REVIEW

Instant Replay Is an All-or-Nothing Affair

In Super Bowl XL, Ben Roethlisberger scored a dramatic one-yard touchdown just before halftime. On that play, it was initially ruled that Roethlisberger carried the ball into the end zone, and that call was upheld upon review. Many people, myself included, thought it was very clear upon review that the ball did not break the plane of the goal line, and therefore the run should not have been ruled a touchdown. But it was, and the Steelers went on to win the Super Bowl.

Scenarios like this illustrate how instant replay plays an important role in professional football in the United States. Oregon's controversial onside kick recovery against Oklahoma in 2006 in which review ultimately gave Oregon the win shows that replay's importance extends to the college ranks, as well. Cases like these abound and stir controversy about instant replay's role in football.

Some people suggest that instant replay belongs and allows us to ensure that the game is played according to the rules. Others suggest that instant replay ruins the flow of the game. Another reason replay is controversial is that some plays are reviewable, but others are not. The distinction between reviewable and nonreviewable plays is not as clear as one might hope, and the aim of this chapter is to suggest that the distinction is seriously problematic. Once we see that this distinction cannot be made in any interesting way, we shall see that either every play must be reviewable, or no play is reviewable.

This discussion will center around the NFL's use of instant replay. But what is said here about instant replay can also be said regarding the

NCAA's use of replay, and of any other football organization that employs instant replay.

Consistency

Were a member of the officiating crew to call holding on one player over and over again throughout the course of a game but not call it on other players who are blocking in exactly the same way, we would think that there was something very wrong with the way that official was calling the game. The problem would be that the official was applying a rule inconsistently. The official would, in effect, be maintaining that some instances of blocking in a particular way are holding, while other instances of blocking in that way are not. That would be like a police officer claiming that sometimes driving seventy miles per hour in a school zone is speeding, but other times it is not. We think that rules should be applied consistently.

Not only should the rules themselves be applied consistently, but the motivations for the rules should also be applied consistently. For instance, we would find it odd if the NFL were to make it illegal to tackle the quarterback out of concern for player safety but still allow wide receivers going across the middle to be tackled by an opponent they do not see coming. To make rules like this would be to apply the motivation for a rule (in this case, player safety) inconsistently. But when the NFL makes so-called horse-collar tackles illegal because there are serious safety concerns about such tackles (rule 12, section 2, article 1 [12.2.1])[1] and also makes hitting a passer below the knees illegal (12.2.12), we can appreciate that in both cases the concern is for catastrophic lower-leg injuries to players. Terrell Owens was the victim of a horse-collar tackle late in 2004 that resulted in his missing most of the playoffs (though, famously, not the Super Bowl). Carson Palmer suffered a serious knee injury in the playoffs against the Steelers (as they were on their way to Super Bowl XL) when Kimo Von Oelhoffen fell into his lower leg. Both of the rules mentioned were new for 2006, due in part to these injuries' making salient ways in which players can unnecessarily be in harm's way during games. The point is that these rules are motivated by the same consideration, and we expect that motivation to be applied consistently.

The Rules

The rules governing instant replay in the NFL are succinct. They appear in section 9 of rule 15. An important aspect in the statement of the rules is the distinction between reviewable and nonreviewable plays. The plays that are reviewable are carefully spelled out, so that plays not covered by the description of reviewable plays are nonreviewable. Reviewable plays are broken down into three categories: (1) plays governed by sideline, goal line, end zone, and end line, (2) passing plays, and (3) other plays. The first category concerns the usual issues, like whether the ball broke the plane of the end zone on an apparent touchdown, whether a ball carrier stepped out of bounds, and so on. The second category concerns things like whether a pass was completed, whether a quarterback fumbled or threw an incomplete pass (because his arm was moving forward when the ball left it), and the like. The third category is new for 2006 and governs things like whether a "runner was ruled not down by defensive contact."

Again, anything that is not a reviewable play as articulated by the rule counts as a nonreviewable play. The rules explicitly mention nine nonreviewable plays, including the status of the clock, the proper down, penalty administration, force-outs (whether a receiver would have come down with the ball in bounds had he not been pushed out by a defensive player), and field goals.

Important to keep in mind here is that this distinction concerns whether plays are reviewable. We're not here concerned to specify exactly which plays are to be reviewed but only which plays it is permissible to review. Many plays that could be reviewed are not. These rules concern which plays could be reviewed.

"Get the Calls Right!"

In a 2003 *Sporting News* article on replay, Paul Attner provides reasons for thinking instant replay is a good idea. He says, "Because football once existed before replay—and before television, for that matter—we still must deal with the grumpy-old-men argument that we shouldn't remove the human element from the game. All that means is we know the officials will make mistakes, but let's not do anything to correct the errors. Nonsense."[2] The idea seems to be that instant replay makes it more likely that the right call will be made; at least, it allows for the correction of officiating mistakes. Since we have definitive rules according to which the game is to be played, why not do everything possible to ensure that the rules are being followed? If we needed a slogan, it could be this: Get the calls right.

But notice that if this is the motivation for including instant replay at all, it does not motivate the NFL's treating such things as field goals as nonreviewable. After all, it would be very easy to tell in a replay whether the ball went over the crossbar and between the uprights. And since it is not at all uncommon for a game to be decided by a field goal, it is certainly important to get those calls right.[3]

Put more generally, if getting calls right is the motivation for instant replay, then we should allow replay on every play. Not to make every play reviewable is to apply the motivation inconsistently. And as we saw above, inconsistent application of the motivations for rules is unacceptable.

One might object at this point that getting the calls right is not important all the time, just on certain calls. But to say this is to allow that inconsistency in the application of the rules is acceptable, which, as we saw above, it is not. So to be consistent, given the motivation for using instant replay, all plays should be reviewable.

Reasons against Instant Replay

In opposition to Attner's position, Steve Greenberg argues that the NFL should give up on instant replay. He says, "There's a blissfully simple explanation why replay should be beanbagged: It's not fun. You know what's fun? Hut-hut-hike, violent tackle. Replay keeps us from that."[4] Greenberg's complaint is a common one among those with whom I watch football: instant replay ruins the flow of the game. One's favorite team can be in the midst of a stimulating drive, which can be disrupted with the throwing of the red flag. Replay, on this view, adds an unnecessary stoppage to the game. Keeping the game exciting is more important than making sure every call is made correctly.

Notice that this line of thought applies to all plays: allowing that any play be reviewed would be to allow the flow of the game to be ruined. So no play should be reviewable. If part of the NFL's motivation for maintaining that certain types of plays are not reviewable because reviewing them would be too time consuming (thereby ruining the flow of the game), their application of the motivation is inconsistent; any replay ruins the flow of the game and so should not be allowed.

Is There a Middle Ground?

So far, we've seen that the reasons for having instant replay are reasons for maintaining that every play is reviewable. We've also seen that a common reason for thinking that some plays should not be reviewable holds for all plays as well. But perhaps there is a middle ground here. Perhaps there is a distinction to be made between those types of plays that are reviewable and those that are not that would allow us to say that the reviewable plays are such that it is more important to get them right than it is to ruin the flow of the game, while the nonreviewable plays are such that it is more important not to ruin the flow of the game than it is to get them right. This would make sense of the way the NFL's rules on instant replay are articulated and would allow the NFL to maintain that the motivations for the rules are indeed consistent. Let us consider, then, what the differences might be.

Judgment Calls

The most commonly held way to distinguish those plays that are reviewable from those that are not is by whether the call is a "judgment call" or not. Consider pass interference penalties (which, being penalties, are not reviewable). Pass interference is defined as follows: "It is pass interference by either team when any player's movement beyond the line of scrimmage significantly hinders the progress of an eligible player or such player's opportunity to catch the ball" (8.2.5). So when an official is considering whether to call pass interference, the official must determine whether a player's movement "significantly hindered" another player's chance at making a catch. But what constitutes significant hindering is up to the official, so this type of call crucially depends on the official's judgment.

Reviewable calls, on this view, do not crucially depend on an official's judging things in a certain way. Only calls that are independent of an official's judgment are reviewable. So consider things like whether the ball has broken the goal line on a short run. This involves no judgment on the official's part, since either the ball has or has not crossed the goal line. Crossing the goal line is not like "significantly hindering" one's chance to make a catch.

There are two problems with this way of distinguishing reviewable from nonreviewable plays, however. The first is that this does not capture the distinction as it is practiced. Surely, for instance, there is no judgment call involved in a field goal; either the ball goes above the crossbar between the uprights or it does not. Field goals are nonreviewable plays that do not depend on there being a judgment call involved. Thus, field goals show that the distinction cannot be made entirely on the basis of whether there is a judgment call involved.

The second and more serious problem with this way of making the distinction is that it is a superficial distinction: on close inspection it becomes difficult to make sense of it. Recall Ben Roethlisberger's one-yard touchdown run in Super Bowl XL. On that play, it was initially ruled that Roethlisberger carried the ball into the end zone, and that call was upheld upon review. Its being upheld means at least that there was insufficient video evidence to overturn the call (as per the rule).[5] Many people, myself included, thought it was very clear upon review that the ball did not break the plane of the goal line, and therefore the run should not have been ruled a touchdown. Somebody is mistaken. It cannot be the case that it was clear that Roethlisberger did not score, and there was insufficient video evidence for overturning the touchdown that was called on the field during the game. How are we to explain this? The best explanation for the controversy surrounding this call seems to be that whether the ball breaks the plane of the goal line is a judgment call.

This might strike some people as shocking. Either the ball broke the plane or it did not, end of story, and the story does not involve anyone's judgment. I am happy to grant that either the ball broke the plane or not, but that isn't really what is at issue. At issue is whether one can determine whether the ball broke the plane. That certainly looks like a judgment call.

One might still be puzzling over the claim that plays like touchdowns involve an official's judgment in the same way pass interference penalties do. To help motivate this idea, let us consider other types of reviewable plays. What becomes apparent is that there are many types of plays that involve a judgment call.

So consider first fumbles. A fumble is defined as "any act, other than a pass or legal kick, which results in loss of player possession" (3.2.4). The crucial notion in the definition of a fumble is that of possession, which is defined as follows. "A player is in possession when he is in firm grip and control of the ball inbounds" (3.2.7). So when, exactly, does a player who fumbles cease having a "firm grip and control" of the ball? This question is especially pressing for situations in which a replay is initiated because there is a question about whether a player was down before losing possession of the ball. If a player is down (7.4.1.e) before losing possession, the loss of possession does not constitute a fumble, and the ball therefore cannot change possession. It is easy enough to imagine situations in which there will be widespread disagreement about whether a player lost control of the ball before going down. This makes it look like whether a player fumbled involves a judgment call.

Or consider whether a player makes a catch, which is defined as occurring when "a player inbounds secures possession of a pass, kick, or fumble in flight" (3.2.7). But on nearly every weekend during the NFL season there are a number of plays about which there is disagreement concerning whether a player had possession of a pass. This suggests that whether a player makes a catch involves a judgment call.

Less frequently, but no less tellingly, there are issues concerning whether a player is down. A player is down when he "is contacted by a defensive player and he touches the ground with any part of his body except his hands or feet" (7.4.1.e). This can be very difficult to determine. For instance, in the second quarter of the 2006 Rose Bowl, Vince Young lateraled the ball to his running back, who took the ball in for the score. Many people thought that Young's knee was down before he pitched the ball. The play was not reviewed, but it is unclear whether the play would have been overturned. Plays like this suggest that determining whether a player is down involves a judgment call.

The last example I offer concerns when a player is out of bounds. Players often step very close to the sidelines, and any contact with those lines constitutes the player's being out of bounds. But it is often very difficult to determine whether a player did or did not make contact with the sideline. Such cases involve a judgment call.

The point of these examples is, again, to show that the notion of a judgment call is not able to make the distinction the NFL would like with replay. Given the nature of an official's imperfect connection to the truth of exactly what happens on the football field, all calls are essentially judgment calls. Some types of calls (like pass interference) are clear less often than other types of calls (like when a player is out of bounds). But that doesn't mean that the two types of plays are essentially different. So to maintain consistency, the NFL cannot motivate the distinction between reviewable and nonreviewable plays in terms of whether there is a judgment call involved.

Correctable Calls

Another way in which one might try to motivate the distinction is in terms of whether a call is correctable; that is, whether a play's outcome could be corrected. Imagine a situation in which an official blows the play dead because the official rules that the player stepped out of bounds, when in fact the player did not.[6] Suppose further that the runner had plenty of room to run and was likely to have gained at least twenty yards on the play.

There is no way to tell exactly what would have happened had the official not blown his whistle. Therefore, there really is no way to correct the play, and so there is no point in reviewing it. Plays like whether the ball crossed the goal line are correctable, and so are reviewable.

This distinction will not work, either. It suffers from two defects. The first is familiar: this distinction does not capture what the NFL actually does. Field goals are surely correctable, even though they are not reviewable.

There is yet a more serious problem: this distinction also fails. There is no such thing as an uncorrectable call. Some calls are easier to correct than others, but every call is correctable. One might wonder how the imagined scenario above, in which the player is ruled out of bounds when he is not, might be corrected. After all, the ball could not be moved to where the runner might have wound up, because we simply cannot determine where that is (the runner might have broken all the tackles and scored, or the runner might have tripped and fallen out of bounds). So such a call is not correctable. The NFL's rules allow for such plays to be corrected, though not in the same way other plays are corrected. Suppose that the running play imagined was a reverse and the ruling was that the runner stepped out of bounds behind the line of scrimmage, resulting in a loss of yards. A mistaken call like this could well prove costly. And while the team on offense cannot regain whatever result would have happened on the play, it surely need not be made to suffer the losses it incurs because of the errant call. Rule 7.4.3.a says that if an official inadvertently blows his whistle (thereby ending the play), "the team in possession may elect to put the ball in play where it has been declared dead or to replay the down." When rulings are mistaken and seem uncorrectable, the play could be treated in exactly the same way an inadvertent whistle is treated. This would allow the team to minimize the effects of a bad call. They need not lose a down, as it could be replayed. And they need not lose yardage, as the down could be replayed. So such plays are indeed correctable, even though the correction is not as obvious as it might be in other types of plays.

Well worth noticing is that every play is so correctable. No play is such that it couldn't be corrected in at least this manner. But if this is so, then whether a play is correctable would not allow us to distinguish reviewable from nonreviewable plays.

Whether a play involves a judgment call or is correctable will not allow one to draw the distinction between reviewable and nonreviewable calls. There seems not to be any other way to make the distinction, so to maintain the distinction on either the motivation of getting calls right or to keep the flow of the game going is to be inconsistent with respect to the motivation for the rule. As we saw above, this is unacceptable. Instant replay, therefore, is an all-or-nothing affair: either every play is reviewable, or no play is.

A Glance at a Different World

One last stumbling block for this position, in some people's eyes, might be the logistics of exactly how it would work for every play to be reviewable, or for no play to be reviewable. In actuality, neither situation is too difficult to imagine.

Consider first it being the case that no play is reviewable. Since football was played for a long time before the use of replay, we are quite familiar with football without replay. There are issues about getting calls right, but for many, consistency and maintaining the flow of the game are well worth the cost of a few bad calls. Football and football fans survived for years with bad calls, so there is little reason to think that a world without replay would be all that chaotic.

A world in which every play is reviewable is not that difficult to imagine either. In the NFL, during the last two minutes of each half and overtime periods, replays are initiated by a replay assistant who is in a booth watching video of the game, rather than being on the field. And as rule 15.9 indicates, "there is no limit to the number of Referee Reviews that may be initiated by the Replay Assistant." If all plays are reviewable, the replay assistant's job becomes much more involved. The replay assistant could initiate reviews from the booth throughout the game, which would help to ensure that calls are made correctly.

Conclusion: All or Nothing

There is no middle ground to take regarding instant replay. Either all plays are reviewable or none are, and in either case, the change to the game need not be that dramatic. But considerations of consistency should motivate the NFL and other organizations that use or are considering using instant replay to adopt an all-or-nothing approach.

Notes

I am indebted to George Schumm, David Merli, Nicholaos Jones, Ryan Jordan, and Mike Austin for helpful discussions about instant replay and comments on earlier drafts of this work.

1. All reference to rules follow the order rule, section, article with only the numbers mentioned. All such references are to the Official Rules of the NFL for 2006. See Larry Upson, ed., *Official Rules of the NFL* (Chicago: Triumph Books, 2006).

2. Paul Attner and Steve Greenberg, "Should NFL Instant Replay Stay or Go?" *Sporting News,* 17 November 2003; available at http://findarticles.com/p/articles/mi_m1208/is_46_227/ai_110314522.

3. Recall Phil Dawson's game-tying field goal against the Ravens on November 18, 2007. The initial call was that the kick was no good, and the Ravens thought the game was theirs. After a lengthy conference, the officials changed their decision, and the game went to overtime. The Browns wound up winning.

4. Attner and Greenberg, "NFL Instant Replay."

5. The referee might well have thought it was clear, however, from the replay that Roethlisberger did indeed carry the ball into the end zone. But for present purposes, that is neither here nor there.

6. Plays in which the runner is not ruled out are reviewable, but the type of play in question is not.

Daniel Collins-Cavanaugh

DOES THE SALARY CAP MAKE THE NFL A FAIRER LEAGUE?

One of the things that fans love about professional football in America is the fact that the National Football League is such a fair league. By "fair," I mean each team seems to have a legitimate chance to win each year. No team is forever out of the running before each season starts—no matter how poorly that team performed the year before. And no team is so completely lacking in talent that it has no chance to win any given game. This keeps the fans interested before the season, during the season, and through the long off-season. The phrase "Wait until next year," which became popular in sports like baseball, seems to ring truer in football, where teams are thought to be able to go from last place to first place in a year or two with much less difficulty than in any other sport.

Take the 2001 Carolina Panthers as an example. They put on one of the greatest shows of futility ever seen in the NFL (at least since the league went to a sixteen-game schedule thirty years ago). They won their first game—and then lost fifteen games in a row. It is a truly remarkable feat to be that bad for that long. Even franchises that have been downright pathetic in the last few years (the Detroit Lions and Oakland Raiders come to mind) have not been able to match that attention to losing! But two years after posting the last one-win record in the NFL, the Carolina Panthers were playing in Superbowl XXXVIII—and had the game tied with only two minutes to go. This is only one example of a team that went from "rags to riches." Every year, it seems, a team that was in last place, or close to it, comes back with a winning record, makes the play-offs, or something similar. Conversely, a team like the Pittsburgh Steelers can be 15–1 in 2004, 11–5 in 2005 and win the Super Bowl, and then wind up 8–8 in 2006 and miss the playoffs. So not only does every team have a chance to be good each year; each team has a chance to be bad, too!

One of the primary causes of this kind of fairness is the salary cap—an absolute limit on how much money each team can spend on total player payroll each year. This means that no team in the NFL can spend significantly more than any other team. And this in turn means that all the teams should have roughly the same level of talent from year to year. Of course, the players make a little less money than perhaps they would if there were not a salary cap. And maybe the owners make a little bit more money than they would if there were no cap. But the fans, who don't get any of this revenue, do get a fairer league because of it. So the distribution of money in the NFL causes the most happiness to all concerned—including the fans.

I believe this makes the NFL a model for a certain theory of distributive justice: utilitarianism. Justice itself is a species of moral philosophy that deals with things like fairness, rights, and whether or not people deserve what they get. Distributive justice is the branch of justice that deals with these things as far as money or other economic resources are concerned. And utilitarianism is a moral theory that concerns itself with the production of happiness. So a utilitarian theory of distributive justice would be one in which the distribution of money, or resources that could be translated easily into money, causes the most happiness. This is what I think many people believe the salary cap does.

There is just one small catch. If the salary cap makes the NFL a fair league, or increases the fairness in the league, then there should be some way to tell that this is actually the case. This is important for utilitarianism, because the theory wouldn't be much of a theory if pretend or imagined or misconceived happiness really counted for something. It would seem that, for this to work, the salary cap (in this case) actually has to do what it claims to do. Otherwise, the fans' happiness isn't really affected by it, which means that this happiness cannot serve as a justification for the harm it does to the players (even if the owners are a bit happier for it—and the harm isn't all that tremendous, anyway).

In this chapter, I will show how the NFL's salary cap can be described by using the utilitarian theory of distributive justice. I will then show that there doesn't seem to be a lot of good evidence that the salary cap is actually doing what people think it does—making the league fairer. This will cause some problems for the attempt to justify the salary cap on utilitarian grounds.

The Salary Cap and the Greatest Happiness Principle

In his seminal work *Utilitarianism,* John Stuart Mill (1806–1873), considered by most to be the principal figure in the history of the theory, defines the theory of utilitarianism very simply as the following: "The creed which accepts as the foundation of morals *utility,* or the *greatest happiness principle,* holds that actions are right in proportion as they tend to promote happiness, wrong as they tend to produce the reverse of happiness. By 'happiness' is intended pleasure, and the absence of pain; by 'unhappiness,' pain, and the privation of pleasure."[1] The happiness being promoted is the happiness of all affected by the action in question. The unhappiness to be avoided is the unhappiness of the same. Anyone capable of feeling pleasure or pain who can be said to be affected by the action needs to be equally considered when computing what Mill calls the "moral calculus."[2] The moral calculus is itself just the adding up of pleasure on one side and pain on the other, and if the pleasure side is greater, or enough greater, then the action should be undertaken.

When it comes to justice, the general principle of utilitarianism is applied as follows. First, we must determine the type of justice we are dealing with. In the present case, we are dealing with distributive justice, which is the type of justice that deals with the allocation of things (or actions) with an economic (which is to say, monetary) value. The utilitarian version of distributive justice would want a distribution that caused the maximum amount of happiness to all those affected by the distribution. In practical terms, this means neither absolute equality of distribution nor a one-to-one match of return for effort to the effort put forth. In fact, Mill himself addresses this very point toward the end of the work, in the chapter on justice. He claims that the actual distribution would have to be decided on the basis of what makes all of the actual parties to it the happiest.

The Cap's Impact on Players, Owners, and Fans

Of the three major parties affected by the distribution of revenue in the NFL, two are affected directly: the players and the owners, insofar as they actually receive the revenue we're talking about. The third party, the fans, is not directly affected by the revenue itself but by the effect the distribution of the revenue has on the fairness of the league. Fans are still affected, however, and in a significant way as regards happiness, so their happiness must be considered. Now in utilitarianism, the action, or in this case, the distribution, has to cause the most good while causing the least harm. It is important to keep in mind that "most" good does not mean the same thing as "absolute" or "perfect" good. Everyone does not have to be completely or perfectly satisfied by the action. We just need to cause the most happiness on balance. This means we can also live with a bit of unhappiness, so long as it does not outweigh the happiness caused.

With the way revenue is distributed in the NFL with the salary cap and the revenue-sharing plan, the owners seem to be very happy. Although some owners might be happier if they didn't have to share so much revenue, they are still happy to have a guaranteed amount of revenue each year because of the salary cap. That is, even the owners of what are often referred to as "large-market" teams (the ones who would supposedly be the most disadvantaged by the salary cap, since they couldn't use their larger market power to get better players through free agency) are happier because they don't have to worry about losing money to the escalating cost of unlimited free-agent contracts. And even if some of the owners of the teams with the most revenue might want to chance a nonsharing, no-cap system, in the end the actual happiness of a guaranteed income would seem to outweigh the potential happiness of maybe having a bit more money—or a better chance to win each year.

When it comes to the players, though, the effect of the salary cap might not be as favorable, because the salary cap effectively limits how much money the players collectively can earn. As economist John Vrooman points out, "the cap could serve as a collusive attempt to control total player costs, and it would allow the maximization of profits *for the league as a whole*."[3] This means that players get less money than they would likely get under a different system of revenue distribution, such as the one enjoyed by players in Major League Baseball.[4] How much less is a matter of some dispute, but it is not unrealistic to think that it is probably something like $2 billion per contract cycle (the contract cycles are seven years). This money goes to the owners instead.

As staggering as this sounds, though, it isn't as if the players in the NFL are what most would consider impoverished. The average NFL salary is still around $1.4 million—not exactly starvation wages.[5] Sure, it's less than the $2.867 million earned by MLB players (who don't have any kind of salary cap to contend with)[6] and the $4.9 million earned by players in the National Basketball Association (who earn this despite having both a team salary cap and an individual salary cap).[7] But it's still a lot of money. And they get free agency after four years of NFL service. So although we could say that they are harmed by the salary cap somewhat, it doesn't seem like a significant amount of harm at first glance.

Fans do not get to share in the revenue of the league. In fact, it's the fans themselves who contribute to the revenue that will be shared by the players and owners. This happens both directly, through ticket and merchandise sales, and indirectly, through television viewing that yields high ratings and leads to the NFL's enormous television contracts. So if the fans aren't benefited by the revenue, what benefit do they derive?

The benefit they derive concerns the thing that fans want from the contests themselves. If you ask most fans, they will tell you that what they want most of all is for their team to win. Now each week, when fans go to their games or watch them on television, the team they support will either win or lose. So fans tend to expect that what they want most of all, the win, will not happen every week. If fans believe their team has a chance to win any particular game, though, they are much more likely to be spectators of that contest. The more they believe this, the happier they will be with the league. This means that fairness, in terms of the competition, will be important because this will lead to the happiness, or potential happiness, of the largest number of fans each year with each team. This overall sum of happiness on the part of the fans needs to be considered as part of the moral calculus that goes into determining whether or not the distribution of revenue under the salary cap is just, according to utilitarianism. So, on the one side, we add up the fans' happiness and the owners' happiness, even though the way in which each party is made happy by the distribution is a bit different. And on the other side, we subtract the players' unhappiness that results from not getting as big a share of the revenue collectively as they would without a salary cap. When we do this, and we can under utilitarianism, we notice that there is a lot more happiness than unhappiness. And since the salary cap seems to be a major cause for this overall result, we can say that it is justified on utilitarian grounds. In fact, we can even say that the way it works seems to serve as a model for a just utilitarian distribution.

Does the Cap Work?

Now that I have laid out how all of this works from a utilitarian point of view, I think it is time to see if there is any way to check whether the salary cap is doing what it is supposed to be doing, namely, making the NFL a fairer league. There are three ways to measure this, I think: competitive balance, distribution of playoff spots, and distribution of championships. If the NFL is fairer with the salary cap than without it, then there should be an improvement in these things that can only be explained, or is only likely to be explained, by the presence of the salary cap. If there is no difference, then we could try looking at a comparison between the NFL and other professional sports leagues. If neither of these provides evidence, though, then I think we would not be justified in claiming the salary cap has the effect that it is thought to have. This would not mean that it definitely does not have this effect. It would just mean that we lack a lot of evidence for the claim right now—and usually, when we lack evidence for a claim, we shouldn't make that claim (that is, until we get better evidence).

Competitive balance, as defined by Vrooman and others, is a measure of the relative strengths and weaknesses of teams on the field, as gauged by winning percentage. The formula to determine this is to take the standard deviation of winning percentages and divide that number by the ideal standard deviation. The ideal standard deviation is a winning percentage of .500 divided by the square root of the number of games played. The closer the number that results from dividing the latter into the former is to 1, the more competitively balanced the league in question is.[8]

If every team's having a chance to win is fair, then an increase in fairness should correspond to a decrease in the number that represents competitive balance, so that a fair league is a league with a score closer to 1. So if the NFL is fairer in the salary cap era than it was prior to the salary cap, we would have some justification for saying that the salary cap had made the league fairer. Unfortunately, if we go all the way back to the merger with the American Football League, which is a period of almost forty years, we don't see this occurring. In fact, the competitive balance in the NFL appears to be quite stable over the whole period. The average for the entire period is around 1.55. The average competitive balance number for any period of five years or so is 1.55. The variation from this number between high and low isn't even that great. And it happens that two of the greatest variations, scores of 1.7 or more, have come during the years of the salary cap.[9] The league has had a competitive balance score of 1.7 or higher the same number of times under the salary cap as it did between the advent of the sixteen-game regular season and the start of the salary cap period.

There is one important thing to keep in mind about the competitive balance score, though. Because the NFL only plays a sixteen-game regular-season schedule, it is almost statistically impossible for it to score higher than something in the low 1.7s. And it does this only rarely, and usually because a few teams happen to have very bad years. Besides, winning and losing in the regular season are really only a means to an end. The goal of teams is to make the playoffs. So in a fair league, each team should make the playoffs at least once a decade or so. And almost every team does do this—at least since the NFL has gone to the wild-card format. But there doesn't seem to be much difference in the rate of teams making at least one playoff appearance otherwise.

Consider the following. In the last ten seasons, only one team, the Houston Texans, has not made a playoff appearance (and to be fair to them, they are only in their fifth year in the league). In the previous ten years, though, only two teams, the Tampa Bay Buccaneers and the Arizona Cardinals, failed to make the playoffs. And in the decade before that, only one team, the New Orleans Saints, failed to make the playoffs at least once. So again, it seems that the salary cap has not made any significant impact on the league. Or, to address the same issue in a different way, we would seem at least as justified in saying that any increases in the number of teams participating in the playoffs in a given period of time is just as easily explained by the inclusion of additional playoff spots, which would, on the surface, be a simpler explanation than some league-wide effect brought on by a salary cap.

There is one more measure we can look at in determining the fairness of a league: the number of franchises that win championships. Presumably, in a balanced league where teams don't have big advantages over each other, there would be many different champions, rather than only a few. And if the salary cap has an impact on this, then we should notice some noteworthy difference between the number of teams that won championships before the salary cap and the number of teams that have won championships after.

Once again, the difference isn't as striking as we might expect. If we break the Super Bowl era up into four decades, the last of which occurred completely during the salary cap era, we do not notice much difference in the number of teams that won championships during each ten-year period. In three out of the four decades, including those two decades or so when the fewest teams made the playoffs each year, seven different teams won championships. The only exception to this was the period from 1987 to 1996, when only five different teams won. One keeps hearing that we are at the end of the dynasty era in professional football, but three out of the last six Super Bowls were won by the same team. So again, there does not appear to be much evidence that the salary cap is causing what it claims to be causing, namely, a fairer league.[10]

There is one last place we can look for evidence. If there doesn't seem to be much of a difference between the NFL before and after the salary cap, perhaps we can compare it to the other two major professional sports leagues. (This comparison is shown in the appendix on pages 178–79.) If we find that the NFL is fairer than these other leagues, and that this fairness seems to be a result of the salary cap, then we may be justified in thinking that the cap is the cause of this greater fairness.

This sort of comparison is problematic, since there are important differences between the leagues. For one thing, each league plays a different number of regular-season games. For another, each league admits a different number of teams to its playoffs each year. But even with these differences, it may be possible to make some comparisons and so arrive at some kind of conclusion. If we look at the other two major professional leagues, MLB and the NBA, we see that both have free agency, but only one, the NBA, has a salary cap. If both the NFL and the NBA are more balanced competitively than MLB, which does not have a cap and is widely thought of as the league with the greatest imbalance, then that would be some kind of evidence in favor of the cap. The same could be said if those leagues produce more different champions in a given period of time. And perhaps the number of teams that make the playoffs would be useful, too.

Unfortunately for proponents of the salary cap, the evidence for its effectiveness is lacking again. It is true that the NFL is more balanced than MLB. But it isn't that much more balanced. And considering that the ideal standard deviation for the NFL is .125, whereas the ideal standard deviation for MLB is .039, the fact that MLB is so close to the NFL seems to speak more highly of baseball than of football in this case. And the NBA, which also has a salary cap (two, in fact, one on total team payroll and one on individual player salaries), and which has had the cap the longest, also has the worst competitive balance score of the three leagues. As a matter of fact, if we look at the competitive balance scores of all three leagues going back to the NFL-AFL merger, the NFL stayed the same over the entire period, MLB improved its competitive balance with free agency and no salary cap, and the NBA's competitive balance actually got worse after it adopted its salary cap system.[11] I will admit, though, that since the NBA went to individual player salary caps (which the NFL does not have), competitive balance in the league has improved somewhat—although the number of different teams winning championships is still smaller (four in nine years) than in the other two sports. This will bear watching over the next ten years or so, particularly if either of the other two major professional sports adopts such a system (which seems doubtful).

If we look at playoff berths and championships won among the three leagues, we do notice one disparity that would seem to favor leagues with salary caps. Both the NBA and the NFL have been able to get nearly all their teams into the playoffs in any given ten-year period. This is not the case with MLB. There is a relatively simple explanation for this: the NFL and the NBA both have one more round of playoffs than does MLB. Since they let more teams in (the NFL has four more teams in the playoffs each year, and the NBA has eight more), it isn't really all that surprising that a higher percentage of teams make the playoffs. In fact, if MLB had an extra round—and it would have to adopt the NBA's model if it did (it wouldn't make sense to give MLB teams a bye week)— then in the last ten years, every MLB team would have had at least one playoff appearance.

This leaves championships for a point of comparison. Here, during the Super Bowl era, MLB comes out on top, with nineteen teams winning championships in the last forty years. The NFL is second with sixteen, and the NBA is last with fourteen. It has also happened that twice in the last twenty-five years MLB has had six teams win consecutive titles. That has happened only once during the Super Bowl era in the NFL (Super Bowl II–Super Bowl VII) and once in the NBA (1975–1980). So in terms of championship distribution, MLB, with free agency but no salary cap, comes out ahead of both leagues with salary caps. Once again, evidence for the impact of the salary cap seems to be lacking.

Now it could be objected that my argument is a bit too speculative. It may be the case that none of these things shows a direct relationship, but I haven't shown that there definitely isn't one either. And since the NFL has never had an uncapped system with free agency (that is, it has never had MLB's system), we can't say that the cap hasn't had an impact. This would be easy enough to test. All we would have to do is have an experimental period, say, ten to fifteen years or so, of no cap and free agency in the NFL. If the competitive balance grew noticeably and consistently worse, if a larger number of teams missed the playoffs entirely, and if, say, only five or six teams won championships in the period, then we would have some evidence that it was the salary cap making the league fairer than it was (or would have been) without it. Somehow, though, I don't think the owners would agree to that type of experiment.

Conclusion: Cause, Effect, and the Cap

This in turn points out a serious problem with the theory of utilitarianism in general, and with its application to distributive justice in particular. If we are going to use the consequences of our actions to gauge their moral worth, then we need an accurate way to measure those consequences. This means that we need to know that things are actually the causes of the things that they purport to be the causes of; our belief or imagination cannot be sufficient. If I want to say that doing something, like building a highway where your farm is, will bring more happiness, then I have to be able to show that this will actually cause more happiness than the available alternatives. If I cannot do this, then my actions are not justified from a utilitarian perspective.

With respect to the NFL salary cap, the mere fact that people believe the salary cap makes the league fairer than it was or would be without it is insufficient to justify its use as a tool of utilitarian distributive justice. Some evidence is needed. And unless we are presented with evidence more compelling than what has been shown hitherto, I don't see any reason why a utilitarian should accept the premise that the salary cap is a good model of the theory. This in turn means that we can consider only the parties who are obviously affected by it: the players and owners. Here, the net unhappiness that results from players' not getting what they would in a more open market is not offset by the increased happiness of owners' getting more money than they would if they had to offer more competitive salaries. Why? Because the owners are thirty-two billionaires, and the players are fifteen hundred semi- or actual millionaires. So the players' net happiness outweighs the owners' net happiness on a straight moral calculus.

Do I think this means that there will be a great outcry by the fans on behalf of the players? Do I believe that, if my analysis were widely accepted, fans would demand an end to the salary cap when they call in to their talk-radio shows or write to the executives of their teams? No, I don't. Sadly for the players, it seems that most fans believe that players should make much less than they do (without a corresponding feeling about how much the owners make). But this is a completely different topic for another discussion.

I would like to close with two pieces of speculation as to why so many people so readily believe that the cap makes the league fair. The first concerns what I take to be the strange relationship sports fans have to the athletes they watch (in whom they invest a lot of time and money watching). It seems to me that there is a certain underlying resentment toward the athletes who make so much more money than most of the fans who watch them. I don't find this resentment to be the case with other highly paid folks, such as actors, singers, and other entertainers. But it really does seem to be there with athletes. How often have you heard the phrase "spoiled rich athlete," or something like it? Because the salary cap limits how much money players can make, fans seem to be pleased by it. There is also a kind of persistent belief that the more players make, the less they care about winning (and not caring about winning is about the worst character trait a player can have, from a fan's perspective). This is ironic in a way, because one of the purposes of the cap is to keep large-market teams from getting all the good players, who cost more money, so that they can win more often.

This in turn leads to the other piece of speculation, which is really more of an intuition based on a particular understanding of the history of another sport, baseball. I believe that the love of the salary cap in the NFL, and the general angst over the absence of a cap in MLB, has more to do with the recent dominance of the New York Yankees than anything else. I base this view on the following. From 1981 to 1994, the Yankees did not make the postseason. They had some decent teams, but never good enough. They finished in last place in 1990 and finished twenty or more games back two other times in the 1990s, although they generally spent more than any other team. Of course in those days (which include the period in the late 1980s when the owners were thought to be colluding to keep player costs down), the difference wasn't as stark as it has since become (or so we're told). But the Yankees became a dominant team again on the heels of a widely unpopular strike in which the players successfully resisted the owners' attempt to impose a salary cap on the league. (I find it amusing, by the way, that the teams that wanted the cap were the large-market teams, since they were, and are, the ones who bear the brunt of escalating player costs under free agency.) And they spend a lot of money. And they are the team that historically has provoked the most reaction, positive and negative, among MLB fans. If the most dominant team since the 1994 MLB players' strike had been the Los Angeles Dodgers or the Los Angeles Angels, and especially if it had been one of the historically "cursed" franchises like the Cubs or the Red Sox (whose large spending almost never provokes comment—but then, they do spend only about 75 percent of what the Yankees spend), then I don't believe one would observe so much hand-wringing over those small-market teams. I believe this is particularly true of the Cubs and the Red Sox. If they—and especially the Cubs, who were not big spenders on player payroll until recently—had spent a lot of money to win championships, I believe they would have been applauded and held up as examples of owners who really cared about their fans.

Is there a comparable team to the Yankees in the NFL? Yes: the Dallas Cowboys. But in the salary cap era of the NFL, except for very early on (when they still had all their good players), the Cowboys have not been a dominant team. In fact, they have been mediocre at best. This doesn't mean that there haven't been dominant teams. The New England Patriots have been about as dominant a team as any in the Super Bowl era. Yet instead of lamenting their dominance, people often express puzzlement that the Patriots can keep their winning ways going and admiration for their excellence in an "age of parity." I doubt that there would be such admiration if we took the entire organization, person for person, and the whole team, player for player, and the whole coaching staff, and the owner too, picked them up out of New England and put them down in Dallas. If the Cowboys had Tom Brady, Bill Belichick, and Bob Kraft and had won three out of four Super Bowls in the last six years, I firmly believe that there would be a lot of consternation over the salary cap. In fact, I wouldn't be at all surprised if, should the Cowboys become a dominant team again in the salary cap era, you heard a lot of the following on your local (or national) sports talk radio: "I hate that salary cap—no one can build a team to beat the Cowboys!"

Appendix

Below are the competitive balance scores for the professional sports leagues in baseball, football, and basketball in the United States, going back to 1970. These scores were obtained by taking the standard deviation of winning percentages for a league in a given year and dividing that number by the ideal standard deviation (.500 divided by the square root of the number of games played). The closer the number is to 1, the more balanced a league is. These figures represent regular-season play only.

Professional baseball is represented by two columns prior to 1999, and three columns beginning in 1999, when interleague play started. Prior to 1999, teams from the American League and National League did not play each other in the regular season.

Competitive Balance Scores for Professional Sports Leagues

Year	AL	MLB	NL		NBA		NFL
1970	2.41		1.56		2.18		1.54
1971	2.13		1.64		2.66		1.40
1972	1.74		2.10		3.40		1.70
1973	1.72		1.64		3.60		1.72
1974	1.15		1.97		2.42		1.48
1975	1.90		1.90		2.15		1.87
1976	1.56		2.05		1.91		1.87
1977	2.51		2.05		1.78		1.59
1978	2.23		1.62		2.02		1.38
1979	2.33		1.82		1.87		1.39
1980	2.05		1.59		2.76		1.50
1981	1.95		2.18		2.98		1.39
1982	1.77		1.59		2.78		1.70
1983	1.87		1.56		2.93		1.39
1984	1.49		1.39		2.09		1.68
1985	1.87		2.23		2.66		1.57
1986	1.41		1.92		2.62		1.67
1987	1.64		1.51		2.80		1.40
1988	1.95		1.95		2.87		1.34
1989	1.67		1.51		2.95		1.44
1990	1.46		1.46		3.16		1.62
1991	1.56		1.56		2.87		1.74
1992	1.62		1.69		2.89		1.66
1993	1.40		2.39		2.87		1.28
1994	1.44		1.52		2.93		1.22
1995	1.99		1.42		2.76		1.47
1996	1.78		1.43		3.47		1.46
1997	1.58		1.50		3.45		1.71
1998	2.08		2.25		2.24		1.50

Year	AL	MLB	NL		NBA		NFL
1999	1.94	1.96	2.03		2.93		1.58
2000	1.38	1.58	1.78		2.85		1.62
2001	2.51	2.06	1.66		2.45		1.32
2002	2.72	2.35	2.07		2.62		1.54
2003	2.50	2.18	1.79		2.47		1.54
2004	2.12	2.14	2.22		2.82		1.54
2005	2.06	1.71	1.39		2.47		1.70
2006	1.90	1.59	1.27		2.40		1.45
2007	1.73	1.47	1.25				1.66

Notes

1. John Stuart Mill, *Utilitarianism* (New York: Prometheus Books, 1987), 116–17.

2. Some utilitarians, such as Mill's mentor Jeremy Bentham and contemporary utilitarians like Peter Singer, extend the moral calculus to anything at all that can feel pleasure or pain, not just people.

3. John Vrooman, "A General Theory of Professional Sports Leagues," *Southern Economic Journal* 61, no. 4 (1995): 980.

4. In MLB, players become free agents after six years of MLB service (or their release, of course). And although there is a luxury tax on payrolls over $100 million, there is no hard-and-fast cap on a team's payroll, as there is in the NFL. This means that the large-market teams, such as the New York Yankees, can, and do, have payrolls as much as ten times that of some of the small-market teams, such as the Florida Marlins or Tampa Bay Devil Rays. This economic disparity is often cited as a cause for MLB's being much less fair than the NFL, even though those cash-strapped Marlins won a World Series over the Yankees (whose payroll that year was something like three times the Marlins') in 2003.

5. Information on average NFL salaries is available at http://www.usatoday.com/sports/football/nfl/2006-07-07-salary-report_x.htm.

6. Information on average MLB salaries is available at http://sportsline.com/mlb/salaries/avgsalaries.

7. Information on average NBA salaries is available at http://www.insidehoops.com/nbasalaries.shtml.

8. Vrooman, "General Theory of Professional Sports Leagues," 983–88.

9. The competitive balance number for the 2005–2006 season was 1.7; the number for the 1997–1998 season was 1.71.

10. It may also be worth noting that the single-elimination model makes repeating more difficult than the "best of x" series model used in the NBA and MLB. Even without the salary cap, no team in the entire Super Bowl era has ever won three straight Super Bowls. In fact, only two teams have ever been to three or more straight Super Bowls: the 1971–1973 Miami Dolphins, who won two, and the 1990–1993 Buffalo Bills, who lost all four.

11. See the table in the appendix (pages 178–79), which has competitive balance scores for the three leagues going back to 1970.

FOURTH QUARTER

METAPHYSICAL MOJO

Mark Hamilton

IS THE GRIDIRON HOLY GROUND?

Football reigns, football is king . . . In Odessa, it's God, country, and Mojo football.
—School board member in Odessa, Texas, *Friday Night Lights*

It is Odessa, Texas, and the kickoff between the Odessa Permian Panthers and the Midland Lee Rebels swiftly approaches. "Outside the Midland High band, dressed in its purple and gold costumes, play[s] the national anthem. An announcer's voice then [comes] over the public address system, asking the sell out crowd of eleven thousand to rise for the prayer, which everyone eagerly [does]."[1] This illustrates the ceremonial triad of God, America, and football occurring in high school stadiums throughout America every fall Friday night.

John Lennon was criticized for saying that the Beatles had become more popular than Jesus. Well, the Beatles were long ago eclipsed by football, which is now America's most popular cultural icon. On scores of Sundays many fans "sacrifice" attendance at church for opportunities to attend a professional football game. On ESPN the Super Bowl has become an American holy day complete with sermons and cult rituals from sunrise until kickoff. We are regaled with stories of how these teams have pilgrimaged to the holy land. Sunday evening services are rescheduled around the Super Bowl as it draws all Americans together. It has become the Church of Football, or more cynically the First Church of the Last Down.

Though American Christianity seems steamrollered by this national zest for football, conflict with American Christianity is not the only way of understanding their relationship. Many have proclaimed a sacred alliance between the two. Football players proclaim their religious conversions, crowds call upon God before games, and teams have organized Bible studies and chapels or meet to pray at midfield after the contest. Who has not heard a football celebrity endorsement of Jesus by Deion Sanders, Reggie White, Tom Landry, and others? The parts are so seamless that one cannot tell where the service ends and the games begin.

What have various philosophical thinkers said about the nature and value of religion that can help us analyze this practice of what is often called a civil religion? Are there moral conflicts that make an oxymoron of the term "Christian football player"? And if so, how does a Christian who plays football deal with these conflicts?

American Civil Religion

The relationship between public religion and football could be considered an expression of civil religion. The modern concept of civil religion originated in the philosophy of Jean-Jacques Rousseau's (1712–1778) *Social Contract*. He says the following about civil religion:

> Religion . . . can be divided into two categories, the religion of the man and the religion of the citizen. The first, without temples, altars, or rituals, and limited to inward devotion to the supreme God and the eternal obligations of morality, is the pure and simple religion of the Gospel, the religion of the citizens is the religion established in a single country; it gives that country its Gods and its special tutelary deities; it has its dogmas, its rituals, its external forms of worship laid down by law; and to the one nation which practices this religion, everything outside is infidel, alien, barbarous; and it extends the rights and duties of man only so far as it extends its altars. Such were the religions of all the early peoples; and we might give it the name of civil or positive divine law. [2]

Rousseau believed that in the ideal society the social contract was between humans and not between a person and a government. He writes, "Each of us places his person under the supreme direction of the general will, and the group receives each individual as an indivisible part of the whole."[3] Rousseau was critical of traditional Christianity because unity in civil society was disrupted by revealed religion, as it created conflict through intolerance; but by drawing on the strength of a civic religion (the religion of the citizen, as described above by Rousseau), relational harmony could be improved. He believed the basic religious ideas that could perform this unifying social bond were considered universal and could be summarized in three dogmas: as a general belief in an infinite God, as belief in an afterlife where justice prevails with virtue being rewarded and vice punished, and tolerance in religious affairs.

Robert Bellah revived interest in this topic in his 1967 essay "Civil Religion in America."[4] Bellah describes how Americans embrace a common "civil religion" in the Judeo-Christian tradition with commonly agreed-upon beliefs, values, and rituals. It binds the nation's most deeply held values with transcendent meaning.

Civil religion frequently includes offerings of public prayers or invocations of God in political speeches or ritualistic recitations of oaths and pledges or a politician's irreligiously saying, "God bless America." It can be called a sociological practice of the folk religion of a people or culture that often includes ritual expressions of patriotism. Prayers prior to football games alongside the national anthem fit this image perfectly. Civil religion has no real moral impact but, rather, reinforces the nationalistic values already embraced.

Football as Civil Religion

Civil religion reigns in American sport and, in particular, in football. The religion is so prominent that many fail even to see it. For civil religion involves social approval of such religion without concern for content; thus it embraces an anti-intellectual approach to life. Certain events, such as wars or Pearl Harbor or 9/11, foster its emergence. Far too often it finds expression in ways like those portrayed in Odessa, Texas. Odessa is described as "still a place that seemed on the edge of the frontier, a paradoxical mixture of the Old South and the Wild West, friendly to a fault but fiercely independent, God-fearing and propped up by the Baptist beliefs in family and flag, but hell-raising, spiced with the edge of violence but naive and thoroughly unpretentious."[5] Here there is a divorce between religious ritual and genuine Christian living. Even the church signs in town provide football-inspired messages such as, "How Do You Spell Defense? Mojo."[6] Such "cheerleading churches" can subtly diminish their prophetic social function. People are capable of clinging to football as if it possesses an innate sacred value, as if there were nothing else in life, so that watching the game in Odessa becomes a "quasi-religious experience."[7] But of course this is Texas, and in Texas, football is religion; who hasn't heard the joke that Texas Stadium was built with an opening in the center so that God could watch the Cowboys play?

This passionate combination of religion, nationalism, and football extends beyond Texas, however. Andrew Miracle and Roger Rees, in their book *Lessons of the Locker Room,* describe how throughout the country, high school football delivers a series of ritual events that demonstrate a community's shared "beliefs about particular ways of thinking and feeling. These myths . . . are cultural blueprints for understanding our society. . . . Ritual is sacred because it denotes a special time in which we do things that confirm the importance of deeply held beliefs. . . . High school sport . . . has these characteristics, whether boys' football in Texas or girls' basketball in Iowa."[8]

Paul Brown Stadium in Massillon, Ohio, is known as "the Temple," but high school is not the only place where the football experience seems religious. Colleges and universities also participate in this sacred pageantry and reenact these holy rites. "Every fall weekend thousands of students and alumni drape themselves in sacred colors, bear on their bodies images of their religious totem . . . in their journey to houses of worship [football stadiums], to sing hymns and participate in rituals"[9] and to cheer the gods of spectacle. The holiest event is homecoming, which provides a sense of place and history. It affirms a sense of belonging, of membership in the tribe. Football is seen as social cement to instill American and ultimately religious beliefs, values, and foundations. At the most intense religious level, the following might occur:

> During the crucial moments of the game, especially a game that is perceived to be particularly important and is closely contested, players and spectators are as one; the individual gives way to the collective. Hundreds or thousands of voices become as one. Almost simultaneously, many individuals may experience ecstasy, that is, an altered state of consciousness, a tremendous natural high. It is the force of public ritual that gives sport the kind of cultural power usually attached to religion. As the anthropologist Clifford Geertz notes with regard to religion, it is a system that acts to "establish powerful, persuasive and long-lasting moods and motivations" by "formulating conceptions of a general order of existence and clothing

these conceptions with such an aura of factuality that the moods and motivations seem uniquely realistic." Sport has done this for American culture in a way that traditional religion could not.[10]

This is obviously an expression of the civil religious ideas held by a wide cross section of Americans. There is an invoking of God to be on our team or an assumption that he is for our nation. Is there a criterion to distinguish good religion from bad religion when civil religion is involved?

The Sacred Prominence of Football

Prior to replying to the question of whether the mix is good or not, we have to ask why football has risen to such sacred prominence. First, the number of games is very limited. There are too many baseball, basketball, or soccer games to create a social civil religion. Every Super Bowl is a one-game, winner-take-all event equivalent to the seventh game of the World Series. With only five to eight home football games a year, a team can establish a historical familial tradition that unites the people in a common bond. Going to the stadium becomes a pilgrimage, and the pregame meal is a time of preparation, festivity, and feasting where communion is experienced with other tailgaters. The game is the service, with the national anthem and opening prayer serving as a call to worship. The final gun begins the benediction as the players shake hands (invoking God's blessing or curse on one another) upon leaving the consecrated turf; some elect are joyous about their standing and others are remorseful that they, the reprobate and rejected, have fallen short.

Existential Experiences in Football and in War

Football players seem to need religion more than the athletes who participate in less demanding activities. More than most team sports, football is governed by emotion. Football shares with warfare similar emotions. It is not emotion run amok but passionate sentiment. The really good player must have some fire in his belly because of the extremely strenuous nature of the game. It is a game of intense bodily contact that at times can become violent. There are numerous hard collisions in the game. An athlete must be mentally and emotionally prepared to assault and be assaulted. To face this boldly without fear, knowing that he is in a dangerous situation, the football player may well call upon God and even depend upon God for safety and protection. It is hard not to seek transcendent meaning while under the threat of being smashed by a fast 320-pound lineman.

Many war images are used in football. In an old monologue, George Carlin comments that in football you blitz, bomb, spear, shiver, march, and score with players possessing nicknames like Tank, the Assassin, Hacksaw, and Mean Joe Green. This is the language of war with the nicknames of warriors. The physical punishment, threat of serious injury, the emotional intensity, and exhausting strain can prompt an emotional outpouring by the football player. As longtime NFL coach Vince Lombardi stated, "I firmly believe that any man's finest hour, the greatest fulfillment of all he holds dear, is that moment when he has worked his heart out in a good cause and lies exhausted on the field of battle—victorious." The football game can be a truly existential experience where one experiences the absurdity of the threat of injury or even of personal destruction—an experience not unlike that of the combat infantryman. There is a need for eternal strength and for a confidant to whom to pour out one's emotions. This frequently is God. This also makes the football player more interested in the valiant knightly approach to religion than the caring shepherd motif.

Does God Belong in the Game?

Robert Higgs, in his book *God in the Stadium,* begins with the observation that "wherever we look in American society we see links between sports and religion and even the confusion of one with the other. . . . They have served one another and have become almost inseparable."[11] He describes this partnership and argues that this mixture has not been good because sports and Christianity are ostensibly incompatible because of the negative effect of sports on Christianity, as sports present the archetype of the Knight over and against the model of the Shepherd. He states "that to modernize Jesus is to muscularize Him and the culture of our time, and to muscularize is to militarize, as the long alliance of military drills, exercises, sports, and religion in the United States amply illustrates."[12] Higgs seems to want to eliminate this perverting combination and remove religion from sport. This is certainly an understandable perspective. Much of what has been produced by this amalgamation has been detrimental. It is my contention, however, that this problem could be remedied, not by seeing sports and Christianity as incompatible, but rather by approaching sports in general and football in particular from a Christian worldview rather than an experiential, fragmented civil religious viewpoint. The problem is not their incompatibility or an imbalance of focus, but rather that the way they have been united has distorted religion and harmed football.

A Worldview Approach to Faith and Football

Martin Marty, a prominent historian of religion, concludes that religion primarily serves two functions: it provides a message of individual salvation, telling us "how to get right with God," and it is a "lens for interpreting the world."[13] Many do not think it is possible to provide an interpretation of the world, a philosophy of sports, or a Christian philosophy of football. But the failure to do so creates a two-worlds mentality resulting in the compartmentalizing of life into the sacred and the secular. Civil religion is conducive to both compartmentalization and superficial unity. It places demands upon certain specific ritualistic behaviors and thereby lessens or precludes understanding and growth of authentic faith that encompasses all of life.

It is impossible to make civil religion a prophetic pulpit for rebuking the sins of a populace or its institutions, because civil religion exists to make them (in this case patriots and football fans) feel sanctified in themselves. This particular temptation is tailor-made for the mind of the athlete. Most of contemporary American Christianity restricts religion to the heart (pietism) and makes religious belief largely irrelevant to real life, including to the games we play. There can be a prayer before the game over the loudspeaker, but who ever heard of anyone being impacted by such a prayer? The obscenities screamed at refs, the dehumanization of opponents and officials, and the encouragement to provoke a violent collision that eliminates the opposing team's best player do not testify to a sanctified audience. The same crowd that prays may moments later be cheering as the opponent's quarterback lies mangled on the gridiron. Prayer can create the illusion of having sanctified the proceedings, but the civil religious context keeps the religious from impacting the secular in any meaningful way. When such bifurcation occurs in the academic community, a religious anti-intellectualism is created. With regard to sports, thinking slides toward pragmatic morality (or immorality).

Beyond football, consider my personal academic experience in a graduate course in pastoral counseling. The intellectual approach was like any other therapeutic counseling program except that we were taught to pray with each client before each session. Of course the prayer could comfort the distressed. But its perfunctory nature did not necessarily sanctify what followed. There was little or no discussion about approaching the subject matter in a theistic manner or from a Christian framework to determine its congruence with Christianity. No one dared ask whether there is an ethical problem in using active-listening methods to fake empathy.

My experience in that context seems analogous to the public prayer before a game. This public prayer ends up supporting the public/private dichotomy. Without a Judeo-Christian interpretation of the sport and its trappings, there cannot be a consistent approach to sport or to the ideal character profile of the athletes, and there is no basis for how to properly evaluate how the game is played or when to cheer a worthy opponent. The Christian coach or Christian football player is seen simply as someone who prays with the team, practices good values off the field or decent sportsmanship on it, and provides a testimony when the camera appears on him. Seldom do we hear anyone calling the sport into question from a Christian ethical framework.

Christianity should be a visionary anchor from which to critique a culture's social structures. Civil religion shows respect for religion, but because of its cultic tendencies, it denies any real relevance to anything substantive. It is pseudofaith with an emotional response without any challenge to lifestyle, morality, or other daily practices. This type of tokenism even allows non-Christians to participate in quasi-religious activity with impunity and without principled demands set before them. This

restricts faith to the religious sphere while adopting whatever views are current in [Christians'] professional or social circles. We probably all know of Christian teachers who uncritically accept the latest secular theories of education; Christian businessmen who run their operations by accepted secular management theories; Christian ministries that mirror the commercial world's marketing techniques; Christian families where the teenagers watch the same movies and listen to the same music as their nonbelieving friends. While sincere in their faith, they have absorbed their views on just about everything else by osmosis from the surrounding culture.[14]

Worldviews author Nancy Pearcy states: "In Christian schools, the typical strategy is to inject a few narrowly defined 'religious' elements into the classroom, like prayer and Bible memorization—and then teach exactly the same things as the secular schools. The curriculum merely spreads a layer of spiritual devotion over the subject matter like icing on a cake, while the content itself stays the same."[15]

The professor and the coach were once considered examples of moral integrity, but that day has long passed. As the gap widened between personal piety and learning as its own end, teaching and coaching began to fail the student and the player alike, causing them not to approach life from a Christian worldview. Civil religion emerged to fill this spiritual vacuum, minimizing values yet allowing football players to continue to feel as if they are practicing some valid form of Christianity. When Christianity becomes restricted to the public prayer over the speaker system at a game or a rote team prayer in the locker room, then there is no impulse, much less urgency, to explore the riches of a thoroughgoing Christian worldview that could actually transform the athlete and the contest. No longer is there Christian thinking that attempts to give the truth about the whole of reality or a viewpoint for interpreting every subject matter, including football. To lack a Christian worldview is to lack "any sense of how Christianity functions as a unified, overarching system of truth that applies to social issues, history, politics, anthropology, and all the other subject areas"[16]—including sports and football. It creates a sacred/secular split that Martin Marty describes as the Modern Schism, saying that "we are living in the first time in history where Christianity has been boxed into the private sphere and has largely stopped speaking to the public sphere."[17]

Civil religion surrounding football events trivializes authentic religious practice. Jesus commanded his followers to love God with heart, strength, and mind. This means there must be a distinctively Christian way of thinking that would involve understanding football from a Christian vantage point while entering into the fun and excitement of the game on its own terms as a legitimate activity. Is it possible there could be something truly redemptive in sport and in football? Indeed, if God has everything to do with everything, then he has everything to do with football.

"How can a simple prayer harm anyone?" a fan asks. Though one may pray and express dependence upon God for the contest, a verbal expression of faith prior to the game is not enough. It may only reinforce civil religion. God is interested in sport because it is part of life, and no part of life is divorced from God. A worldview approach is needed for sport and for football. The Christian football player should be different, not just because he leads the team in prayer, but because he thinks and applies his faith to the game.

Spiritual growth would include character development and candid renunciation of dehumanizing immoral elements and practices. It goes without saying that the Christian football player should be a good person as a role model, but he should also think deeply about applying his faith to football. He must examine violence, language, the role of anger, respect for opponents and officials, the value of the activity, and how to make the sport morally good. A Christian view of football rejects the view that the purpose of the game is to obtain fame and money or exemplify selfishness and greed. It is not to create an idol of the fame and money made or to be selfish or greedy. The avarice and egoism in football must be questioned.

The Love of the Game

The Christian philosopher Augustine (354–430) describes how evil is a disordering of our priorities. Every object is a legitimate object of love, but we must not expect more from it than its nature can provide. To fail in this creates evil. What a person loves, and how he or she loves, will determine the character of life. Consequently, the whole person is to be loved more than just the body, while God is to be loved more than the self. Hence, virtue, Augustine says, is a form of "rightly ordered love," while vice is disordered love.[18] The more the affections are distorted, the more cancerous evil becomes.

Football is one of the lower things in life. It is not as important as pure religion, family, and character. Yet it has muscled into a position of great prominence, often trumping these objects of affection. Civil religion seems to affirm this trumping. The cause of evil in the limited microcosm of sport is an expression of the cosmic cause of evil. The athlete craves some limited good in an absolute way and is enslaved by his disordered longing. The body is valuable, but virtue is more valuable. And if this is so, we must love the body and love virtue more. A sense of virtue, including humility, sportsmanship, and love and respect for the opponent (loving one's neighbor) are aspects of sport that ought to be considered more important than a public generic prayer before a game.

Other questions that ought to be pursued from a Christian mindset could be: Should playing with pain be viewed as a badge of courage? How should one approach the desire to intentionally harm an opponent? Is there a place for verbally abusing a player, a coach, a referee? Are not values more important than winning? How should one evaluate issues of race or of economic prosperity? What responsibilities do athletes have as role models? Look at the coaches in Super Bowl XLI, Lovie Smith and Tony Dungy. These are men of strong Christian character. Concerning his victory in the Super Bowl, Dungy stated, "I'm proud to be representing African-American coaches, to be the first African-American to win this. . . . But again, more than anything, I've said it before, Lovie Smith and I are not only the first two African-Americans, but Christian coaches showing that you can win doing it the Lord's way. And we're more proud of that."[19] Both men are soft-spoken, God-fearing coaches who demonstrate that one can get to the top of the coaching profession without being a miserable human being, without being a raving, screaming, paranoid, lunatic, workaholic madman. They are men of humility, men of God who never trash-talk. And the greatest shock is that they actually do put their families first.[20] They know the proper priority of sport, instead of worshipping at its feet. Dungy's Christian beliefs carry over into how he treats his players (his respectful, non-yelling approach) and how he carries himself. Because of his lack of ego, Dungy can say of Smith, "I'm so happy for Lovie, who does things the right way, without cursing and shows things can be done differently. We give God all the credit."[21] Both want people to know that who they are on the inside is what matters most.[22]

Conclusion: The Best of All Possible Games

In the book *Season of Life,* Jeffrey Marx probes the philosophy of football of the coaches at Baltimore's Gilman High School, including former

NFL star Joe Ehrman, who is now a pastor. They are coaching in a climate where they are limited in speaking about their Christian faith directly to the players; nevertheless, they approach their coaching as Christian men and are thinking "Christianly" about football. In that regard they consider their most important responsibility to be teaching these young men how to become "men for others." As the boys take the field, the following exchange is heard:

> "What is our job as coaches?" he [Joe Erhman] asked.
> "To love us," the boys yelled back in unison.
> "What is your job?" Joe shot back.
> "To love each other," the boys responded.[23]

Their goal is to teach these young men to love each other, to live in community, and to serve others. Ehrman states, "So I am part of a football program in Baltimore, and we use this as our base philosophy. Our understanding is that sports—football—is nothing more than a context to help connect with boys and teach them, one, a clear and compelling definition of what it means to be a man. Second is to give them a code of conduct for manhood. And the third is to help them figure out what their own unique, transcendent cause should be or could be in this world."[24] This is congruent with the Shepherd rather than only the Knightly archetype, and combining these creates a holistic approach that does not invalidate the game of football. This is a consistent Christian worldview approach that does not see football as an end in itself but as a means to a greater end. It does not negate proclamation, but it makes personal faith more important and sees it as a deeper well than civil religion. This holistic approach has the power to transform men and in the process raise football into the "best of all possible games." In this way, then, the gridiron can truly be holy ground.

Notes

1. H. G. Bissinger, *Friday Night Lights* (New York: Harper Perennial, 1990), 175.

2. Jean-Jacques Rousseau, *The Social Contract* (London: Penguin Classics, 1968), 181.

3. Rousseau, *The Social Contract*, 61.

4. This chapter was first published in the journal *Daedalus* (Winter 1967). Many

others have since written upon this topic, including Martin Marty, Sidney Mead, R. C. Wimberly, and John F. Wilson.

5. Bissinger, *Friday Night Lights,* 32.

6. Bissinger, *Friday Night Lights,* 47.

7. Bissinger, *Friday Night Lights,* 182.

8. Andrew W. Miracle Jr. and C. Roger Rees, *Lessons of the Locker Room* (Buffalo, NY: Prometheus Books, 1994), 13.

9. David Hackett, "Is Gator Football a Religion?" http://clasnews.clas.ufl.edu/clasnotes/alumninotes/00spring/hackett.html, 1.

10. Miracle and Rees, *Lessons of the Locker Room,* 20.

11. Robert J. Higgs, *God in the Stadium: Sports and Religion in America* (Lexington: University Press of Kentucky, 1995), 1.

12. Higgs, *God in the Stadium,* 333.

13. Quoted in Nancy Pearcy, *Total Truth: Liberating Christianity from Its Cultural Captivity* (Wheaton, IL: Crossway Books, 2005), 35.

14. Pearcy, *Total Truth,* 33.

15. Pearcy, *Total Truth,* 37.

16. Pearcy, *Total Truth,* 33.

17. Quoted in Pearcy, *Total Truth,* 35.

18. Augustine, *City of God* (London: Penguin Books, 1984), 637.

19. Dave Daubenmire, "Faith Triumphs over Race," http://www.newswithviews.com/Daubenmire/dave59.htm, 2.

20. Mike Bianchi, "Character, Not Color, Defines Dungy, Smith," *Orlando (FL) Sentinel,* http://www.orlandosentinel.com/sports/columnists/orl-bianchi2807ja, 1.

21. Richard Land, "Faith by Example—Dungy, Smith," http://erlc.com/article/faith-by-example-dungy-smith, 2.

22. Daubenmire, "Faith Triumphs over Race," 4.

23. Jeffrey Marx, *Season of Life* (New York: Simon & Schuster, 2003), 3.

24. Marx, *Season of Life,* 34.

Joseph Keim Campbell

TOUCHDOWNS, TIME, AND TRUTH

Consider the *truthmaker theory,* which claims that "for every truth there is a truthmaker" (Fox 1987, 189). In some cases truthmakers are individuals. Peyton Manning is the truthmaker for the claim that Peyton Manning exists. In other cases, truthmakers are events, like falling on a football in the end zone. The primary question of this essay is, What are the truthmakers for *touchdown truths,* that is, truths about touchdowns?

According to the NFL definition of "touchdown," a touchdown occurs "when any part of the ball, legally in possession of a player inbounds, breaks the plane of the opponent's goal line, provided it is not a touchback" (NFL 2007). Thus, truthmakers for touchdown truths appear to be worldly events, like Devin Hester's crossing the goal line after a ninety-two-yard kickoff return to open Super Bowl XLI.[1] Call this view, which combines the NFL definition of a touchdown with the truthmaker theory, the "traditional theory of touchdown truths." In this chapter, I show that the traditional theory is incorrect.

In the first half of this chapter, I develop the traditional theory of touchdown truths. I also draw distinctions between some key metaphysical concepts and dispel a fatalistic worry about the truthmaker theory. In the second half, I argue that, given the traditional theory, NFL touchdowns are not *real* touchdowns. Referees miss plays and make bad calls, yet ultimately something is or is not a touchdown only if it is registered in the final score. The NFL definition is fine as a guide for referees, but it fails as an indicator of the truthmakers for touchdown truths, which are events involving referees, not football players. In the final section, I explore the consequences of this observation and show that they are not as dire as one might think.

Truthmakers for Touchdown Truths

Given the NFL definition of a touchdown, what are the truthmakers for touchdown truths? First, let's distinguish between truthmakers and truthbearers. *Truthbearers* are the ultimate bearers of truth-value, the things that are true or false.[2] Truthbearers appear to be *sentences* like

(D) Devin scored a touchdown.

I won't deny that (D) has a truth-value. On the other hand, as (D) stands, it is incomplete. What game? Which Devin? Given our *context,* things seem clear enough. Above I indicated that Devin Hester scored the first touchdown in Super Bowl XLI, and that has a lot to do with how one understands (D). Given this context, anyone who remembers the game correctly would say that (D) is true.

The truth or falsity of (D), though, appears to be independent of our ability to determine its truth-value. Provisionally, at least, we want to be *realists* about touchdowns and accept that

- The world exists objectively, independently of the ways we think about it or describe it.
- Our thoughts and claims are about that world. (Glanzberg 2006)

Touchdowns are a part of the world and are independent of our thoughts about the world. Touchdown truths should be similarly independent of our thoughts and descriptions.

If this is the case, then (D) is not the ultimate bearer of truth-value. At most, (D) is true in a context and its truth is dependent upon something else. Perhaps it is dependent upon the truth of another sentence.

(D') Devin Hester scored a touchdown in Super Bowl XLI.

Even here, context plays a role. It distinguishes, for instance, Devin Hester, the return specialist for the Chicago Bears, from anyone else who happens to have the same name. In order to find the ultimate bearer of truth, we'll need to go to further. Consider:

(D") Devin Hester, the return specialist for the Chicago Bears, scored a touchdown in Super Bowl XLI.

Context still plays a role, though, for when assessing the truth of (D") we wouldn't consider football games played in another country or galaxy that happened to be called the "Super Bowl." It seems that no matter how much information we include in a sentence, context always plays a role in how we understand it. Our judgments about (D), (D'), and (D") depend on something more than the mere words on the page together with linguistic conventions. Sentences are not the ultimate bearers of truth-value.

I find the above argument compelling. For this reason, I believe that *propositions* are the ultimate bearers of truth-value. Propositions are abstract entities like numbers, as opposed to concrete entities like sentences or numerals. However, it is not essential that the reader agree with me on this point. One may think of propositions as *eternalized sentences*—what you get once you record all of the salient information provided by context (Quine 1960)—if such a thing is possible. Or one might think of propositions as declarative sentences *in a context*. Or one might regard the term *proposition* as synonymous with "truthbearer." What is important is that propositions are something more than the mere words that I use to express them.

Propositions are truthbearers, but what are *truthmakers;* that is, what are the things that make truthbearers true (or false)? We're concerned with only a subset of true propositions, namely, those that express contingent facts about the world. A *contingent fact* about the world is one that is true but could have been false: for instance, that Devin exists or that Devin scored a touchdown. We're not interested in what makes it the case that all bachelors are men or that $7 + 5 = 12$. These latter claims are *necessarily true* and could not have been false. Thus, the truthmaker thesis is the claim that *every contingent proposition has a truthmaker.* What are the truthmakers for touchdown truths?

There are, potentially, three kinds of truthmakers. First, *individuals,* like Devin Hester, seem to be the truthmakers for certain propositions. Devin Hester is an obvious choice as the truthmaker for the proposition that Devin Hester exists. On the other hand, Devin is not the truthmaker for the proposition that Devin Hester was the first person to score a touchdown in Super Bowl XLI. Scoring a touchdown is not something Devin can do alone. This is a metaphysical point, not a mere cliché like "There is no 'I' in 'team'!" Truthmakers are usually something more than mere individuals. Additional candidates for truthmakers are *events* and *facts*.

Events come in all sizes. There is an event for every touchdown, for example, Logan Mankins recovering a Tom Brady fumble, Asante Samuel intercepting a Peyton Manning pass. On the other hand, Super Bowl XLI was itself an event. Events are like individuals in that both are "concrete, temporally and spatially located entities organized into part-whole hierarchies. Both can be counted, compared, quantified over, referred to, and variously described and re-described" (Casati and Varzi 2006). One can count the number of scorings just as one can count the number of individual players who score.

Events are appropriate candidates for truthmakers of touchdown truths, given the NFL definition. Consider these true propositions.

- Asante Samuel scored in the 2007 AFC Championship.
- Jeff Saturday's touchdown led to a tie in the same game.
- Joseph Addai scored the final touchdown of Super Bowl XLI.

According to the truthmaker theory, corresponding to each proposition is some worldly event that was its truthmaker. For instance:

- Asante Samuel's intercepting a Peyton Manning pass and then running across his opponent's goal line.
- Jeff Saturday's recovering a fumble in the end zone.
- Joseph Addai's crossing the plane of the goal line after a three-yard run.

These examples lend support to the traditional theory of touchdown truths.

One might just as easily say that facts are the truthmakers for touchdown truths: the fact that Jeff Saturday recovered a fumble in the end zone, or the fact that Joseph Addai crossed the plane of the goal line while possessing the football. Facts are not events. For one thing, the event of Jeff Saturday's scoring a touchdown during Super Bowl XLI occurred at a particular time in the past, whereas that he scored the touchdown is just as much a fact today as it was then.

As I see it, touchdowns are *things that happen* and are more closely linked to events than they are to facts. For this reason, I take events to be the truthmakers for touchdown truths. I remain neutral as to whether events are more fundamental constituents of reality than individuals or facts. I merely recognize the need for events in our final story about the world, for in the final story we'll need to talk about football.[3]

The truthmaker theory sketched above is a version of the *correspondence theory* of truth, which claims that truth is a matter of correspondence between propositions and the world. According to our version, what makes a contingent proposition true is its correspondence with some worldly event. I am not going to argue for the truthmaker theory or explain what I mean by "correspondence." Nor do I wish to discount competitors to the truthmaker theory, or even claim that it is always easy to distinguish the truthmaker theory from its competitors (Lewis 2001). I'm more interested in exploring the consequences of applying the truthmaker theory given the NFL definition.

Making Propositions True

An *NFL touchdown* occurs "when any part of the ball, legally in possession of a player inbounds, breaks the plane of the opponent's goal line, provided it is not a touchback" (NFL 2007). Applying this to the truthmaker theory, we get the traditional theory of touchdown truth: the truthmakers for touchdown truths are events, like a running back's crossing the goal line with the ball, or a wide receiver's catching the ball with both feet in the end zone. Certain events occur, and that's what makes some claim about a touchdown true.

Of course, individual players like Devin Hester, Jeff Saturday, and Peyton Manning play a significant role in scoring touchdowns. Doesn't Devin *make it the case* that Devin scores a touchdown? Aren't playmakers the *real* truthmakers for touchdown truths? These questions reveal an ambiguity with the word "make." According to the truthmaker view, events are truth*make*rs for propositions. We might also recognize that some agents—who are kinds of individuals—*make* it the case that a proposition is true. There are two different senses of "make" noted here.

The primary influence of agents is through their actions and the consequences of those actions. Actions are types of events, so the consequences of our actions often come in the form of other events. For instance, Devin runs back the opening kickoff, and that causes the crowd to burst into cheers. Since events are truthmakers for propositions, our influence on the world may be extended to propositions (van Inwagen 1983; Perry 2004). By scoring the touchdown, Devin made it the case that the Bears had an early lead.

There is a difference, though, between Devin's making it the case that a touchdown is scored and Devin's being a truthmaker for the proposition that Devin exists. In the latter case, Devin doesn't *do* anything. His mere existence makes it the case that he exists. Following John Fox, we say that truthmakers *necessitate* propositions. In other words, when an individual is a truthmaker for a proposition, then that the person exists entails that the proposition is true (see Fox 1987, 189).

Yet individuals rarely necessitate propositions. There are unusual examples, like claims about an individual's existence, but in most cases, truthmakers are larger portions of the world, like events. Barry Smith puts it nicely: "There are parts of reality which necessitate the truth of corresponding judgments. Thus if 'John is kissing Mary' is true, then a certain process, a kissing event *k,* necessitates this truth. John himself is not a necessitator for the given judgment, though he is a necessitator for the judgment 'John exists'" (Smith 1999, 276). In general, when a person *makes it the case that* some proposition is true, he is not the necessitator for the proposition. For example, Devin made it the case that the Chicago Bears had an early lead in Super Bowl XLI. Devin performed an action, and that action had as a consequence the truth of a certain proposition: that Chicago scored the first touchdown of Super Bowl XLI. Yet Devin was not the proposition's truthmaker. He scored the touchdown, to be sure, but the necessitator was some larger part of reality, like the event of Devin's crossing the goal line.

Philosophers often use the phrase "make it the case that" in an effort to capture the notion of an action's being genuinely *up to* an agent. This way of speaking is especially helpful in clarifying debates about free will and moral responsibility (Campbell 2005). Devin made it the case that Chicago had an early lead in Super Bowl XLI. Many would agree that Devin is praiseworthy for his action precisely because it had that consequence. Yet this is not the same thing as Devin's being the necessitator for the proposition, even if his control over the event was absolute. Smith writes: "Suppose God wills that John kiss Mary now. . . . God's act is not a truthmaker for this judgment" (Smith 1999, 278). Truthmakers are the parts of the world that correspond to true propositions, thereby making them true. Even if we admit that God plays a causal role in every event, it does not follow that he is the truthmaker for all propositions. Perhaps God made it the case that John kisses Mary. Nonetheless, he does not *correspond* to that proposition.[4]

We may summarize the traditional theory of touchdown truths as follows:

- Events—possessing the ball in the end zone, carrying the ball over the goal line—are truthmakers for touchdown truths.

Other important results from this section include the following:

- Given the relationship between events and propositions and the fact that some events are up to us, it follows that some propositions are up to us.
- Individuals often make it the case that certain propositions are true.
- Individuals are generally not truthmakers for propositions.

Some Provisional Worries about Time and Truth

How does time fit into this picture? Events occur at times, whereas propositions are timeless, or so it seems. The event of Devin's scoring the first touchdown of Super Bowl XLI is past, but that Devin scored the touchdown is just as true today as it was then.[5] Did the proposition *become* true once the event occurred? Or was it always true that Devin would score the first touchdown of Super Bowl XLI? Does the admission that the proposition was always true commit us to fatalism about football?[6]

There are a variety of worries noted in the above paragraph, but I think that they may be dealt with rather easily. Consider first the following view about time and truth: the *tenseless view of semantics*. According to this view:

1. Propositions have truth values *simpliciter* rather than having truth values *at times*.

2. The fundamental semantic locution is "p is v" (where the expression in place of "p" refers to a proposition and expression in place of "v" refers to a truth value).

3. It is not possible for a proposition to have different truth values at different times. (Markosian 2002)

This theory may be explained rather easily with an example. Consider this proposition:

(F) Devin Hester scored the first touchdown of Super Bowl XLI.

(F) is true. Note, corresponding to (2), that "(F) is true" has the same form as "*p* is *v*," where *p* is the proposition (F) and *v* is the truth-value "true." According to (3), if (F) is true, then it was always true. Thus, in keeping with (1), we can't say that (F) didn't have a truth-value until Devin made it the case by crossing the goal line.

According to the tenseless view of semantics, (F) has no *time of truth;* that is, there is no time that the proposition *became* true, for propositions cannot change their truth-values: if it is true, then it was always true and will always be true. Does this mean that (F) was fated, up to neither Devin nor anyone else? Following John Perry (2004), we may distinguish between a proposition's *being true*—which is a timeless property of the proposition—and the property of a proposition's *being made true*—which occurs at a time. According to the tenseless view, propositions have the property of being true timelessly. There is no time of truth for (F), no time that the proposition became true.

Still, there was a time that (F) was made the case. According to the traditional theory, (F) was made the case by the event of Devin's crossing the plane of the goal line after running back the opening kickoff of Super Bowl XLI. This event occurred at a specific time, fourteen seconds into the game. Since propositions are eternally true or false, this is not the time of truth for (F). Rather it is the *time of event* for (F), the time of the occurrence of the truthmaking event.

Given Perry's distinction, we cannot immediately conclude that (F) was fated even if (F) was eternally true. Presumably, (F) was up to Devin, for he made it the case that (F). Note that I'm not claiming that (F) was not fated, nor am I claiming that (F) was up to Devin. I don't see any reason to deny these claims, but my point is simply that we cannot conclude that (F) was fated *given* the tenseless view of semantics.[7] It might be that the tenseless view together with some *other consideration* entails fatalism. That is a different matter.

NFL Touchdowns Are Not Real Touchdowns

The problem of fatalism is not a serious problem for the traditional theory of touchdown truth. Yet in this section, I argue that the traditional theory is false since NFL touchdowns are not *real* touchdowns. In the final section, I show that this is not a substantive worry.

The main argument of this section concludes that NFL touchdowns are not *real* touchdowns, given the truthmaker view. The argument rests on this assumption:

(R) Real touchdowns are reflected in the final score.

(R) is grounded on the intuition that saying "The New York Giants scored five touchdowns but still lost to the Dallas Cowboys 30–0" conveys a failure to deal with reality. It is the final score that settles issues about touchdown truths. If the final score reveals that your team did not score any touchdowns, then they did not score any *real* touchdowns. If your team lost even though they scored NFL touchdowns that were not reflected in the final score, then they still lost. Sometimes NFL touchdowns are not reflected in the final score, so NFL touchdowns are not *real* touchdowns, given (R).

I'm not suggesting the NFL definition is irrelevant. Certainly referees make use of it when determining whether something is a real touchdown. But referees often make mistakes. Perhaps Philip Rivers completed a pass to Vincent Jackson in a 2007 AFC playoff game between the San Diego Chargers and the New England Patriots. The event might have been the truthmaker for an NFL touchdown truth, one that would have entailed that the Chargers won were it recorded in the final score. Yet the final score remains the same, and the Chargers lost in part because this alleged NFL touchdown did not count as a *real* touchdown. As long as something is not reflected in the final score, it is not a *real* touchdown, whether it is an NFL touchdown or not.

Note that we need not give up the truthmaker theory. We may agree that the truthmakers for touchdown truths are events involving individuals. What we must reject is that the relevant individuals are football players. Rather, they are referees. More specifically, events involving the *beliefs* of referees play the role of truthmaker for touchdown truths.[8]

Antirealism about Touchdown Truths

Recall our provisional acceptance of *realism,* the view that

- The world exists objectively, independently of the ways we think about it or describe it.
- Our thoughts and claims are about that world. (Glanzberg 2006)

This definition specifies two considerations: independence and existence (cf. Miller 2005). There is no reason to doubt that touchdowns exist or *happen,* given that they are events. Yet *real* touchdowns are not independent of the ways that people think about the world. *Real* touchdowns depend upon the ways that referees think about the world. Real touchdowns violate the independence condition of realism.

Let me explain this point in another way. Consider first the following realist view of touchdown truth:

- *Touchdown Realism:* Touchdowns exist in the mind-independent world, and the fact that they exist and have properties such as winning a game or putting one team ahead of another is independent of anyone's beliefs, linguistic practices, conceptual schemes, and so on (cf. Miller 2005).

It appears that Touchdown Realism is false. This leaves us with two alternatives:

- *Modest Touchdown Antirealism:* Touchdowns exist, but the fact that they exist and have the properties that they have is *dependent* on certain beliefs, linguistic practices, conceptual schemes, and so on of referees.
- *Touchdown Relativism:* Touchdowns do not exist in a mind-independent world, for the fact that they exist and have the properties that they have is *relative* to the beliefs of certain individuals.

I move that we accept Modest Touchdown Antirealism.

It is not as if something is a touchdown if you are a Chargers fan yet not if you are a Patriots fan. Something is a *real* touchdown if it is registered in the final score. Thus, the truthmakers for *real* touchdowns are not *relative* to individual belief. There is only one set of beliefs that matters: the beliefs of the referee. You may argue about NFL touchdowns all you want, but the final score is the final arbiter for *real* touchdowns, and this matter depends on the beliefs of referees.

Finally, consider the *semantic realism* of Michael Dummett. Miller (2005) discusses an unknown principle of mathematics, the truth of which "we have no guaranteed method of ascertaining":

(G) Every even number is the sum of two primes.

He then writes:

> A semantic realist, in Dummett's sense, is one who holds that our understanding of a sentence like (G) consists in knowledge of its truth-condition, where the notion of truth involved is *potentially recognition-transcendent* or *bivalent*. To say that the notion of truth involved is potentially recognition-transcendent is to say that (G) may be true (or false) even though there is no guarantee that we will be able, in principle, to recognise that that is so. To say that the notion of truth involved is bivalent is to accept the unrestricted applicability of the law of bivalence, that every meaningful sentence is determinately either true or false. Thus the semantic realist is prepared to assert that (G) is determinately either true or false, regardless of the fact that we have no guaranteed method of ascertaining which.

Bivalence is the thesis that there are only two truth-values: true and false. Semantic realists believe that every proposition has a truth-value, independent of our ability to determine whether or not it does. We've been accepting bivalence from the very beginning, and thus far it hasn't been problematic. There is no reason to reject semantic realism about touchdown truths.

Realism about touchdowns has taken a blow, for touchdowns are not independent of human reflection. Yet this is no reason to believe that touchdowns do not exist in the mind-independent world. Nor is it a reason to be a relativist about touchdown truth or to reject all forms of realism. To put it another way, Devin Hester scored a real touchdown on the first play of Super Bowl XLI, as reflected in the game's final score.

Notes

1. Or facts about the world, like the fact that Logan Mankins recovered a fumble in the end zone during the 2007 AFC Championship. See below.

2. Bivalence is the view that there are only two truth-values—true and false—and that every proposition is either true or false.

3. Note that, for any event that occurs, there is a corresponding fact, namely, the

fact that the event occurred. For this reason, one may just as easily say that facts are the truthmakers for touchdown truths.

4. I'm not claiming that the makes-it-the-case-that relation is a causal relation. Maybe it is. Maybe it is merely an explanatory relation. Maybe it is something else altogether. This is a topic for another paper.

5. Notice the similar point about the difference between events and facts above.

6. A proposition is *fated* if it is not up to anyone.

7. See Markosian 2002 for a different view.

8. One might argue that the truthmakers for touchdown truths are certain actions of referees, for example, the event of one referee's holding up both hands. In the end, I don't think that this view holds up either, since not all of these results are reflected in the final score.

References

Armstrong, David M. 1997. *A World of States of Affairs*. Cambridge, UK: Cambridge University Press.

Campbell, Joseph Keim. 2005. "Compatibilist Alternatives." *Canadian Journal of Philosophy* 35: 387–406. An earlier version of this paper is on *The Determinism and Freedom Philosophy Website*, Ted Honderich (ed.). URL: http://www.ucl.ac.uk/~uctytho/dfwIntroIndex.htm.

Casati, Roberto, and Achille Varzi. 2006. "Events." *Stanford Encyclopedia of Philosophy (Summer 2006 Edition)*, Edward N. Zalta (ed.). URL: http://plato.stanford.edu/archives/sum2006/entries/events/.

David, Marian. 2005. "The Correspondence Theory of Truth." *Stanford Encyclopedia of Philosophy (Fall 2005 Edition)*, Edward N. Zalta (ed.). URL: http://plato.stanford.edu/archives/fall2005/entries/truth-correspondence/.

Fox, John. 1987. "Truthmaker." *Australasian Journal of Philosophy* 65: 188–207.

Glanzberg, Michael. 2006. "Truth." *Stanford Encyclopedia of Philosophy (Summer 2006 Edition)*, Edward N. Zalta (ed.). URL: http://plato.stanford.edu/archives/sum2006/entries/truth/.

Lewis, David. 2001. "Forget about the 'Correspondence Theory of Truth." *Analysis* 61: 275–80.

Markosian, Ned. 2002. "Time." *Stanford Encyclopedia of Philosophy (Winter 2002 Edition)*, Edward N. Zalta (ed.). URL: http://plato.stanford.edu/archives/win2002/entries/time/.

Miller, Alexander. 2005. "Realism." *Stanford Encyclopedia of Philosophy (Fall 2005 Edition)*, Edward N. Zalta (ed.). URL: http://plato.stanford.edu/archives/fall2005/entries/realism/.

NFL. 2007. "NFL Fans Digest of Rules." URL: http://www.nfl.com/fans/rules.

Perry, John. 2004. "Compatibilist Options." *Freedom and Determinism,* Joseph

Keim Campbell, Michael O'Rourke, and David Shier (eds.). Cambridge, MA: MIT Press.

Quine, Willard Van Orman. 1960. *Word and Object.* Cambridge, MA: MIT Press.

Smith, Barry. 1999. "Truthmaker Realism." *Australasian Journal of Philosophy* 77: 274–91.

van Inwagen, P. 1983. *An Essay on Free Will.* Oxford: Clarendon Press.

Ben Letson

FEEL THE BIG MO'

In the 1993 AFC wild-card game, the Buffalo Bills mounted the greatest comeback in NFL history, posting a 41–38 win over the Houston Oilers after trailing by thirty-two points just a few minutes into the third quarter. The Oilers had been up 28–3 in the first half, and the Bills outscored them 35–3 after the last Oilers touchdown early in the third quarter to pull out the victory. A one-yard run for a Buffalo touchdown followed by a successful onside kick marked the beginning of the comeback.[1] It would be tempting to explain the dramatic turnaround in this game as the result of a shift in momentum, possibly started by the touchdown and the recovered onside kick. Certainly the game contained what would appear to be two different demonstrations of momentum—the Oilers dominated the first half, whereas the Bills rolled to victory in the second—and we can say that there was a shift in the patterns of scoring. Is momentum indeed part of the explanation of what happened in this historic game?

The typical discussion of momentum in football goes something like this: "Coach Jones would sure like to make this field goal before halftime so the Panthers can go into the locker room with the momentum on their side." Or: "Well, we've just seen a pretty dramatic shift in the momentum of the game after the Owls coughed up that fumble in the last series, Coach." But what *is* momentum? It seems to be something that can shift. It seems to be something that can be conserved between games and can perhaps be conserved even between the end of one season and the beginning of the next. Does it refer to anything real at all? Does it, instead, refer to an event that normally would be described in other terms? Can momentum be more than a matter of playing well or of having the breaks go your way in a football game?

Momentum and Success

Whatever else it refers to, the idea of momentum is often used as an explanation of things going well on the field. We never, or almost never, appeal to the idea of momentum when things are going badly. It would be very strange to hear an announcer refer to momentum during a stretch of bad play—dropped passes, missed blocks, interceptions. This much is obvious, but it is just this feature of momentum-talk that should make us suspicious, at least if we would like momentum to do some explanatory work. Why should this be so? The problem is that if momentum is going to explain successful football playing—if it is to *be* something other than successful football playing—then we need a way of identifying momentum that is independent of the evidence offered for its presence. So it would be good if we could find some way of separating momentum from the evidence for momentum, and doing this seems to be difficult. And there is another feature that complicates things for us: why is it that, in common usage, only one football team in a given game can exhibit momentum at a time? At the very least, this fact about the way that we use this term should give us pause, for if momentum is a separate phenomenon, if it refers to something more than success itself, then why couldn't two teams have it at the same time? We could imagine two teams in a well-played, hard-fought game playing to a standstill, but no one would think that the two teams in this imagined situation were exhibiting momentum. It would seem that one team can have momentum only if the other team lacks it, and so we have another piece of our puzzle: a team is said to have momentum when it is playing well and the other team is not. Are there other components to this concept? Perhaps, but let us see whether we can make sense of what we've got.

The Mystery of Momentum

It is possible that talking about momentum is nothing more than a shorthand way of pointing out that one team is playing well while its opponent is not. If this is true, then we can forgive announcers and others who routinely discuss momentum and find them innocent of the charge of appealing to mysterious or even superstitious explanations. Of course coaches and players want momentum, on this view, since having momentum would be the same thing as playing well while your opponent does not. But a careful look at how we actually use this concept seems to point to something beyond this alternative way of expressing the obvious. It seems that the concept of momentum is intended to *explain* something and that the concept means more than simply playing well. Let's try again.

It might be that some mysterious force or power is being pressed into service here. How literally should we take the claim that the Bills are playing well *because* they have the momentum? True, we do talk about momentum shifting and about teams gaining and regaining momentum, and this might mean that momentum is a *something* that can be gained and lost. Now, not every noun indicates the existence of a thing, and perhaps momentum is like, say, talent: talent is not a something in the way that a can of beer is a something, but the term might refer to a condition or a potential or a power. Is momentum like this?

The idea of talent is promising here, because it shares another feature with momentum: having talent is also indistinguishable, mostly, from the evidence for talent. Even so, most of us talk freely about artists and athletes as though they either are or are not talented. So maybe talent and momentum will stand or fall together: either we can use both with good conscience or we can use neither. But *does* the concept of talent explain anything? To be sure, talent is not absolutely indistinguishable from the evidence for talent. We do talk about persons who squander their talent, and this seems to open up enough daylight between the concept and the evidence for the concept so that perhaps the concept does some work. But even here, when we talk about talent that is wasted, we are generally basing our belief in that talent on a demonstrated ability to do something, and so there isn't that much daylight, perhaps, after all. And the situation is worse for momentum, because it is hard to imagine the existence of *any* daylight between the concept of momentum and the evidence for momentum.

Still, every football player I have talked with about this subject has maintained a devout belief in the existence of momentum, and it seems mean-spirited to dismiss these players' beliefs so easily. Could it be that momentum refers to a complex but real phenomenon that is shown in successful performance but that refers to something more than successful performance itself?

One key element in the idea of momentum is that success leads to continued success. Momentum on this psychological account would refer to successful performance that is at least partly explained by confidence on the part of players. To this we might add a corresponding lessening of confidence on the part of the opponents: as one team believes in itself, the other begins to have doubts about its ability to withstand the efforts of the other. The "confidence" explanation seems to make sense of other features of the momentum phenomenon, the fact that momentum can come and go and that we don't normally attribute momentum to both teams at once. It stands to reason that as the deficit between the Bills and the Oilers began to shrink, the Bills would gain confidence and the Oilers would lose it. Additionally, the confidence explanation helps us to make sense of the way in which shifts in momentum seem to have an element of randomness; they occur as if dispensed as a matter of grace and not of desert.

What empirical support is there for the hypothesis that confidence causes success?

Though there are numerous explanations for the phenomenon of momentum and a growing body of research, no scientific consensus has been reached as to the preferred explanatory model to be used, and the actual empirical research to date is less than conclusive.

A Model for Understanding Momentum

Jim Taylor and Andrew Demick propose a theoretical model of momentum that uses the idea of a "momentum chain," a series of changes that result in momentum:

a. Precipitating event or events

b. Change in cognition, affect, and physiology

c. Change in behavior

d. The resulting increase or decrease in performance consistent with the above changes

e. A contiguous and opposing change in the previous factors on the part of the opponent (for sports with head-to-head competition)

f. A resultant change in the immediate outcome.[2]

Item (b) would include the confidence that results from a precipitating event, so this model clearly makes room for a psychological explanation of momentum. One benefit of this model is that it explains why momentum fails to occur even when we might expect it to following an appropriate precipitating event: Taylor and Demick suggest that the disconnect between expected momentum shifts and actual outcomes is the result of failure at different links of the chain. To show that there is in fact a correlation between precipitating events and performance outcomes, they conducted two preliminary studies. One study involved basketball, and the other involved tennis. Interestingly, though their model predicts that momentum will be less likely to occur in a team sport because individual players will traverse the momentum chain at different rates of speed, it was in basketball that they were able to show that precipitating effects were important for the production of changes in immediate outcomes. In tennis, by contrast, no statistically significant differences were observed between the presence and absence of precipitating events and immediate outcomes.[3]

David Romer has created a stir recently by publishing an analysis that, if correct, shows that NFL coaches are far too careful when it comes to punting on fourth down, and his analysis has something to say about momentum, too. Romer found that the expected average advantage of going for a first down on fourth down is greater than the expected disadvantage. So in the long run, a coach who always goes for it on fourth down will win more games than he would have won if he had punted most of the time and gone for it only occasionally.[4] One objection that Romer considers is whether his analysis is undercut by the possibility of a team's losing momentum if they go for it on fourth down and fail. It might turn out that the expected advantage of always going for it won't materialize because his argument has not taken into consideration the likelihood of the damaging effects of being on the losing end of a momentum shift. So Romer provides a rebuttal to this potential objection, and his response is simple: momentum does not exist.[5]

Romer's methodology resembles that of other studies of momentum. He looks at expected outcomes following very good or very bad plays to see whether there is a tendency for a good play to generate further good plays or a bad play to generate further bad plays. He finds no such statistically significant tendency. In fact, there is a slight tendency for teams that have endured very bad plays (which in this case means they have lost possession of the ball) to do somewhat better than average in the situation that follows the bad play.[6]

So far the evidence of the existence of momentum is equivocal. Some studies are able to make an impressive case for momentum, though the definitions of course vary somewhat, and others appear to show that any correlations between events that jump-start momentum and subsequent performance can easily be explained as occurring by chance. Still, in some cases at least, the evidence for momentum, no matter what the model, demands a second look.

One difficulty in developing a model with testable predictive value is that it is difficult to include the subjective experiences of athletes in real time. We might interview athletes during games, but that presents a number of challenges, the most obvious being that players will be unable to stop play so that they can answer questions. Physiological monitoring shows more promise, and Taylor and Demick's model already contains the physiological as a link in the chain. But why are the subjective experiences of athletes important?

Momentum under the Helmet

We need to get at the subjective experience of athletes because, intuitively, momentum is thought to be a feeling of mastery and success at achieving athletic goals. The psychological models of momentum seek to link the experience of mastery and success with previous and current performance, and if we removed the subjective side of things, we would be left with no obvious causal mechanism for the linkage of present and future success. Subjective experience without actual positive performance would not be momentum, and a mere linkage of earlier and later positive performance without appeal to the subjective experience of mastery and success might be of little value, for at least two reasons. First, athletes hope to be able to understand momentum and *use* it. A number of sports advisers purport to be able to teach athletes how to initiate positive "jump starts" or to take advantage of positive events when they happen randomly. If momentum can't be manipulated, then athletes won't be able to profit from studying it. Second, correlations that make no use of the athletes' conscious responses to events during a game just seem plain uninteresting. Whatever the connection might be, if there is no causal connection that runs through the athletes' own conscious experience, it is not momentum.

What we need here is a way to access a team's collective sense of momentum (in the case of football) and a way of marking the initiation or change of momentum; we need a way of defining a momentum-initiating event. But why should this be the case? Couldn't we say that a team might enter a game with the requisite feelings of mastery and success and then go on to dominate its opponent with ease? The many one-sided Super Bowls in the history of the NFL serve as examples of this possibility. Why wouldn't these be cases of momentum? And how would we recognize the difference between a team's beginning a game with solid play because it is a superior team and a team's entering a game and getting a lucky break that, because of the power of momentum, it then turns into a dominant performance?

Most of the studies seem to think of momentum as something whose existence begins as a result of a particular episode, but how should we think of the early episodes of dominant teams in games? Are we to say that excellent teams *always* or nearly always exhibit momentum? Excellent teams certainly seem to fulfill most if not all of the requirements sometimes listed for momentum: a sense of confidence, mastery, flow, and success. Should momentum require that a particular event cause or intensify these qualities? But if momentum ends up being displayed in just *any* performance that exhibits these characteristics, then we run the risk of using momentum to say no more than that a team is playing well. There is some appeal, then, in the idea that momentum requires an initiating event.

Is Momentum a Metaphysical Reality?

It might seem that if there is at least some case for the existence of momentum, then use of the idea of momentum by athletes, sportscasters, and fans is also justified. But this isn't necessarily so. It all depends on how large the momentum effect might be. It might turn out that, though there is statistical reason for thinking that success does breed success, the real question is how much momentum explains relative to other factors, including sheer randomness. Given the uncertain nature of the studies done on momentum so far, and the relatively small momentum effects claimed, it appears that momentum, especially in some sports, will turn out to be less likely as an explanation than the combined effects of other explanations—chance, principally—and even less likely than other single causes. So perhaps there is some boost in success rates that occurs as a result of athletes' responding well to precipitating events; even so, unless that success is greater than the studies to date seem to support, then we will usually be wrong when we refer to momentum as a significant explanation. The situation is like cigarette smoking: we know that smoking increases your chance of having a heart attack, but we are unable in any particular case to say that smoking was the cause, since many other factors are generally at work as well.

So, even if momentum is real, its appeal is greatly overrated, given its relative unimportance as an explanation for athletic success. The amount of success caused by momentum—even according to the studies that support its existence—is usually small in comparison with the sum total attributable to the other causal factors involved, so appeals to momentum as explanations of a team's success will often be unjustifiable. Since the best evidence for momentum is almost always going to involve statistics unavailable to the casual observer, appealing to momentum will be like the wife of a victim appealing to smoking as a cause of her husband's heart attack. She may feel that she just knows that smoking did it, but she will not be in a position to establish her case in any plausible way.

Let us sum up the points made so far. In at least a few sports, momentum would appear to be real. There appears to be a phenomenon in which success makes it more likely that success will follow, though even here there are questions about definition: does momentum as measured by social scientists match its usage by athletes, sportscasters, and fans? In any given case, the evidence—typically statistical in nature—needed to justify an attribution of momentum in a football game will be lacking, so that any appeal to that concept as an explanation of a particular shift in the fortunes of a particular team will be suspect.

Consider, now, a typical scenario. The Tigers score a touchdown on a thirty-yard pass and take a narrow lead of 10 to 7. They then score another touchdown just before the half. In addition, their fans and perhaps the sportscasters feel that they can see improved body language in the players: they are hustling, they're in a groove, they are not getting procedure penalties, they're protecting the quarterback, and so on. Things are going their way and they seem to be confident, though earlier in the game they appeared hesitant and out of sync somehow. Now, do the Tigers have the momentum going into the locker room? Further, suppose that researchers have reached a consensus that, for a well-defined list of momentum initiators, a team receives a 20 percent momentum premium. In other words, suppose that a team is 20 percent more likely to score if the players have been jump-started with one of the items on the list—recovered fumble, interception, and so on—than if they had simply received a kickoff (since just having the ball in itself makes it more likely that a team will score, obviously). Would we be justified in saying that the Tigers have momentum?

Assume that the "evidence" is appropriate; that is, assume that what we are observing in this case is just what our ideal researchers say we should observe if we hope to observe momentum as described in someone's ideal model of what momentum is. In other words, this would be an ideal case: we are observing the kind of event that, when observed hundreds of times, say, would be expected to yield a statistically significant momentum effect. In this case, can we say that the Tigers have momentum?

Unfortunately, my purely hypothetical 20 percent momentum premium would represent only an average, and we would expect it to be spread out in an unpredictable way through most games. Perhaps in some games momentum accounts for more than 20 percent of scoring, and in other games it accounts for less. This means that, though momentum might on occasion be a significant explanation for the success of a football team, in general we will not be in a position to say that it is a significant factor. Given the size of the momentum effects we would expect to discover statistically, we would be well advised to be cautious in appealing to momentum in any given case.

Conclusion: Don't Punt on Fourth Down

Finally, let us return to the possibility that David Romer is right in saying that momentum plays no role in football. If he *is* right, then it is important for coaches and players to know that. Romer's conclusion about punting on fourth down is a good example of how our belief in momentum may lead us to play too conservatively, since we will factor in the possibility of losing momentum if we fail to make a first down. Removing the threat of a momentum loss might also enable players of other sports to be more aggressive in situations that might not obviously justify taking risks. Paradoxically, if Romer is right and we would win more games by playing more aggressively, then our belief in momentum and the possibility of losing it might actually lead us to lose games that we would otherwise have won.

Notes

1. Pro Football Hall of Fame, *The NFL's Greatest Comeback,* http://www.profootballhof.com/history/.

2. Jim Taylor and Andrew Demick, "A Multidimensional Model of Momentum in Sports," *Journal of Applied Sport Psychology* 6 (1994): 51–70, http://www.drjimtaylor.com/articles/scholarly.html.

3. Taylor and Demick, "Multidimensional Model," 51–70.

4. David Romer, "Do Firms Maximize? Evidence from Professional Football," *Journal of Political Economy* 114, no. 2 (April 2006): 342, http://find.galegroup.com.

5. Romer, "Do Firms Maximize?" 358.

6. Romer, "Do Firms Maximize?" 358.

CONTRIBUTORS

Michael W. Austin is associate professor of philosophy at Eastern Kentucky University. He has published articles in ethics and philosophy of religion. His two other books are *Conceptions of Parenthood: Ethics and the Family* (Ashgate, 2007) and *Running and Philosophy: A Marathon for the Mind* (Blackwell, 2007).

Raymond Angelo Belliotti, distinguished teaching professor of philosophy at State University of New York, Fredonia, has published books on law and philosophy, ethnic and personal identity, sexual ethics, Nietzsche, human happiness, the meaning of life, the philosophy of baseball, and the connections between great philosophers and famous ballplayers.

Myles Brand assumed his duties as president of the National Collegiate Athletic Association on January 1, 2003. Termed by some the "education president," he has presided over passage of the most comprehensive academic reform package for intercollegiate athletics in recent history and has also changed the national dialogue on college sports to emphasize the educational value of athletics participation and the integration of intercollegiate athletics with the academic mission of higher education. President at both the University of Oregon and Indiana University, he has a PhD in philosophy from the University of Rochester. He has also served on various boards and executive committees for higher-education organizations.

Joseph Keim Campbell is associate professor of philosophy at Washington State University. His main areas of research are skepticism, free will, and the metaphysics of moral responsibility. He is a cofounder of the Inland Northwest Philosophy Conference and coeditor of the Contemporary Topics in Philosophy series from MIT Press.

Daniel Collins-Cavanaugh is an adjunct instructor in humanities and philosophy at the University of Maryland, University College and in philosophy at Prince George's Community College. His teaching and research interests include ethics and philosophy of sport.

Scott A. Davison is professor of philosophy at Morehead State University. His areas of research include ethics, metaphysics, and the philosophy of religion. He earned degrees in philosophy from two football powerhouses, Ohio State University and the University of Notre Dame.

Jeffrey P. Fry is assistant professor in the Department of Philosophy and Religious Studies at Ball State University. His recent work has examined the intersection of sport, ethics, and religion. He is the author of "Running Religiously," in *Running and Philosophy: A Marathon for the Mind,* edited by Michael W. Austin (Blackwell, 2007).

Daniel B. Gallagher is assistant professor of philosophy and theology at Sacred Heart Major Seminary. He has previously contributed to *Basketball and Philosophy: Thinking Outside the Paint* (University Press of Kentucky, 2007) and Lost *and Philosophy: The Island Has Its Reasons* (Blackwell, 2007).

R. Douglas Geivett is professor of philosophy at Biola Univeristy. He has contributed chapters to such edited volumes as *The Rationality of Theism* (Routledge, 2003) and *Does God Exist? The Craig-Flew Debate* (Ashgate, 2003). He authored *Evil and the Evidence for God: The Challenge of John Hick's Theodicy* (Temple, 1993) and coedited *Contemporary Perspectives on Religious Epistemology* (Oxford, 1992) and *In Defense of Miracles* (InterVarsity, 1997). His most recent book, coedited with James Spiegel, is *Faith, Film, and Philosophy: Big Ideas on the Big Screen* (InterVarsity, 2007).

Mark Hamilton is associate professor of philosophy and faculty representative to the NCAA at Ashland University, where he teaches courses in philosophy of religion, ancient and medieval philosophy, sports ethics, and C. S. Lewis. He has contributed to *Baseball and Philosophy* (Open Court, 2004).

M. Andrew Holowchak is assistant professor of philosophy at Wilkes University in Pennsylvania. He has authored many books, including *Happiness and Greek Ethics, Critical Reasoning and Philosophy, Ancient Science and Dreams: Oneirology in Greco-Roman Antiquity, Philosophy of Sport: Crucial Readings, Critical Issues,* and *The Stoics: A Guide for the Perplexed,* and numerous papers.

Stephen Kershnar is professor of philosophy at State University of New York at Fredonia. He has published articles on torture, sex, discrimination, and religion and has written two books: *Justice for the Past* (SUNY Press, 2004) and *Desert, Retribution, and Torture* (University Press of America, 2001).

Ben Letson is chair of the Department of Philosophy at Emory and Henry College. He is the author of *Davidson's Theory of Truth and Its Implications for Rorty's Pragmatism* (Peter Lang, 1997).

Scott F. Parker is a graduate student at Portland State University. He has contributed to Lost *and Philosophy* (Blackwell, 2007).

Joe Posnanski is a sports columnist for the *Kansas City Star.* He has twice been named best sports columnist in America by the Associated Press Sports Editors. A selection of his columns about the magic of sports is compiled in the book *The Good Stuff* (Kansas City Star Books, 2001). His newest book is *The Soul of Baseball: A Road Trip through Buck O'Neil's America* (William Morrow, 2007).

Heather L. Reid is associate professor of philosophy at Morningside College in Sioux City, Iowa. She is former president of the International Association for the Philosophy of Sport and serves on the editorial boards of the *Journal of the Philosophy of Sport* and *Sport, Ethics and Philosophy.* She has published articles in ancient philosophy, philosophy of sport, and Olympic studies. Her most recent book is *The Philosophical Athlete* (Carolina Academic Press, 2002).

Sharon Ryan is associate professor and chair of the philosophy department at West Virginia University. She works on philosophical problems in epistemology, metaphysics, philosophy of religion, ethics, philosophy of sport, and philosophy for children. She is the creator of The Question (thequestion.blogs.wvu.edu), an inviting blog that encourages everyone, including young children, to share ideas on deep philosophical questions that really matter. This project was featured in a full-page article in *Sports Illustrated.*

Joshua A. Smith is assistant professor of philosophy at Central Michigan University. He has published articles in epistemology.

Marshall Swain is professor emeritus and former chair in the Department of Philosophy at Ohio State University. He has published numerous articles in epistemology and metaphysics, including an early paper on causality coauthored with Myles Brand (his coauthor in the current volume). He also has written or edited several books, including *Reasons and Knowledge* (Cornell Press, 1979), *Essays on Knowledge and Justification* (with George S. Pappas, Cornell Press, 1978), and *Induction, Acceptance, and Rational Belief* (Reidel Press, 1970).

INDEX